THE CHOICE Wine™

7 STEPS TO A SUPERABUNDANT MARRIAGE

STEVE BOLLMAN

GREENLEAF
BOOK GROUP PRESS

This publication is designed to provide accurate and authoritative information in regard to the subject matter covered. It is sold with the understanding that the publisher and author are not engaged in rendering legal, accounting, or other professional services. If legal advice or other expert assistance is required, the services of a competent professional should be sought.

Published by Greenleaf Book Group Press
Austin, Texas
www.gbgpress.com

Distributed by Greenleaf Book Group

For ordering information or special discounts for bulk purchases, please contact Greenleaf Book Group at PO Box 91869, Austin, TX 78709, 512.891.6100.

Design and composition by Greenleaf Book Group and Debbie Berne
Cover design by Greenleaf Book Group, Debbie Berne, and Kimberly Guerre

Cataloging-in-Publication data is available.

Print ISBN: 978-1-62634-249-1

eBook ISBN: 978-1-62634-250-7

Part of the Tree Neutral® program, which offsets the number of trees consumed in the production and printing of this book by taking proactive steps, such as planting trees in direct proportion to the number of trees used: www.treeneutral.com

TreeNeutral®

Printed in the United States of America on acid-free paper

15 16 17 18 19 20   10 9 8 7 6 5 4 3 2 1

First Edition

For Shelly

Contents

Acknowledgments

The material in the 7 Steps to a Superabundant Marriage has been in development for over a decade and has been seen by tens of thousands of people. As such, I owe a debt of gratitude to more people than I could ever mention. Of critical importance was a small couples' group where it all began, which included Allan and Connie Klenke, John and Kathleen O'Connor, Robert and Laura Lee Vaio, Bill and Lauren Granberry, Emery and Ann Biro, David and CeeCee Sladic, and Mark and Aileen Hansen.

Throughout the entire process, I have received incredible support and encouragement from the Paradisus Dei staff and program participants. Without question, Mark Hartfiel has provided untold support to me personally during the past ten years in his hidden, humble way. May you be forever blessed. Together with his staff, he has done an incredible job coordinating the nationwide That Man is You! program. James Pinedo and the media department has done an incredible job putting together a DVD series to bring the science and stories to life. Brian Topping has provided invaluable advice and expertise in the preparation and publication of the manuscript.

Special thanks go the St. Cecilia That Man is You! and She Shall be Called Woman groups. We have met together for twenty-six weeks a year for the past twelve years! Thank you for your patience in our long and winding road. Without you, this material would have never made it to a wider audience.

Special thanks also go to the Leggett family for sharing Riley and Rose Mary. It is now my great joy to share them with you. You are in for a treat.

Above all, very special thanks go to my own family: Shelly, Anne Marie, and Mary Rose. I love you more than you will ever know. Thank you for making my life superabundant.

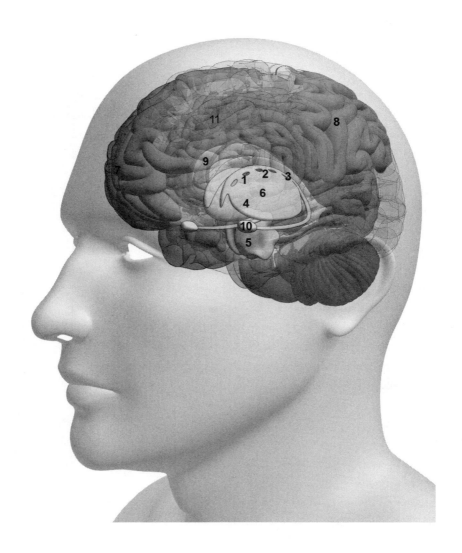

Brain Structures Important in Marriage

1. CAUDATE NUCLEUS: Forms part of the brain's reward circuitry by helping individuals identify and select specific rewards.

2. VENTRAL TEGMENTAL AREA (VTA): Forms part of the brain's reward circuitry. Contains dopamine producing cells.

3. NUCLEUS ACCUMBENS: Forms part of the brain's reward circuitry. Site where dopamine is released.

4. HYPOTHALAMUS: Contains sexual centers and secretes oxytocin and vasopressin, which are critical in the bonding between spouses.

5. MIDBRAIN: Contains trust centers and helps process fear.

6. DORSAL STRIATUM: Contains trust centers and provides a feedback loop to guide future behavior.

7. PREFRONTAL CORTEX: Center for decision making and planning complex cognitive behavior.

8. PARIETIAL LOBE: Processes sensory information and helps to determine a sense of self relative to surroundings.

9. ANTERIOR CINGULATE CORTEX: Center for empathy and compassion.

10. AMYGDALA: Processes emotion, especially fear and anxiety.

11. INSULA: Helps to control the body's homeostasis and perceives pain.

CHAPTER ONE

Tasting the Choice Wine

Is it possible to be truly happily married?

I'll be honest. I never gave the question much thought. I just assumed the answer was yes. I have a basically positive outlook on life and more or less accept the notion that you can accomplish whatever you set your mind to. I've read all the books and watched all the movies. The difficult part is up front when the boy meets the girl but can't have her. Once the boy gets the girl, they live happily ever after.

I first truly confronted the question when Shelly and I became engaged. To be polite, we were more mature than most people entering a first marriage. To be honest, we were old. I was almost 39, and Shelly was 37. When I announced our engagement to the other men at the office, I fully expected to go through the typical male ritual.

"Steve, have you lost your mind?"

"My condolences."

"Guys, Steve's getting ready for the ball and chain."

"Why would you throw away a great life to do that?"

Nonetheless, I had expected these joking comments to give way to more sincere expressions of congratulations. They never did. After a week or so, I began to suspect that behind the half smiles, something more was at work.

At the time, I was trading energy derivatives and nearing the end of a fifteen-year career in the oil industry in Texas. The oil industry has a history filled with colorful characters, with rugged individuals willing to risk everything in the hopes of striking it big and making millions. They thrive on risk and pride themselves on their ability to live life on the edge, both profession-ally and personally. It showed in their personal lives. Many were divorced. Some several times. Others had very difficult relationships with their wives and children. Truth be told, I didn't see many people truly happily married. Eventually, I wearied of the sarcastic comments and decided to push back.

"Come on, guys. It can't be that bad. Some of you must be happy." To my surprise, they universally agreed that no one was happily married. Let me make sure that I do not *understate* their response. First, they were not personally happily married. Second, no one they knew was happily married. Finally, they believed it was impossible for anyone to remain happily mar-ried. It soon became obvious that they had given up hope of happiness in married life.

Before long, my buddies decided to prove their point to this "starry-eyed lover." They began to ask one another the question, "How long were you happily married before it went bad?" The shortest answer was less than a day.

"We had a horrible fight on our wedding night, and it got worse from there."

The longest answer was a year, which was then very heavily qualified as a theoretical goal to be desired.

"My own marriage wasn't bad through six months, but by a year it had certainly gone down."

Although the answers varied in the length of time given, there was a very clear theme. For these men, happiness in marriage consisted of one thing: good sex. When the "newlywed sex" ended, the happy marriage ended. It then descended into an unwritten point system. To get what you truly wanted you had to give something to your spouse that she truly wanted. "I'll let you go out drinking with the boys if I get to . . ." According to my bud-dies, your greatest hope in married life was to master this unwritten point system so that the payback never cost more than the joy received from doing what you truly wanted to do.

I'll be honest. I was a bit shaken by the extent of their skepticism. These men had abandoned any hope of "living happily ever after." Nonetheless, the more I pondered their responses, the more I realized they sounded a lot like another group of men—the apostles of Jesus Christ.

Near the end of Christ's public ministry, the leaders of the Jewish community came up to Jesus and asked him a simple question:

"Is it lawful to divorce one's wife for any cause?" (Matthew 19:3). Jesus responded, "Have you not read that he who made them from the beginning made them male and female, and said, 'For this reason a man shall leave his father and mother and be joined to his wife, and the two shall become one'? So they are no longer two but one. What therefore God has joined together, let no man put asunder" (Matthew 19:4–6).

Throughout history, this verse has been critically important in forming Christianity's teaching on marriage and divorce. At least indirectly, reformations and wars can be tied to the interpretation of this verse. However, I would like to simply focus on the response of the apostles:

"If such is the case of a man with his wife, it is not expedient to marry" (Matthew 19:10).

It is easy to read the apostle's response without giving it much thought, so let me put it into context. This scene occurs not long before the end of Christ's life. Therefore, the apostles have been living and traveling with Christ for almost three years. They have seen him walk on the water and multiply the loaves. They have seen him give sight to the blind and hearing to the deaf. They have even seen him raise the dead to life. They have heard him define his moral code in the Sermon on the Mount. They have even identified him as the "son of God." Nonetheless, as soon as Christ says that once you get married, you have to stay married, they effectively respond by saying, "Fine, then we won't get married!" Apparently, the thought of living happily ever after wasn't on the radar screen for the apostles either.

Marriage as a Pathway to Superabundance

It was easy for me to write off the skepticism of the men in the oil industry, but Christ's own apostles? I loved Shelly and couldn't imagine it would ever come to an end. What was a not-so-young, starry-eyed lover to do? Well, if you have an MBA on top of an undergraduate engineering degree, you set out to find some objective data. I quickly discovered that in the past generation, a mountain of research has been conducted on marriage. This research reveals that marriage is really good for you. Indeed, married people are significantly happier, healthier, and wealthier than people who are not married. That's not a bad start. Who doesn't want to be happy, healthy, and wealthy?

Furthermore, the data revealed a very interesting pattern, which I've come to call the *marriage premium*. Let's call the never-married state the base state since everyone begins life as a single person. When you get married, there is a significant increase in happiness, health, and wealth. However, if you get divorced, you lose the marriage premium, and your happiness, health, and wealth fall back to the never-married starting state.

Happiness

Data from one of the largest sociological databanks in the country, the General Social Survey, indicates that married people are happier than single, divorced, separated, or widowed people (see Figure 1.1). Indeed, married people are almost twice as likely as people from the other marital categories to be "very happy" with their lives. This is the marriage premium for happiness. Furthermore, according to the General Social Survey, single, divorced, separated, or widowed people are significantly more likely to be "not too happy" with their lives versus married people.[1]

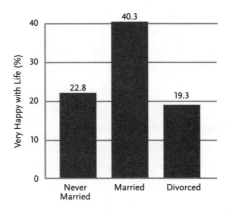

Figure 1.1: Marital Status and Happiness
Source: General Social Survey, 1972–2012.

Health

The data also reveals a marriage premium for health. When the General Social Survey asked respondents for a self-assessment of their general health (excellent, good, fair, or poor), there was a very clear relationship to marital status (see Figure 1.2). On the surface, the marriage premium on health seems fairly small—especially relative to the marriage premium on happiness. But let's take a look at it from another perspective—those who are struggling with their health. According to the survey, only 2.9 percent of married adults between ages 36–50 are in poor health. Yet, 5.1 percent of never-married adults and 5.5 percent of divorced adults of similar ages are in poor health.[2] This equates to a 75 percent increase in poor health for those who have never been married and a 90 percent increase for those who have been divorced. That's a significant change.

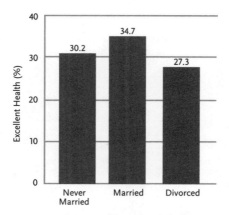

Figure 1.2: Marital Status and Health
Source: General Social Survey, 1972–2012.

This subjective assessment of general health is manifested in real-life experience. When the survey asked the respondents, "How many days of poor physical health did you experience in the past 30 days?" we once again encounter the marriage premium. The average 36- to 50-year-old who has never been married experiences 1.13 additional poor physical health days each month compared to the average 36- to 50-year-old married person. That translates into 13.5 additional poor health days each year, or almost two weeks of additional poor health! This is a very big number, especially for men and women who are usually in their prime productive years between the ages of 36 and 50.

This correlation between health and marital status endures throughout life until the moment we die. Data from the US Department of Health and Human Services indicates that married people are only half as likely to die in a given year as those in all other marital status categories. This relationship holds true across all age groups.[3]

Wealth

The data also reveals a marriage premium for wealth. Janet Wilmoth and Gregor Koso from Purdue University tracked 9,824 individuals throughout their adult life history to determine the impact of marital status on preretirement wealth accumulation. Their study indicates that individuals who marry once and remain married their entire adult life accumulate significantly more wealth than any other marital history (see Figure 1.3).

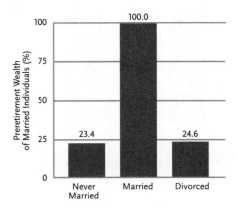

Figure 1.3: Marital Status and Wealth
Source: Wilmoth, J., and Koso, G., "Does Marital History Matter? Marital Status and Wealth Outcomes Among Preretirement Adults," *Journal of Marriage and Family*, 64 (2002): 254–268.

The magnitude of the difference is almost shocking. Continuously married individuals accumulate approximately four times the net wealth of those individuals who have never been married or who are divorced.[4] Interestingly, if a divorced person remarries, they are able to make up much of this lost ground. Their preretirement net wealth is only 30 percent lower than that of continuously married couples.[5] However, if they get divorced a second time, it's a double whammy. Their accumulated net wealth is approximately five times lower than continuously married individuals.[6] That's significant!

Other researchers have also discovered the huge financial advantage enjoyed by married individuals. It is frequently assumed that economies of scale largely explain this financial marriage premium. In other words, a married couple has only one house payment as opposed to two, they can specialize in tasks, and so on. Interestingly, Wilmoth and Koso tracked individuals who were never married but were cohabitating. In theory, these cohabitating couples would enjoy the same economies of scale as married couples. Nonetheless, the study indicated that married couples still amass more than four times the preretirement net wealth of never-married but cohabitating couples.[7] The data clearly indicates that marriage is good for your pocketbook.

The Black Cloud in Marriage Statistics

When it comes to the research on marriage, this is truly just the tip of the iceberg. The good news is that it all points in the same direction. Marriage is really good for you. As such, how can I explain the general skepticism regarding marriage I encountered when Shelly and I got engaged? Simply put, a good portion of my coworkers were either divorced or in very difficult marriages that seemed to be headed toward divorce. They were not experiencing the marriage premium on happiness, health, or wealth. Indeed, many of them had fallen back to their starting point in terms of happiness, health, and wealth, but now they were ten, twenty, or even thirty years older.

I wish I could say that their experience was the exception to the rule. But it's not. To be honest, their experience of marriage is all too common. Indeed, to gain a more complete understanding of the impact of marriage on the individual, we need to consider some additional data. According to data published by the US Census Bureau, approximately 40 percent of all first marriages in the United States will end in divorce (see Figure 1.4).[8] Indeed, 20 percent of first marriages end within 10 years.[9] The failure rate for second marriages is even higher.[10]

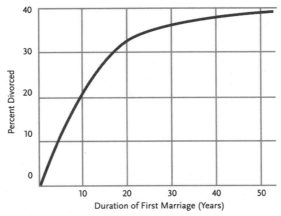

Figure 1.4: First Marriages Ending in Divorce
Source: US Census Bureau, "Number, Timing, and Duration of Marriages and Divorces, 2009," (May 2011).

Furthermore, when you consider the data on divorce, it is obvious that staying married has gotten more difficult over time. Returning to survey data, fewer than one in five (18.8 percent) marriages begun during the 1930s ended in divorce.

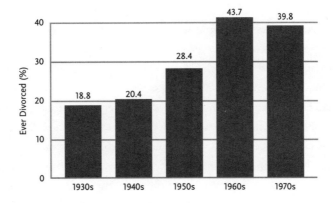

Figure 1.5: Changes in Divorce Rate
Source: US Census Bureau, "Number, Timing and Duration of Marriages and Divorces, 2009," (May 2011).

This number more than doubled to over 40 percent for marriages begun during the 1960s or later. Although we haven't seen the complete picture for marriages begun more recently, the data indicates that the divorce rate for first marriages remains at essentially 40 percent.[11]

Suddenly, the skepticism I encountered regarding marriage began to make more sense. Marriage can be a risky proposition. When it works out, you experience a marriage premium in terms of happiness, health, and wealth. Unfortunately, there is no guarantee that it will work out. Indeed, two in five marriages fail; and when they fail, you fall to a level below your starting point. Although my buddies didn't say it in such simple terms, the conclusion was simple: Marriage just isn't worth the risk.

A Simple Answer to a Difficult Problem

Sifting through the mountains of studies and data on marriage, I was able to better grasp the true issue at hand. Marriage is really good for you when it works, but unfortunately a substantial number of marriages don't work. How was a not-so-young, starry-eyed lover to find the secret to marital success? Fortunately, I knew a great place to turn to: my future father-in-law and mother-in-law.

E. Riley Leggett and Rose Mary Pellerin married on April 27, 1957. They were old enough to be part of what is now called *the Greatest Generation*. Riley was an incredible man. He lived the American Dream to the fullest. Born in a small farming town in East Texas in 1915, Riley was old enough to have personally experienced the harsh reality of the Great Depression. As he said, "I know what it is to hoe a row of cotton in the Texas heat and I know what it is like to go to bed hungry."

When the war came, Riley stayed home to care for his aging parents while his brothers were fully engaged in battle. After the war, Riley set about obtaining an education so that he could escape the harsh reality of his youth. He enrolled at the University of Texas in Austin. He truly walked several miles to school every day, from his aunt's house, where the board was free, to his classes, to his job at a local auto parts dealer, and then back to his aunt's house. Rain or shine, blistering heat or biting cold, the path was always the same. Eventually, the stress of attending classes, working, and walking several miles every day took its toll, and Riley was unable to finish his degree.

Down but not out, Riley landed on his feet—literally. He hit the streets of Houston in 1952. In coat and tie, Riley trudged through the heat and humidity of Houston to work.

As he put it, "If you don't have a nickel, you can't pay the toll to ride the bus."

After work, he began attending classes at the University of Houston and eventually completed his degree. He tried his hand at teaching, but the small town in which he was teaching ran out of money and dismissed classes early for the year. Realizing teaching would be a hard way to support a family, Riley got a job at a light manufacturing company in Houston. In time, he was able to buy into the partnership and Riley became a successful businessman.

Along the way Riley met the love of his life, Rose Mary Pellerin. Born in New Orleans in 1922, she too knew the struggles of the Great Depression. Her family moved to Houston when she just five years old. Times were difficult and Rose Mary had to wear hand-me-down tennis shoes (black high-tops) given to her by a boy. She was mortified. Rose Mary worked hard and put herself through college, graduating from the University of Houston in 1955—long before college degrees were common for young ladies. Rose Mary was beautiful and charming with a flair for culture and the arts. She traveled internationally when such behavior merited coverage by the Houston papers. Indeed, Rose Mary would grace the society pages of the Houston newspapers on more than one occasion.

When Riley and Rose Mary were married in 1957, she brought a joy into his life that is difficult to put into words, but was easily seen in the sparkle in their eyes. To be in their presence was to experience the joy of a couple in love. Together, they had four children and sixteen grandchildren.

When I met Shelly, Riley and Rose Mary were already living the golden years, fully reaping the rewards of the marriage premium. Their children were busy raising their own families. Riley was retired after a successful career. They were both in good health and had the financial resources and time to enjoy travel together. Indeed, the night Shelly and I went on our first date, Riley and Rose Mary were busy chaperoning their oldest granddaughter's school trip to Europe! In Riley and Rose Mary, I knew I had a couple that could tell me the secret to their success in marriage.

An opportunity presented itself shortly before Shelly and I married. I found myself sitting on the couch next to Riley and Rose Mary without anyone else around. I thought I had the perfect opportunity to receive a little advice and score big-time with my future father-in-law. I mean, who wouldn't love a future son-in-law who has the humility to ask for a little advice? I asked what I thought was a perfectly brilliant question.

"Riley, in about a month, I'm going to marry your daughter. Considering how well you raised your family, do you have any advice for me?"

Very bad choice! Riley looked at me like I was from another planet. I could see the wheels spinning in Riley's mind: "This guy wants to marry my daughter and he doesn't have a clue what to do? What a dumb question! I can't tell him how to do it. You just do it."

He leaned over to Rose Mary and said, "You tell him. You did all the work."

Rose Mary promptly hit him and was just beginning to answer. But, before a word escaped her lips, Riley got a sparkle in his eye. The kind of sparkle someone gets when they are really proud of themselves. I could tell Riley was quite impressed with himself for coming up with an answer he didn't think he knew.

"I'll tell you what to do. Eat dinner with your family every night and sit in church with your family every Sunday. That just about covers it. Do that and everything will be just fine."

Rose Mary suddenly got a big smile. She didn't know Riley had it in him.

My response? That's a different story. I think it would be accurate to say that I progressed from one awkward moment to another. I mean, how do you respond to such advice? I think I came up with something incredibly brilliant along the lines of "Okay." The couch suddenly seemed very crowded and I began looking for an exit strategy.

I didn't realize it at the time, but I had just had a "Naaman the Syrian moment." Naaman was a general in the Syrian army, famous for fighting and winning battles. Unfortunately, he had the most dreaded disease of his day, leprosy. One day a little servant girl to his wife suggested that Naaman go to the prophet Elisha in Israel to be cured of his leprosy. Naaman did what every important man of the day would do. He got a letter of introduction from the king and packed the camels with gold, silver, and festal garments.

When Naaman arrived, Elisha was not impressed. Indeed, he refused to go out to meet Naaman. Instead, he sent a note to Naaman telling him to go jump in the river: "Go and wash in the Jordan seven times, and your flesh shall be restored, and you shall be clean" (2 Kings 5:10).

Not surprisingly, Naaman went off in a very big huff. Fortunately, one of his servants reasoned with him, "My father, if the prophet had commanded you to do some great thing, would you not have done it? How much rather, then, when he says to you, 'Wash, and be clean'?" (2 Kings 5:13).

Naaman listened to the advice of his servant and cooled off—literally. He went and jumped in the river! When he came out his flesh was like that of a little child.

Truth be told, we all have more of Naaman the Syrian in us than we would like to admit. On the one hand, most of us are truly willing to move mountains to make life better for ourselves and those whom we love. On the other hand, that's the problem. We keep looking for mountains to move. Frequently, small things—if they are the right small things—can make a very big difference. This is the wisdom that Riley Leggett understood and it is the wisdom he proposed to me.

The Wisdom of Riley

Let's consider some data regarding Riley's two suggestions to me. First, Riley suggested that I come home and eat dinner with my family every night. Believe it or not, every couple of years, researchers from Columbia University publish a study on the impact of eating dinner together. Amazingly, eating dinner together has a positive impact on just about every measure of a family's life. Let's specifically look at the impact on a family's ability to live harmoniously together. Only 7 percent of families that eat dinner together five or more times a week experience a great deal of tension. However, 19 percent of families who eat dinner together twice or less every week experience a great deal of tension—an increase of more than 170 percent (see Figure 1.6).[12]

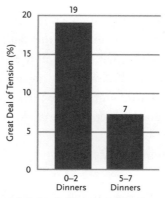

Figure 1.6: Family Dinner and Tension
Source: The National Center on Addiction and Substance Abuse at Columbia University, "The Importance of Family Dinners II" (September 2005): p. 8.

Now let's consider Riley's second suggestion, to "sit in church together with your family every Sunday." Once again, a tremendous amount of research has been done regarding the impact of church attendance on marriage and family life. This research indicates that formal participation in organized worship services has a very strong relationship to marital stability. Returning to data from the General Social Survey, more than 40 percent of the people who never attend formal worship services have been divorced, whereas only 17 percent of those who attend worship services on a weekly basis have been divorced (see Figure 1.7).[13]

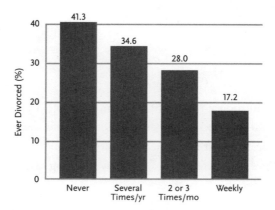

Figure 1.7: Church Attendance and Divorce
Source: General Social Survey, 1972–2012.

Looking at the data, there was good reason for Riley to have a sparkle in his eye. He nailed it. "Sitting in church together with your family every week" and "eating dinner together with your family every night" will profoundly change your family life. Without doing any research, Riley was on to something. He gained his wisdom from the life he had lived. We will continue to encounter this simple wisdom as we progress.

The 7 Steps to a Superabundant Marriage

Although Riley mentioned only two requirements for a happy marriage, there were certainly other things he just took for granted. Being part of the Greatest Generation, he lived by a moral and ethical code that was unquestioned. For instance, he took for granted that you would be a man of your word. In the case of marriage, if you stood at the altar promising to be faithful to his daughter while "forsaking all others," he expected you to live by your word. If you didn't, Riley would love to show you his hunting trophies. Indeed, he might just turn you into one of them!

Over time I expanded Riley's list a bit. Indeed, I have identified seven steps that will truly make your marriage superabundant.

1. Honor your wedding vows.
2. Use money for other people.
3. Give God some of your time.
4. Set your mind on the things above.
5. Find God in yourself.
6. Find God in other people.
7. Make it easy to be good and hard to be bad.

Whenever I introduce these 7 Steps to an audience, I most frequently receive a room full of blank stares—not unlike the one I gave Riley. I can almost hear their internal thoughts:

"I can't believe I got up early on a Saturday morning to drive all the way over here to listen to this."

To which I reply, "Oh, go jump in a river!"

As we consider these 7 Steps, we will discover an amazing depth hidden beneath their simplicity. To unpack this depth, we'll need to use everything at our disposal. As such, we will move freely between the findings of modern science and the theology of the ages. To many modern readers, this may seem strange. In our modern culture we have built a solid wall separating scientific knowledge and religion. Indeed, in many circles there is subtle antagonism, if not outright hostility, between the two. Some may trace this situation to Charles Darwin and the theory of evolution.[14] Others may point to the Catholic Church's handling of the Galileo case in the seventeenth century.[15] Still others will select some other event in the past. Nevertheless, if we look closely we will see that the tension between science and religion—or, as others would say, the tension between faith and reason—has existed for millennia.

When addressing the Christian community at Corinth, the apostle Paul would complain: "Jews demand signs and Greeks seek wisdom" (1 Corinthians 1:22). There you have it. "Signs" is the code word for "faith," and "wisdom" is the code word for "reason" or "science." The tension between faith and reason goes all the way back to the founding of Christianity, two thousand years ago—if not further.

Interestingly enough, the apostle Paul did not take sides. Instead, he boldly proclaimed that Christianity introduced a wisdom based on Christ that breaks down the wall separating Jew and Greek. It therefore breaks down the wall separating faith from reason. It was from this perspective that one of the earliest and most influential Christian writers, St. Augustine of Hippo, could proclaim,

> Some people read books in order to find God. Yet there is a great book, the very appearance of created things. Look above you; look below you! Note it; read it! God, whom you wish to find, never wrote that book with ink. Instead, he set before your eyes the things that he had made. Can you ask for a louder voice than that? Why, heaven and earth cry out to you: "God made me!"[16]

We will do our best to read from both books. We will consider some of the best research conducted by some of the top minds at some of the best universities from around the world. We will be particularly interested in research from the social and medical sciences. At the same time, we will happily consider the wisdom that has been handed down through the ages in the Judeo-Christian tradition. In considering both books, we will allow each field its appropriate autonomy. Very frequently, we will be amazed at the harmony that exists between them.

As we progress through the 7 Steps we will discover a certain hierarchy among the steps. The first three steps (honor your wedding vows; use money for others; and give God some of your time) lay a foundation and help to "divorceproof" your marriage. The second three steps (set your mind on the things above; find God in yourself; and find God in other people) allow your marriage to move beyond surviving to become truly thriving. This is the level of superabundance. The final step (make it easy to be good and hard to be bad) will allow you to experience something of a foretaste of Paradise. Yes, our goal is to go to the very end of love to experience its depth and beauty.

To Expand the Human Heart

To achieve this goal, we must be willing to expand our hearts beyond the confines of our broken, wounded world. Believe it or not, God has been working to expand the human heart from the very beginning. Indeed, in the story of Paradise, God leads the man through a type of divine lesson where he teaches humanity what it means to be human.[17]

The story begins with God placing humanity in a Paradise that has every "manner of tree, fair to behold, and pleasant to eat of" (Genesis 2:9). Ah! Who has not been struck at some point by the beauty of creation? For me, it is to stand at the summit of Vail Mountain and look out across the back bowls and a valley that seems to stretch for hundreds of miles. It is to stand on the shore of the sea and watch the sun slowly set across the waters. It is to stand on a cool, cloudless, moonless night and gaze at the stars of the Milky Way. During such moments, God seems very near.

In the story of Paradise, God then asks the man to "till the soil" (Genesis 2:15). In other words, God asks man to work. Since this is before temptation and sin, which is mentioned in the following chapter, humanity's call to work is not to be seen as a punishment for sin nor as part of the fallen world. Rather, humanity is given the dignity to work as a sign of its cooperation with God in the work of creation. Yes, as much as I hate to admit it, there is incredible joy when—after days of pounding my head against the computer screen—it all comes together, the clouds part, there is light, and I remember to plug in my computer! It is the thrill of little victories!

Nonetheless, it is precisely at this moment that God grieves "that the man should be alone" (Genesis 2:18). In other words, God wants even more for you. The beauty of creation and the thrill of little victories at work aren't enough. Your heart was created for more. It was created for love, which means it was created for communion with another person. Therefore, God creates woman from the heart of man, which is symbolized by the rib enclosing the heart. He brings woman to the man and we hear

> "This, at last, is bone of my bones and flesh of my flesh; she shall be called Woman, because she was taken out of Man." Therefore, a man leaves his father and mother and cleaves to his wife, and they become one flesh (Genesis 2:23–24).

These verses have been incredibly important in Judeo-Christian history. They give to us the final vision of humanity in Paradise before the introduction of evil. It is a vision of a man and a woman in a union so intimate that they are one. Furthermore, this union is so profound that it brings the couple out of themselves and opens them to an encounter with God.[18] This is the dignity of the human heart. It was created for a union so profound that it transcends the limits of this material world.

Unfortunately, this incredibly beautiful vision does not long endure. In the following chapter of Genesis, humanity encounters evil. Immediately after this encounter, we see the first disruption of the union of man and woman: "Then the eyes of both were opened, and they knew that they were naked, and they sewed together fig leaves and made themselves clothes" (Genesis 3:7). Obviously, this is very symbolic language and volumes have been written about this moment. Let us simply note that in the previous chapter Adam and Eve lived in such intimate union that they were "naked and unashamed," and now they have introduced something in the middle of their union that separates them from each other—fig leaves. The union of man and woman has experienced difficulties ever since.

Tasting the Choice Wine

The Good News is that Christ came to restore to humanity that which was lost in the Garden of Eden. This is why he answered the question regarding divorce by referring to humanity in its innocence:

> Have you not read that he who made them from the beginning made them male and female, and said, "For this reason a man shall leave his father and mother and be joined to his wife, and the two shall become one?" (Matthew 19:4–5).

Christ wishes to give couples the superabundant joy that was experienced by man and woman in Paradise.

This is manifest in Christ's first public miracle. Jesus was invited to a wedding feast along with his apostles. His mother is also there and she notices that they have run out of wine. So she says to Jesus: "They have no wine" (John 2:3).

Jesus responds by asking the waiters to fill six jars[19] with water and to take a sample to the steward of the feast. When the steward tastes the water turned into wine, he is amazed—so amazed that he runs to the bridegroom and tells him that he is doing everything all wrong: "Every man serves the good wine first; and when men have drunk freely, then the poor wine; but you have kept the good wine until now" (John 2:10).

Let's put this miracle in perspective. The bridegroom and bride ordered what they thought was enough wine for the party. But, it's not. It has been a really great party and the guests seem to be lingering. Jesus responds by transforming the water in "six stone jars . . . each holding twenty to thirty gallons" (John 2:6) into the choicest of wines. That's approximately 150 gallons of wine. Considering that the entire town is believed to have had about 600 total inhabitants (men, women, and children) at the time of Christ,[20]

150 gallons of additional wine is truly superabundant. God does not relate to us at the level of sufficiency. He relates to us at the level of superabundance.

It is interesting to note that the account of Christ's first public miracle ends with, "His disciples believed in him" (John 2:11). Transforming 150 gallons of water into the choicest of wines is certainly impressive. But, let's go a little further. In Scripture, "wine gladdens the heart of man" (Psalm 104:15). If the couple has no wine, then they have no joy in their heart.[21] That's the issue! Outside of Paradise, where humanity is subjected to temptation and sin, husband and wife experience struggle. This is the experience underlying the skepticism of modern culture. This is the experience of Christ's own apostles. But Christ has an answer: He gives the couple superabundant, choice wine—which is to say that Christ renews in the heart of the couple superabundant joy. Perhaps this is the greater miracle.

Jesus Christ wants you and your spouse to personally experience this miracle. He wants you to experience superabundant joy. He wants you to taste the choice wine. That's what these 7 Steps are all about. If you faithfully live them, they will truly transform your life. If you have a good marriage, they can make it great. If you have a great marriage, they can help you have a foretaste of Paradise. If you are in a very difficult situation, they can provide a pathway to a better future. Indeed, if faithfully lived, these steps can transform the almost certainty of divorce into a strong possibility of true happiness. Furthermore, the ability to live these steps is totally within your control. They don't depend on someone or something else. A happier, more superabundant future is within your grasp.

We have an incredible journey before us. It is a journey that will allow us to depart from the skepticism born of wounded hearts to cross the threshold of hope. It is a hope that believes authentic love truly exists, and that it is within our grasp. Let us begin our journey.

CHAPTER TWO

STEP ONE:
Honor Your Wedding Vows

The first step to a superabundant marriage is to honor your wedding vows. I know. Talk about a yawner for an opener! It is so obvious and mundane, why bother? Certainly, Riley took it for granted and never felt the need to mention it. And I basically agree except for one small detail: *No one knows their wedding vows!* How do I know? Because I have asked thousands of people across this country. Sure, the women do slightly better than the men, but they both fail miserably.

Mind you, they remember everything else about their wedding. The location of the rehearsal dinner. The menu. Who drank too much and was obnoxious. The number and names of the wedding party. The church or venue. The music that was played. All the details of the reception—food, music, alcohol, location, *costs*. They can tell you everything about the wedding night and honeymoon (well, not everything, please).

But ask them about the wedding vows; ask if they are able to recite them word for word. Let's put this in context. This is obviously a very important moment. They have found the person with whom they hope to spend the rest of their life. They have prepared for months—if not longer. They have invited all of their family and friends to this big moment. They have spent way too much money. Tears will almost certainly be shed. The photographer and videographer are primed to catch the all-important moment when they look deeply into each other's eyes and their voices fill with emotion. They will replay this moment countless times as they watch the video across the years.

Nonetheless, ask them if they can recite their wedding vows without aid and suddenly you get a look very different from the one Riley had. There is no sparkle in the eye, no pride in the voice. Worse, they know that this is something really important. They know that they should know it. And they know that they don't know it. A small reddish flush comes to the face. A little embarrassed smile. A half chuckle—from the men. Finally, "Uh, no. Not really. I mean, not word for word."

So I follow with, "Okay. You don't really remember the words—at least not word for word. Can you tell me what the wedding vow means?" After a brief, awkward silence, most people, especially the men, respond along this line: "You know. It means that it's like just the two of us. I won't mess around on her with other women."

The Fruitfulness of the One Flesh Union

Although not stated in very eloquent terms, the intuitive understanding of "it's just the two of us . . . I won't mess around with someone else" is actually quite good. Indeed, it takes us right back to the very first union between man and woman as recorded in the Garden of Eden. However, Scripture uses more eloquent language: "Therefore a man leaves his father and mother and cleaves to wife and the two become one flesh" (Genesis 2:24).

"One flesh," that's the most fundamental understanding of the union between husband and wife. Furthermore, the "one flesh" union is absolutely foundational to the marriage premium regarding happiness, health, and wealth that the couple will experience. Both of these realities find expression in the wedding vows.

It is interesting to note that on those occasions when someone actually attempts to recite his or her wedding vows, the most frequent response I receive is "With this ring, I thee wed . . . " Suddenly, the voice trails off and I receive an inquisitive glance pleading, "Am I on the right track?"

These words are found in the Anglican Book of Common Prayer dating to the middle of the sixteenth century and are part of the ring ceremony— the moment that the bridegroom and bride place the wedding ring on each other's finger. Since these words were traditionally recited by Anglicans, Episcopalians, Methodists, and others, they found their way into popular culture. The complete phase is

> With this Ring I thee wed, with my body I thee worship, and with all my worldly goods I thee endow: In the name of the Father, and of the Son, and of the Holy Ghost. Amen.[1]

Notwithstanding the old English that is a bit challenging for all of us, these words make a very important connection. When the couple seals their marriage by the exchange of wedding rings, their words point to the importance of the bodily union of husband and wife. Although it sounds strange to modern ears, the words "With my body I thee worship" definitely correspond to the "gut level" understanding that the "one flesh" union of husband and wife is the foundation of the marital bond.

Catholics recite different words during the exchange of wedding rings. Nonetheless, the words still point to the centrality of the "one flesh" union in the life of the couple.

> (Name), receive this ring as a sign of my love and fidelity. In the name of the Father, and of the Son, and of the Holy Spirit. Amen.[2]

Fidelity. The word remains hanging in the air. The meaning is so clear that there is no need to ask the question, "Fidelity to what?" Fidelity. "You know. It means that it's like just the two of us. I won't mess around on her with other women." This intuitive understanding of the foundation of marriage is accurate and it finds expression in the marriage ceremony.

However, we must go further. The "one flesh" union of husband and wife is called to "be fruitful and multiply" (Genesis 1:28). Throughout history, the fruitfulness of the spousal union has been primarily considered relative to children. Indeed, every young married couple quickly learns "new math." In marriage, 1 plus 1 does *not* equal 2. It equals 3 or 4 or 5. The fruitfulness of the "one flesh" union of husband and wife certainly relates to children.

Nonetheless, the fruitfulness of the spousal union first relates to the couple themselves. Indeed, it relates to the marriage premium we discovered in the previous chapter. To understand this reality, we must consider the actual wording of the wedding vows. Catholics, Anglicans, Episcopalians, Methodists, and others recite the following wedding vow or something very similar:

> I, (Groom), take thee, (Bride), as my lawful wife, to have and to hold from this day forward, for better for worse, for richer for poorer, in sickness and in health, until death do us part.[3]

If we consider the wording of this wedding vow carefully, we will find hidden in it a reference to the marriage premium. Think about it. "For better or for worse." That's just another way of saying happiness. "For richer or poorer" is obviously about wealth. "In sickness and in health" is obviously about health. The wording of the wedding vow takes us right back to the concept of the marriage premium.

The marriage vow requires bridegroom and bride to remain faithful to each other regardless of their personal circumstances relative to happiness, health, and wealth. Nonetheless, as the data in the first chapter indicated, married people as a group are generally happier, healthier, and wealthier than those who are not married. As such, the married couple is the first one to experience the fruitfulness of the spousal bond. In the first chapter, we called it *superabundance*. For a couple to experience superabundance or fruitfulness in their marriage, they must remain faithful to the "one flesh" union as the channel through which this fruitfulness flows.

The Issue of Infidelity

Given the importance of the "one flesh union" to the well-being of the couple, it is not surprising to find that fidelity to this union is critical to the continued viability of the couple. Researchers from the University of Nebraska followed couples for twelve years to determine the factors leading to divorce.[4] The results are presented in Table 2.1.

This chart lists the increased probability of divorce given certain behaviors or traits. Since women file for divorce more frequently than men, I have

Behavior	Women	Men	Average
Infidelity	299%	363%	331%
Use Money Foolishly	187%	77%	132%
Drug/Alcohol Abuse	183%	216%	200%
Becomes Jealous	130%	101%	116%
Not Home Enough	105%	-NA-	52%
Critical Attitude	98%	93%	96%
Irritating Habits	92%	127%	110%

Table 2.1: Reasons for Divorce
Note: Table values are the percentage change in the odds of divorce. An increased probability of 100% indicates a doubling in the probability of divorce.
Source: Amato, P. R., and Rogers, S. J. "A Longitudinal Study of Marital Problems and Subsequent Divorce," *Journal of Marriage and Family* 59 (1997): 612–624.

listed first the reasons women divorce their husbands. This study clearly indicates that infidelity is the most serious threat to the marital union. It increases the probability that a woman will divorce her husband by almost 300 percent (Note: An increased probability of 300 percent corresponds to a quadrupling of the likelihood of divorce). Men are even less forgiving. If the wife is unfaithful, it increases the probability that a man will divorce his wife by 363 percent.

I have known several couples struggling with the issue of infidelity. I can testify to the validity of these results. Very few couples survive infidelity once it becomes known. Those who do survive usually have a very deep faith in God and a strong support system. Nonetheless, they experience tremendous pain over a fairly prolonged period of time. Simply put: If you wish to have a superabundant marriage, the first place to start is fidelity to the "one flesh" union of husband and wife.

Fortunately, most people get it. Although Western culture experienced a sexual revolution in the past generation that radically altered sexual mores, the vast majority of people still consider sexual infidelity to be wrong. A survey by the Gallup Poll indicated only 7 percent of Americans think it is "morally acceptable" to have an affair.[5] Nonetheless, the actual incidence of infidelity is more than twice that number (16.5 percent).[6] More men are unfaithful to their wedding vows than women: 21.2 percent versus 12.8 percent, respectively.[7] As such, at least one-fifth of all marriages will experience a crisis related to infidelity.

Embracing Fidelity Before Marriage

I'll be honest, the issue of infidelity just wasn't on Riley and Rose Mary's radar screen. Being part of the Greatest Generation, their values on marriage and family life predated the sexual revolution of the 1960s.[8] As such, the thought of breaking your word on something as important as a marriage vow just did not register. However, something else did—sex before marriage.

Shelly told me about a little talk that Rose Mary had with the girls. We will have the opportunity to get to know Rose Mary much better as we progress. She was an incredibly beautiful, wonderful, and gracious woman. As Shelly said, "My mom dined. The rest of us just ate!" Her little talk was consistent with this image.

She asked the girls to think about the family's fine china. It's reserved for the special occasions. Treated with utmost care. Cherished through the years. Eventually, passed to the next generation. Then she asked the girls to think about the paper plates the family used from time to time. They are made to be used once and then thrown out when you're done. She then asked the very simple question, "Are you going to be the fine china that is cherished and respected through the years or are you going to be a paper plate that's used once and then thrown out?" Of course, the girls got the meaning.

Rose Mary and Riley were formed by a value system that believed fidelity to your spouse actually began before marriage. Christ's statement that "every one who looks at a woman lustfully has already committed adultery with her in his heart" (Matthew 5:28) was taken to mean that intimate sexual relations outside of marriage were not permitted. Although it is frequently viewed in a negative light as a prohibition, there is actually a positive orientation. The person was called to proactively "save himself or herself" as a gift to be offered to his or her spouse on the wedding night.

I must admit that this sounds archaic in modern culture. Studies indicate that approximately 10 percent of women are virgins at the time of their marriage[9] and almost seven out of ten never-married 18- to 19-year-old women have had sexual intercourse.[10] Furthermore, cohabitation has become widely practiced and accepted. Indeed, it is estimated that approximately two-thirds of all young people will cohabitate before they get married.[11]

Nonetheless, studies indicate that these activities occurring before marriage have a significant impact on the stability of a future marriage. Indeed, one of the largest surveys ever completed on sexual practices in the United States found that for men, premarital sexual activity increased the probability of divorce by 61 percent and cohabitation increased the probability of divorce by 85 percent.[12] These are significant numbers. Fidelity to your future spouse, even before marriage, can make a huge impact on the superabundance of your marriage.

Pornography as Virtual Infidelity

Another issue impacting a significant portion of couples is pornography. Reliable data about pornography usage based upon scientific surveys is surprisingly sparse. However, we do know that technology—especially the Internet and mobile world—has made pornography consumption easier than ever before.[13] We also know men are more attracted to pornography than women; approximately 35 percent of men versus 16 percent of women have viewed an X-rated movie in the past year.[14] Finally, younger men view pornography more frequently than older men; approximately 62.7 percent of men aged 20–29 have viewed an X-rated movie in the last year versus 23.3 percent of men aged 50–59.[15]

Pornography has become a major issue on college campuses. A survey of 813 college students from six universities across the United States revealed the extent of pornography consumption on campus. Over 86 percent of college men are consuming pornography and almost half, 48.4 percent, are consuming pornography at least weekly if not more frequently. A very different picture emerged for college women. Less than one-third of college women consume pornography at any level and only 3.2 percent consume it at least weekly or more frequently (see Figure 2.1). Given the level of pornography consumption, it is absolutely appropriate to question the impact of pornography consumption on the life of a couple. To illustrate this point, I would like to consider the real-life story of a young college couple.

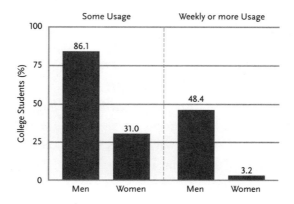

Figure 2.1: Pornography Consumption
Source: Carroll, J. et al., "Generation XXX: Pornography Acceptance and Use Among Emerging Adults," *Journal of Adolescent Research* 23, no. 1 (2008): 6–30.

Harry and Sally are the type of kids every parent hopes for. They were truly outstanding in their youth and high school years. Both were excellent students, active in their faith, and good athletes. Harry was an Eagle Scout and a triple letterman in sports. He was the captain of his high school football and baseball teams. Upon graduation from high school, each enrolled in a small Catholic college.

When they arrived on campus, both remained very active in their faith life and they were excelling academically. Sally was a varsity athlete. Before long, Harry met Sally and they fell madly in love. Nonetheless, they stuck to their moral code and decided to "save themselves until marriage." During their sophomore year, they attended the same study abroad program. Soon, they were certain that they had met the person of their dreams and that there was no need to postpone marriage until after graduation. So Harry and Sally were married during the summer before the start of their junior year.

The anticipated delightful newlywed period was cut short by an unexpected visitor in their home—pornography. Sally discovered Harry looking at pornography during their honeymoon. She felt betrayed; after all, this was their honeymoon. They had saved themselves for this moment. Harry was supposed to be attracted to her. Immediately, tension was introduced into their marriage. Nonetheless, Sally tried to dismiss it as a "guy thing."

Before long, school resumed and Sally was very busy. Between classes, practice, and travel to away games, Sally was frequently away from home. With significant time alone, a computer, and an Internet connection, Harry's pornography consumption skyrocketed. Before long, he discovered that he actually preferred pornography to his physical relationship with Sally. He looked forward to her away games and practices. When she was home, he looked forward to her going to bed so that he could stay awake and spend time on his computer.

Little more than a year into their marriage, Harry and Sally were in trouble. Sally had discovered the truth about Harry's pornography consumption. She began to "hate the moment he walked through the door." Harry's consumption progressed to "harder" forms of pornography. Before long, he began to think he had made a major mistake. After all, he had been quite the athlete himself and girls still took notice. He could be scoring big-time with the ladies right now. Harry thought to himself, "It's never easier than college, right?" Suddenly, Harry and Sally's marriage was on the brink.

At this moment, Harry and Sally received another unexpected guest. Sally conceived a child. Harry's response: "I don't think I'm ready to be a dad. I think I'm going to leave you." Sally miscarried a week later. She told Harry she had had enough. He wasn't the man she fell in love with. He wasn't the man she married.

Harry was a mess. He had a full-blown addiction to pornography. His marriage of two years was done. He was failing most of his classes in college. He had lost most of his friendships, since he preferred time on his computer with pornography to time with them. Furthermore, Harry was guilt stricken. He had been a man of faith his entire life. Pornography was not consistent with his moral code. Yet he felt powerless to do anything about it. Before long, Harry was considering taking his own life.

Fortunately, the story of Harry and Sally has a happy ending. Harry found the help he needed and turned his life around. He reconciled with Sally and eventually completed his college degree. Together, they had children and now live a wonderful family life together.

Is the story of Harry and Sally unique, or does it illustrate a fundamental reality? Let's start with Sally. She felt betrayed. Indeed, she considered Harry's pornography consumption tantamount to infidelity: "I was competing with those girls in Harry's mind. Every time we were together, I knew he was really thinking of them."

Many women respond in a very similar way. A study by the Gallup Poll indicates that fewer than one-third of Americans believe pornography consumption to be "morally acceptable."[16] I conducted a nonrandom, nonscientific survey of practicing Christian married women attending a couples program. Almost four out of five women, 78 percent, considered pornography consumption to be a type of infidelity.[17]

Considering the large portion of women who consider pornography consumption to be infidelity, it is not surprising to discover a correlation between pornography consumption and divorce. Men who view pornography five or more times in a month are over three times more likely to be separated or divorced from their wives versus those who never view pornography—46.5 percent versus 12.7 percent, respectively (see Figure 2.2).[18] Given the prevalence of pornography consumption, it is not surprising to discover that a survey of the American Academy of Matrimonial Lawyers identified "obsessive interest in pornography" to be a contributing factor in over half of all divorces, 56 percent, in the United States.[19]

Amazingly, neurological studies point to the same reality.[20] Pornographic images viewed with the eye travel down the optic nerve to reach the brain, where they are processed as if they were a real event. They bypass the neocortex and go straight from the thalamus to the amygdala, which is the part of the brain that processes emotion. As such, sexually stimulating images are processed by the brain at the emotional level, not at the rational level. Within one-fifth of a second, a neurochemical cocktail is released in the brain that mimics the neurochemicals released during sexual intercourse: testosterone, vasopressin, oxytocin, epinephrine, norepinephrine, and dopamine. The mirror neuron system in the brain activates, and the brain experiences something of a virtual neurochemical sexual encounter.

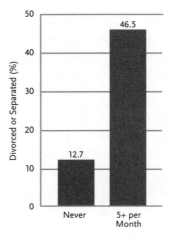

Figure 2.2: Pornography and Marital Disruption
Source: General Social Survey, 1972–2012.

During an actual sexual encounter, the brain's reward circuitry activates and the neurotransmitter dopamine is released.[21] Since we will encounter this reward circuitry and neurotransmitter dopamine on several occasions along our journey, we should take a moment to better understand them. The caudate nucleus helps a person to perceive and distinguish between rewards. The attainment of these rewards triggers the release of dopamine, which is a cocaine-like substance. As such, the brain experiences something of a neurochemical high each time it receives a dumping of dopamine, which reinforces a behavior so that it will be repeated in the future. Dopamine is secreted in the ventral tegmental area and released in the nucleus accumbens.

Regarding sex, our brain is wired to motivate us to find union with the opposite sex. When we attain this union, our brain releases dopamine to reward and reinforce the behavior. Reproduction of the species is a good thing.

Mimicking an actual sexual encounter, pornography consumption also releases dopamine in the brain, which has necessary consequences.[22] First, since our brain's reward circuitry is activated, we are primed to do it again. Second, our brain builds a tolerance to dopamine. As such, when frequently activated, it takes ever-greater quantities of dopamine to achieve the same neurochemical high, which drives the individual to consume greater quantities and harder types of pornography to achieve the same neurochemical impact.

The increased tolerance to dopamine has real consequences for a man's sex life. Dopamine activates the sexual centers in the hypothalamus, which send a signal to the erection centers located in a man's spinal cord. The erection center in the spinal cord then sends a signal so that the man is able to attain an erection. When the brain builds tolerance to dopamine, this pathway is short-circuited. The "normal release" of dopamine doesn't do the trick. The sexual centers in the hypothalamus are not activated, which means no signal is sent to the erection centers in the spinal cord. As counterintuitive as it sounds, consumption of large quantities of pornography leads to a loss of interest in sex. One survey indicated that over half of the men heavily involved in cyberpornography have lost interest in intercourse with a real woman.[23]

Furthermore, the need to consume ever-greater quantities of pornography to achieve the same neurochemical high frequently leads to social isolation. The time spent viewing pornography crowds out all other activities and people. Since social isolation is a major risk factor for depression, it is not surprising that individuals consuming large quantities of pornography are more likely to be depressed. Indeed, data from the General Social Survey indicates that individuals who view pornography five times a month or more are almost four times more likely to be depressed versus those who never view pornography—23.9 percent versus 6.0 percent, respectively (see Figure 2.3).[24]

This is the science behind Harry and Sally's life. Virtual infidelity. Sexual dysfunction. Social isolation. Depression. Pornography takes a toll on individuals and it takes a toll on couples. It's not surprising that half of divorce lawyers say pornography is a major issue in divorces today.

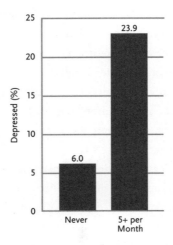

Figure 2.3: Pornography and Depression
Source: General Social Survey, 1972–2012.

Beyond Fidelity to Honor

The "one flesh" union of husband and wife is certainly central to the marriage covenant. However, I do not know any couple that defines marriage simply based upon the physical union of husband and wife. Marriage is about the entire life that the couple shares together. When a couple falls in love, the desire of the heart is to be with the other person as much as possible. It is the desire to share a life together. As such, we must consider the whole life of the couple.

It is interesting that in Catholic wedding ceremonies, the bridegroom and bride are asked three "questions of consent" before they are allowed to pronounce their vows. I'll be honest, I sometimes have a little fun with this one. If you think couples don't remember their wedding vows, imagine their response to this question: "Could you tell me the three questions of consent you were asked in the wedding ceremony?"

The standard response is "What?"

Then I give them a break, realizing that many simply do not recognize the theological jargon. So I begin to explain, "You know. Before you pronounced your vows, the priest asked you some questions."

Suddenly the lights turn on. "Yeah. Yeah. I remember that."

To which I respond, "Okay. Can you tell me the questions?"

The lights turn off—way off. There isn't the faintest glimmer of a sparkle in their eyes. I have yet to find a single person who could recall all three questions! Nonetheless, these three questions are critically important. In many ways, they help us to understand the vows that the bridegroom and bride pronounce.

The first question establishes that the couple is entering into marriage of their own free will, without the coercion of another party: "Have you come here freely and without reservation to give yourselves to each other in marriage?" In ages past and in certain cultures where arranged marriages were the norm, this question was essential. In most Western countries today, it is fairly safe to assume that bridegroom and bride freely choose to enter into marriage with each other. Nonetheless, the question is still absolutely relevant to every couple. The key words are "give yourself." In marriage, we are called to give ourselves away.

The second question helps us to understand why we give ourselves away: "Will you love and honor each other as husband and wife all the days of your life?" The wording of the question is once again critically important. It pairs "love" together with "honor." Love is not simply an emotion. It is more like an interior force that draws me out of myself and drives me to another person. It urges me to be good to the other person. To make the life of the other person better. To build up the other person, which is another way of saying to honor the other person. That's the point. I'm drawn out of a preoccupation with my own interests and desires as I become focused on making someone else's life better. Indeed, I'm called to give my life to make the life of my spouse better.

Now, let's get practical. How am I going to build up or give honor to my spouse? First and foremost, I honor my spouse by the life I choose to live for myself. Indeed, in many ways, the life of husband or wife reflects upon the other person. They share in each other's glory and they share in each other's misery. I promise you that when a man marries an outstanding woman, he takes tremendous pride when his friends tell him, "You certainly married up."

If the life I live gives honor to my spouse, what would happen if I lived a really, really good life? Let's be so bold as to ask, "What would happen if I lived a perfect life?" Interestingly enough, Scripture defines perfection in a surprising way:

> If any one makes no mistakes in what he says he is a perfect man. . . . For every kind of beast . . . can be tamed . . . but no human being can tame the tongue. . . . With it we bless the Lord and Father, and with it we curse men, who are made in the likeness of God. . . . This ought not to be so (James 3:2–10).

That's it? Perfection simply means I control my tongue? Sounds easy, right? Go give it a try! Indeed, your brain—especially the brain of men—has circuitry destined to frustrate you. There's a special area in the male hypothalamus that helps you identify the opportunity to put someone else down and make yourself look good. It is the "one-upmanship" area.[25] It might come in handy in competitive situations, but it can wreak havoc in a marriage. Get it under control and it will transform your life. Let me tell you the story of Edith Stein.

Edith Stein was an amazing woman who lived a life worthy of a major motion picture. She was born in Germany to devout Jewish parents in 1891 on the Jewish feast of Yom Kippur. Nonetheless, by age sixteen, she had become an atheist. She was brilliant from her youth and received a PhD in philosophy at a time when most women received little or no formal education. While staying with some Christian friends, she was unable to sleep and spent the entire night reading the autobiography of St. Teresa of Ávila. In the morning, she declared, "This is the truth." Within six months, she was baptized and entered the Catholic Church.

She desired to become a Carmelite nun like St. Teresa of Ávila, but was dissuaded by a spiritual director. She began teaching history at a Dominican girls' high school and speaking extensively, especially on women's topics. When Hitler's Law for the Restoration of the Professional Civil Service took effect on April 7, 1933, Edith Stein was no longer able to teach. As such, she was free to fulfill her desire to become a Carmelite nun.

Together with her sister Rosa, she set out for the Carmelite convent in Cologne. When Hitler's full fury was directed toward the Jews, she and Rosa were smuggled across the border into the Netherlands. Nonetheless, Edith and Rosa were arrested by the Gestapo on August 2, 1942. They were sent to Auschwitz and died in the gas chambers. Pope John Paul II canonized her as a saint on October 11, 1998.

Talk about a dramatic life! All packed within fifty-one short years! Nonetheless, behind the melodrama and geopolitical events is the story of a young girl learning to use the gifts she had received for the benefit of others. She was learning the art of building other people up.

Edith had been gifted with a brilliant mind. From her youth, she could discern the logic of an argument and discern the path of conversation. Edith was also gifted with a sharp tongue. If you made a mistake in your logic or reasoning, she would run ahead of you in the conversation, wait for you to arrive, and then hand you your head on a silver platter! It was not a particularly endearing trait.

When Edith received her PhD, she was the star student and assistant to Edmund Husserl, one of Europe's leading philosophers. Academic success seemed assured. Nonetheless, she was denied tenure. There were many factors at work, not the least of which were the facts that Edith was Jewish and she was a woman. Edith was crushed. She expected her mentor to share in her shock. Instead, she received a statement that would change her life: "Edith, perhaps it is best for you to move on. Here, you have alienated so many people by your sharp tongue and harsh comments. Perhaps a fresh start for you would be good."

This became a moment of soul searching for Edith. She decided that she had used the gifts she had been given incorrectly. If she had been given a keen intellect and sharp tongue, they were called to protect other people, not tear them down. She promised that henceforth, when she saw someone heading down a line of reasoning that would get them in trouble, she would run in front of them to protect them. She would change the line of reasoning, or change the subject, or deflect criticism. She lived this promise so well that she became a saint.

Imagine the difference it would make in your marriage if you and your spouse both agreed to follow the resolution of Edith Stein. When Shelly and I were dating, I told her this story. I told her that I would always do my best to follow the example of Edith Stein and never consciously use my speech to hurt or tear her down. Shelly later told me that it was at that moment she knew she wanted to marry me.

Shelly made the same promise to me. Through the years, issues invariably arise. Fortunately, we have a promise that prevents the mind from questioning the other person's good intentions. We also have a great starting point for resolution, "Honey, I know that you would never consciously hurt me . . ." Little things, if they are the right little things, can make a big difference—just ask Naaman the Syrian.

"Until Death Do Us Part"

No discussion of the wedding vows would be complete unless we consider those five little words that bring the marriage vow to its conclusion, "Until death do us part." Let's be honest, in the vast, vast majority of marriages, "death" is the furthest thing from the minds of the bride and groom. Truth be told, the bride can't see past the reception. The groom can't see past the honeymoon. Couples simply do not get married thinking about "death." They are in love and it is inconceivable that their love could ever end. Indeed, one of the most popular Scriptural passages read at weddings captures this thought very well:

> If I have not love, I gain nothing. Love is patient and kind; love is not jealous or boastful; it is not arrogant or rude. Love does not insist on its own way; it is not irritable or resentful; it does not rejoice at wrong, but rejoices in the right. Love bears all things, believes all things, hopes all things, endures all things. Love never ends (1 Corinthians 13:3–8).

Couples select this reading because it resonates with the sentiments of their hearts. Deep within the heart is the understanding of a profound truth: true love is permanent. It does not end. The desire of the heart is to personally experience this profound love. To receive it and to give it.

This very deep need has found its way into popular culture. Books and movies abound with tales of men or women who have sacrificed everything for love—fame, family, fortune. Scripture even states, "If a man should give all the substance of his house for love, he shall despise it as nothing" (Song of Solomon 8:7). Very strong words, but they resonate with the heart. Each of us hopes that we would be capable of sacrificing everything for true love and we hope that someone else would be willing to do it for us. Indeed, this is the standard established for marriage:

> Husbands, love your wives, as Christ loved the church and gave himself up for her, that he might sanctify her . . . that he might present the church to himself in splendor, without spot or wrinkle or any such thing, that she might be holy and without blemish" (Ephesians 5:25–27).

Ouch! Surely this is just a goal. A noble idea. Something to be aspired to. Scripture can't possibly be serious. Actually, Scripture is very serious and this noble idea has been lived to the end more frequently than imagined. I would like to mention a couple of stories from one of the most famous tragedies in history, the *Titanic*.

The *Titanic* set sail from Southampton, England, at noon on April 10, 1912. It was the world's largest and most luxurious ocean liner. After brief stops in France and Ireland, the *Titanic* headed into the open waters of the Atlantic carrying 2,224 passengers and crew.

The first three days of the crossing were uneventful until the *Titanic* encountered a major cold front with blustery winds and eight-foot waves. After several hours, the front gave way to a clear, calm, bitterly cold night. In the calm of the night, April 14, 1912, at 11:40 p.m. ship time, the *Titanic* struck an iceberg. The lifeboats on the *Titanic* had a total capacity of 1,178 people, or approximately one-half of the passengers actually on board. The order was given, "Women and children first." As a result, 69 percent of the women and children were saved while only 18 percent of the men were saved. Indeed, many couples arrived at the lifeboats together only to find a seat offered to just one of them.

One such couple was Lucian and Eloise Smith, who were returning from their honeymoon.[26] Lucian was the heir to a prominent mining family and fortune. Eloise was the daughter of West Virginia's Congressman James Hughes. They met in January 1912 and were married within a month. For their honeymoon, they decided to set off for a grand European tour. When Eloise conceived a child, they decided to cut short the honeymoon and head home on the *Titanic*.

When the *Titanic* struck the iceberg, Lucian woke his pregnant wife and asked her to dress warmly. He calmly nudged her out of the stateroom, declaring there was no time to gather her jewels, "just trifles." When they arrived at the lifeboats, she was offered a seat. He was not. She protested. He insisted, "I never expected to ask you to obey, but this is one time that you must." He asked her to get into the lifeboat, stating that he would catch a later boat. As they lowered Lifeboat 6, his parting words to her were "Keep your hands in your pockets—it is very cold weather." After a last wave, Lucian Philip Smith disappeared into the icy waters of the Atlantic along with the *Titanic*. Eloise survived and gave birth to a son, Lucian Smith, Jr., later that year. Lucian Smith was willing to give his life for his bride.

When I tell this story, I get very different reactions from the men and the women. Men love the thought of Lucian giving his life to save the life of his young bride and their future son. The ability to remain calm, to forgo fortune, to remain focused on the lifeboat, the parting words focused on the good of someone else. Men see in this story the image of masculine love.

Women hate this story. They have no problem with Lucian. They have a problem with Eloise. Sure, she's pregnant and she needs to think about the life of the baby, but . . . they hold women to the same standard as men. They expect women to go to the end of love. They expect women to be willing to sacrifice everything for love—fame, family, and fortune. And, yes, life itself. So, I tell them another story from the *Titanic*.

Isidor and Ida Straus were also traveling first class.[27] They had already lived a long and wonderful life together. Isidor was sixty-seven and Ida six-ty-three when they set sail on the *Titanic*. They had been married for for-ty-one years. Together, they had seven children and countless grandchildren.

Isidor had been a congressman from New York and the co-owner of Macy's Department Store in New York City. They were traveling back to the United States after having "wintered" in France.

After the *Titanic* struck the iceberg, Isidor, Ida, and their maid, Ellen Bird, made their way to Lifeboat 8. Ida and Ellen were offered seats. Isidor was denied one. Ida refused to get into the lifeboat and said, "I will not be separated from my husband. As we have lived, so will we die, together." Ida took off her fur coat and handed it to Ellen, stating, "I won't be needing this tonight." Ellen entered the lifeboat and survived. Isidor and Ida joined arms, walked to the upper deck, and were last seen arm in arm shortly before the *Titanic* disappeared into the waters of the Atlantic. "Until death do us part." The survivors of the tragedy were touched by what they called a "most remarkable exhibition of love and devotion."

Once again, I receive very different reactions to this story. Men hate this story. They believe their job is to save the life of their bride—even if it means sacrificing their own life. Women love this story. A woman willing to go to the end of love to remain one with her husband speaks to their hearts.

If you think about the very different reactions of men and women to these two stories, the same mystery is revealed. Deep within the human heart is the desire to experience a love that goes to the end. When we do so, we are transformed and so are others.

* * *

Imagine the profound difference it would make to your life and your marriage if

- Both spouses were faithful to each other in their minds as well as with their bodies?
- Both spouses sought to protect the vulnerabilities of each other and never exploit them?
- Both spouses were willing to go to the end of love, willing to sacrifice everything—fame, family, fortune, and even life itself?

The first step, honor your wedding vows, will certainly help you to "divorceproof" your marriage. It will also point it in the direction of superabundance. We've just begun. We have six steps to go.

CHAPTER THREE

STEP TWO:
Use Money for Others

The second step to a superabundant marriage is to use money for other people. Okay. We've gone from sex to money, which is from bad to worse. You don't think so? One time I was listening to a conversation by a group of men who were discussing the very issue from the previous chapter that gets you an express ticket to the divorce lawyer. They were having a very open conversation about cheating on their wives. Which ones had cheated, which was surprisingly high. Which ones were willing to cheat if the right opportunity presented itself. Which ones were determined to remain faithful, which was disappointingly low. In the midst of the conversation, one of the men spoke up. "I'd love to have a fling, but there's just one problem: my wife. She told me if she ever caught me having sex with another woman, she would divorce me and take half my money. I love money more than sex so I just can't do it!"

People are very sensitive about their money. I remember several years ago, I was newly hired into the petroleum industry. Over dinner with a very successful retail marketer, we were discussing how new government regulations would force the closure of a large number of smaller, family-owned gasoline stations. Armed with a freshly printed MBA and buzzwords such as "efficient market," I was explaining the "magic" of free markets. There were too many small stations in the market depressing prices for everyone. Once these stations closed, prices would increase. The remaining stations would be able to afford the new regulations. Everyone would have gas and everything would be great. Without seeing it coming, I suddenly had a perfectly rational gentleman in my face with a stern warning: "The next time you put your hand in someone else's wallet, you had better think about what you are saying!" Fortunately, things calmed down and the evening turned out fine.

Unfortunately, I still have to talk about money. I know. I've been warned! However, money is really important in the life of a couple. That's why the wedding vows include those five wonderful little words, "for richer or for poorer." The language from the sixteenth-century Book of Common Prayer was even more pointed, "with all my worldly goods I thee endow." Money and how it is used can be a source of great joy or tremendous misery. As such, if you truly want a superabundant marriage, then you simply have to tackle the issue of money.

Money and Marital Stress

Throughout history money has been one of the leading causes of tension between spouses. In the previous chapter, we looked at a study identifying the behaviors that lead to divorce. The results are reproduced in Table 3.1. These results indicate that the improper use of money was the second leading cause for women divorcing their husbands, almost tripling the likelihood of getting divorced. Although husbands were slightly more forgiving, the improper use of money was still a major source of tension in the life of a couple.

Behavior	Women	Men	Average
Infidelity	299%	363%	331%
Use Money Foolishly	187%	77%	132%
Drug/Alcohol Abuse	183%	216%	200%
Becomes Jealous	130%	101%	116%
Not Home Enough	105%	-NA-	52%
Critical Attitude	98%	93%	96%
Irritating Habits	92%	127%	110%

Table 3.1: Reasons for Divorce
Note: Table values are the percentage change in the odds of divorce. An increased probability of 100% indicates a doubling in the probability of divorce.
Source: Amato, P. R., and Rogers, S. J. "A Longitudinal Study of Marital Problems and Subsequent Divorce," *Journal of Marriage and Family* 59 (1997): 612–624.

Although infidelity is the most certain route to divorce court, historically a smaller percentage of couples were impacted by infidelity than by financial stress. According to data from the General Social Survey, 19.4 percent of the individuals married during the 1970s were unfaithful to their spouse at some point during the course of their marriage.[1] By comparison, a recent survey by National Public Radio, the Robert Wood Johnson Foundation, and the Harvard School of Public Health revealed that 49 percent of the respondents had experienced major stress in the past year. Of these, 53 percent cited financial stress as a contributing factor.[2] Put those two numbers together and you discover that approximately one-quarter of all couples experience financial stress *every year*! Let me emphasize, every year almost 25 percent of couples experience financial stress, which means the vast majority of couples will experience financial stress at some point during their married life.

Financial stress can be particularly intense during the newlywed period when bridegroom and bride try to blend two lifestyles and two bank accounts into one married life. A study of over 1,000 newlywed husbands and wives revealed financial issues to be the number one source of tension.[3] The top five issues (including a three-way tie for #5) are listed in Table 3.2.

Behavior	Women	Men	Average
Preexisting Debt	19%	18%	18.5%
Balance Work & Marriage	18%	19%	18.5%
Spousal Relation Frequency	13%	14%	13.5%
Husband's Job	12%	14%	13%
Financial Decisions	13%	12%	12.5%
In-Laws	13%	12%	12.5%
Household Tasks	13%	12%	12.5%

Table 3.2: Source of Newlywed Tension
Source: Schramm, D. et al., "After 'I Do': The Newlywed Transition," *Marriage and Family Review*, 38 (2005): 45–67.

A quick look at this chart reveals that we have indeed gone from bad to worse. Four of the top issues causing tension for newlyweds relate to money in some way: preexisting debt, balancing work and marriage, the husband's job, and financial decision making. Only one of the top five issues related to sex: the frequency of spousal relations. Money is a bigger issue than sex, at least for newlyweds!

At the top of this list is preexisting debt brought into the marriage. Researchers identified four areas of preexisting debt that caused stress: credit card debt, car loans, student loans, and medical expenses.[4] For the moment, let's assume that the medical expenses were necessary and that the student loans were a wise investment in the future. Therefore, let's focus on the first two issues, especially credit card debt.

Surveys indicate that the four leading purchases on credit cards are clothing, gasoline, eating out, and travel.[5] Note that these items are consumable goods—meaning they are "used up" or "consumed" almost immediately. When these goods are purchased on a credit card, the item is consumed almost immediately, but the pain of paying keeps going and going and going. This financial dynamic is really hard on your brain. It can actually give you a headache!

Money on Your Brain

Brain imaging studies reveal that when a person considers purchasing a desirable product, the reward circuitry in the brain activates.[6] Indeed, dopamine, that cocaine-like substance we discussed in the previous chapter, is released in the nucleus accumbens. As such, when the brain considers purchasing a desirable product, it anticipates a reward and it receives a little dopamine high.

However, when a person considers paying for a purchase, an entirely different region of the brain activates, the insula.[7] This region of the brain anticipates pain. Indeed, you will only make the purchase if the anticipated reward is greater than the anticipated pain. Think of the last time you were standing in a store unable to make a decision whether to purchase an item or the last time you were online and just couldn't bring yourself to click the

"Purchase Now" button. This was a real-life experience of two competing regions of your brain slugging out a close call.

The secret to the success of credit cards is that they separate the reward of purchasing from the pain of paying. Suddenly, the wonderful evening out doesn't cost a couple of hundred bucks. It only costs $6.91 for 36 months at 15 percent interest! Unfortunately, a couple of hours later, the evening is over and the reward is gone, but your brain is left with the pain of paying for the next three years. Talk about a headache! Literally. People experiencing financial stress are almost three times more likely to experience migraine headaches compared with those who don't have financial stress.[8]

But here's the really bad news. Preexisting credit card debt is even harder on the newlywed spouse. Think about it. You charge up your credit cards traveling, eating out, entertaining. You have a wonderful time. Then you get married. Your spouse received none of the reward, but he or she receives all of the pain of paying. And it keeps going and going and going. No wonder preexisting debt, especially credit card debt, is at the top of the list of issues for newlywed couples.

However, the consequences of debt and financial stress aren't limited to newlywed couples. The reality is essentially the same for all couples. The decision to reap the reward of purchasing now and delay the pain of paying until later introduces stress into marriages. As such, it is not surprising that studies indicate that debt and financial stress lead to lower levels of marital satisfaction and higher levels of marital discord.[9] Debt is hard on marriages.

It is also very hard on the individual. An Associated Press and America Online poll revealed that financial stress impacts the health of the individual from head to toe.[10] A particularly large toll is taken on the mental and emotional life of the individual. Anxiety increases by 625 percent and depression by 475 percent. The cardiovascular system is impacted. Heart arrhythmias increase by 100 percent and high blood pressure by 27 percent. Generalized stress hits the gut and back in a very powerful way, especially in men. Ulcers and digestive issues increase by 238 percent and back and muscle tension increase by 65 percent. Furthermore, when you try to take a break from your worries, you just can't turn them off. Insomnia increases by

129 percent. As P. T. Barnum reportedly said, "Money is a terrible master, but an excellent servant."[11]

Nonetheless, Americans continue to rack up debt at unprecedented levels. Although the financial crisis of 2008 and the ensuing Great Recession was a wake-up call for many Americans regarding debt, the change in behavior was surprisingly small. On the positive side, Americans seem to have learned that you don't need to accept every credit card application received in the mail and that it's a really bad idea to max out the credit cards once you receive them. As a result, credit card debt, in relative terms, has fallen for the past several years. Unfortunately, credit card debt has frequently been channeled into other areas and consumer debt is now at record levels (see Figure 3.1). Let's put these numbers in perspective. Immediately after World War II, consumer credit in the United States equaled 3.74 percent of personal income. Today, consumer credit stands at 21.86 percent of personal income, an almost sixfold increase! Debt is taking an incredible toll on individuals and couples.

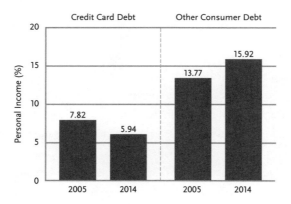

Figure 3.1: Consumer Debt
Source: The Federal Reserve Statistical Release, Series G.19; Bureau of Economic Analysis, Table 2.1: Personal Income and Its Disposition.

Balancing Work and Family

The need to balance work and family demands was the other issue at the top of the survey as a major cause of stress for newlywed couples. Nonetheless, this issue doesn't just impact newlywed couples. Indeed, it is hard to find a single couple in the United States that is not struggling with this issue on some level.

Recent studies indicate that Americans are working harder than ever before. Today the average full-time worker in the United States works approximately 47 hours per week[12] and just over 1,700 hours per year.[13] These amounts are substantially higher than workers in the three largest economies in Europe (see Figure 3.2). Indeed, the average for those three economies is 1,511 hours per year. Americans work almost 5 additional 40-hour weeks per year compared to this average. Furthermore, Americans are bringing more work home, working more frequently on weekends, and skipping more vacation time than other countries.[14, 15]

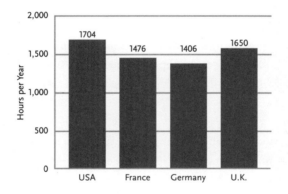

Figure 3.2: Average Annual Hours Worked
Source: Federal Reserve Bank of St. Louis, Economic Research, Average Annual Hours Worked by Persons Engaged in the United States.

Not surprisingly, this creates serious challenges for families. Consider just one important area, the ability to sit down and have dinner together as a family. Just over half of teenagers (57 percent) eat dinner together with their families at least five nights a week or more.[16] Indeed, teenagers actually desire to eat family dinners together more frequently.[17] The number one reason they don't—parents working late.[18]

Nonetheless, the challenges of balancing professional demands with family obligations go further. The digital and technological revolution of the past generation have made it easier than ever for workers to remain plugged in and harder than ever for workers to check out. Surveys[19, 20] indicate that four out of five workers (80 percent) continue to work after they have left the office. Almost seven out of ten of workers (69 percent) will not go to bed without checking their work emails first. Almost three out of five workers (57 percent) check their work emails while they are on family outings. Furthermore, almost one-half (46 percent) of workers check their work email when they are home on a sick day. As such, it is not surprising that almost one-half (49 percent) of workers say that it is hard for them to disconnect from work while they are at home and on weekends. Taken altogether, the average worker spends an additional seven hours per week working from home.

Technology has brought work into our homes on an unprecedented scale, making the need to balance work and family life more important than ever. Nonetheless, many individuals feel trapped. Indeed, almost half of workers report that either their employer or their customers demand that they remain accessible at all times.[21, 22] We need to find another way.

Finding Time for Family

Riley Leggett also faced the challenge of balancing work and family life. Yet he was able to eat dinner with his family every night. A few years after I married his daughter, I had the opportunity to talk with Riley about how he was able to balance these competing demands. Considering my previous poor performance, I waded in cautiously.

"Riley, a few years ago I asked you the secret to a happy marriage. You told me to sit in church with my family every Sunday and eat dinner with my family every night. Shelly and I met in church, so I think we have that one covered. Can you tell me a little more about the need to eat dinner with my family?"

In one of those rare and precious moments, an incredible man opened a bit of his heart.

"You know, I grew up during the Depression. People today can't understand how difficult those days were. My dad owned a small store, but he couldn't turn his back on his friends. He continued to give them what they needed, even when they couldn't pay. Eventually, he gave away everything and had to close the store.

"To say we didn't have much doesn't do it justice. Lots of days, we just didn't have any food. So, we all went to bed hungry. John fainted from hunger one day while he was hoeing a row of cotton. That's what we did to try to get by.

"You know, if you ever go to bed hungry, truly hungry, just once in your life, it will change your life forever. I vowed to myself that not one of my kids would ever go to bed hungry."

Suddenly, Riley's life came into perspective. Working his way through college. Walking miles to school at the University of Texas. Night school at the University of Houston. Pounding the pavement in the heat and humidity of Houston. Working his way into a partnership at a small manufacturing company. The meaning of these events became clear. But Riley continued.

"You know, you don't ever forget days like that. You don't ever get over them. It wasn't hard for me to work really hard. I was putting in all those long hours. Staying at the office late every night. Coming to the office on the weekends. Then one day, I was sitting in my office and it struck me. Just like a bolt of lightning from the sky. All I ever wanted to be in life was a husband and father. With the war and everything, I wasn't sure if it would work out. Now I was a husband and father and I never saw my wife or kids because all I did was work! That very day, I walked out onto the shop floor and called together all the employees and told them, 'From this day forward, we are going to work very hard from 8 a.m. until 5:30 p.m. What we can't get done in that time will have to wait until tomorrow because at 5:30 p.m., I'm locking the door and we're all going home to have dinner with our families.'"

Later I asked Shelly if her dad had kept that promise. She said, "Yeah. Dad pretty much had dinner with us every night. He also made our lunches for school and dropped us off on the way to work every day."

Feeding an Insatiable Appetite

I have no question that had Riley decided to continue working nonstop his business could have been even more successful. Furthermore, Riley was certainly driven to succeed. As such, he had to consciously choose between the motivation for success at work and time with his family. The chemistry in our brain makes this choice more difficult than many people realize.

The motivation to succeed is tied to the brain's reward circuitry. As we've already seen, this system provides the brain with a dumping of dopamine to reward and reinforce a behavior. The body has a host of hormones designed to help drive you to your goal so that your brain can receive its dopamine reward. Key among these is testosterone. Whenever we compete, testosterone is released into the blood stream. Testosterone helps to increase our mental activity and focus our attention on our goal. Furthermore, it also helps to increase energy so that we have an inexhaustible drive to achieve our goal. Once we attain our goal, testosterone levels surge, simultaneously enhancing the effects of dopamine and preparing us to begin the cycle all over again.[23] This is the thrill of victory.

Unfortunately, our brain's reward circuitry is a dual-edged sword. As we saw in the previous chapter, our brain builds a tolerance to dopamine, which means our brain requires an ever-greater victory to produce the same dopamine high. This poses a major problem. What happens when there is no greater victory? This is an issue for many professional athletes and teams that reach the pinnacle—the gold medal in the Olympics or the World Series or the Super Bowl. No greater victory is possible, and winning a second time just isn't the same. Many struggle with the motivation necessary to stay at the very top of their sport.

Money, however, is a different story. Essentially, there is no upper limit. A greater victory is always possible. Suddenly, a dynamic is set up where incredibly successful individuals continue to chase ever-greater successes. They truly become addicted to success. Is this a real issue? Yes! To illustrate, consider a study done by the United Bank of Switzerland of wealthy individuals. Approximately three out of every four individuals (72 percent) with a net wealth between $1 million to $5 million did *not* consider themselves wealthy. Furthermore, 40 percent of the individuals with a net wealth of over $5 million did *not* consider themselves wealthy.[24] Let me put this in context. These individuals are above the 99.9 percentile of the wealthiest individuals in the wealthiest country on Earth during a period of its greatest wealth generation—and almost half of them do *not* think they are wealthy. What's up?

Obviously, there are many factors involved, but a good starting point is to understand how these individuals defined being wealthy. The most common definition was "no financial constraints."[25] Let's think about that definition for a moment. Certainly individuals with $5 million in net wealth have far fewer financial constraints than the average person, but . . . have you seen Tiger Woods's new yacht? It has a $20 million sticker price, which doesn't include staff, maintenance, or docking. How about Larry Ellison, the founder of Oracle? He purchased 98 percent of Hawaii's sixth largest island, Lanai. If the true definition of wealth is "no financial constraints," then $5 million isn't close and that's part of the problem.

Studies indicate that as wealth increases, so do expectations.[26, 27] A person begins by wanting to make $1 million. When they do, they discover it won't get close to buying them the toys of the ultrarich. It won't get close to paying for the maintenance on the toys of the ultrarich. So the goal increases, and then increases again and again and again. I suppose that it is possible to make enough money so that there are no financial constraints, and it appears that a very small group of individuals have attained that goal. Nonetheless, the amount of money it takes to reach that threshold is much higher than most people assume, and the odds of achieving it are incredibly small.

There's another major issue with adopting the philosophy that money is just a means of keeping score in the game of financial success—there is an incredible skew of wealth at the top of the financial charts. Although a net wealth of $5 million will place you above the 99.9 percentile of all Americans, you will only have 0.006 percent of Bill Gates's $80 billion in wealth. Indeed, if your net wealth were $1 billion, making you one of the approximately 1,550 billionaires in the world, your net wealth would still be only 1.2 percent of Bill Gates's wealth. Your net wealth would still be significantly closer to the poorest person on Earth than the richest—not that I'm going to give you much sympathy. If keeping up with the Joneses—or the Gateses—is your game, it is going to be much more difficult than you can imagine.

Indeed, long before brain scanners and the science of neurology, Scripture nailed the fundamental truth we are discussing: "The eye of the covetous [or greedy] man is insatiable . . . he will not be satisfied till he consume his own soul" (Sirach 14:9). Insatiable. Incredibly strong word. Approximately 2,200 years ago, Scripture nailed the neurological truth that if your mind is set upon money, then you will never get enough. Furthermore, the relentless pursuit of money can easily lead to your ruin. Therefore, Scripture advises us, "If riches increase, set not your heart on them" (Psalm 62:10). Fortunately, there is another path.

Money and Happiness

Okay, enough of the bad news about money. Now for some good news. Although it is very hard to win the financial success game, you don't need to. You don't need the money of the ultrarich or their toys to be happy. There is a relationship between money and happiness, but it is much different and less complex than most people expect. Numerous researchers have investigated the relationship between money and happiness. In general, their studies find a very simple and very basic relationship: Increased wealth leads to increased happiness until basic needs are met. After that point, other factors become more important.

Consider one study where researchers looked at the happiness and wealth of different groups of individuals from around the world.[28] A summary of their results is presented in Figure 3.3. Not surprisingly, individuals in the Forbes 400 are generally happy with their lives, averaging 5.8 on a 7-point scale. However, please note that they are not perfectly happy. Earlier we saw that many individuals define wealth as having no financial constraints. Although we didn't define the number, I feel quite confident the billionaires in the Forbes 400 have attained that threshold. Nonetheless, they are not perfectly happy. Furthermore, the Amish in Pennsylvania and a native tribe in Greenland (Inuit) are just as happy as the Forbes 400, scoring 5.8 on the 7-point scale. Even more surprising, a random sampling of Swedish individuals attains almost the same score (5.6). True to our simple principle about meeting needs, college students—who notoriously struggle to make ends meet—report a lower happiness score (4.9). Finally, those individuals not having even their basic needs met—the homeless in California or Calcutta—are not happy at all, scoring 2.9 on the 7-point scale.

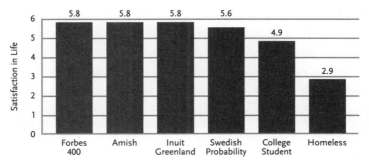

Figure 3.3: Money and Happiness
Source: Diener, E., and Seligman, M. E. P., "Beyond Money: Toward an Economy of Well-Being," *Psychological Science in the Public Interest* 5, no. 1 (2004): 1–31

From this study we clearly see that money is important to a certain level, but then other issues come into play. Before discussing the other issues, let's talk just money. There is obviously a massive difference between the Forbes 400, who are all billionaires, and the Amish, or the native Inuit in Greenland, or a random Swede. As such, it is appropriate to ask, "What is the threshold above which money does *not* influence happiness?" Believe it or not, the number is surprisingly low. You don't need to be a billionaire. You don't need to be a millionaire. You don't even need half a million. According to data from the General Social Survey, individuals with a net wealth of between $250,000 and $500,000 are happier with their lives than individuals with a net wealth above $5 million.[29] That's good news. Although $250,000 to $500,000 is not insignificant, it is within the realm of possibility for a large portion of general society.

Now the *really* good news. The other issues that researchers tie to happiness are actually free. This fact gets lost because researchers use big terms like *social connectedness* and *social interaction*.[30] In layman's terms, the key is family and friends. So forget the toys of the rich and famous. Forget working endless hours and staying plugged in 24/7. Relax. Come home from work and enjoy a little time with family and friends. It will do wonders for your happiness and won't hurt your pocketbook either.

The Life of Riley

This is the truth that Riley Leggett discovered—and he didn't need to plow through all the statistics and studies! Riley kept his promise to have dinner with his family every night and had the time of his life while he did it. Nonetheless, he never forgot his vow that not one of his kids would go to bed hungry. To fulfill that vow, Riley was frugal to a fault and loved to tell his kids, "A dollar saved is a dollar earned." For Riley, it was just the means to fulfill a promise.

This lesson was brought home in a particularly strong way one evening. Shelly and I were taking Riley and Rose Mary out to dinner for Rose Mary's birthday. We were going to one of those fancy restaurants that energy derivatives traders with MBAs visit. As Shelly and I were getting ready for the evening, she said, "I can tell you what my dad is going to order." I said, "Really? I thought your mom and dad have never been there before." Shelly assured me, "They haven't. But I know what my dad will order. The cheapest thing on the menu." I protested, "But what if he doesn't like the cheapest thing on the menu?" Shelly clued me in, "You really don't get it. That's what my dad likes. The cheapest thing on the menu!"

When we arrived at the restaurant, I already knew what I was having. I had eaten there several times before and they had a filet to die for. When they handed us a menu, I scanned down the list as quickly as I could to find the cheapest entrée. It was a chicken dish. To my surprise, Riley was just as fast—and this was his first visit! We both put our menus down at the same time. Boom. When the waiter arrived, sure enough, Riley ordered the cheapest thing on the menu. After he finished, he pushed back from the table and said, "Best meal I ever had."

At a fancy restaurant, you never finish a meal without coffee and dessert. Here come the dessert menus. Even fifteen years ago, dessert was going to run at least $7.50 for a slice of pie. Riley would die before he paid that kind of money for a slice of pie. Mind you, he wanted a piece of pie. This is the same man who ordered pie according to shoe size! In his own home, when he was offered a piece of pie, the standard answer was, "Yes. Give me a piece about the size of my foot." It was size 9. He wanted a big piece of pie.

Shelly is not only a loving wife but also a loving daughter. She came to Riley's rescue. "Dad, they have a blackberry croustade to die for. I'd really like one, but I just don't think I can eat it all. Would you help me?" Riley grabbed the menu. A twinkle returned to his eye. Blackberry croustades were served. Riley was happy and I think he even gave Shelly a bite!

I watched Riley for the rest of his life. When it came to dinner you could count on two things. First, whenever he ate out, Riley ordered the cheapest thing on the menu and it didn't matter if it was a fancy restaurant or McDonald's. Second, after every meal—whether it was at home or out—Riley pushed back from the table and said, "Best meal I ever had."

As he said it, I remembered his other words: "If you ever go to bed hungry just once in your life, it will change you forever."

Riley lived his entire life like this. Shortly before he died, he made a trip to visit an accountant. He took the normal interstate instead of the tollway, which meant sitting in Houston traffic for a long time. I asked him why. His simple answer, "A dollar saved is a dollar earned." I mentioned the story to Shelly and said, "Do you realize your dad is still sacrificing for you kids? At this point, he doesn't have too much longer to live. He doesn't need any money. So every time he makes a sacrifice, it's just so he can give more money as an inheritance. It's still all about his children." Shelly smiled and said, "That's my dad."

Can you imagine the impact that Riley made on his children? Simply put, every one of his children named their firstborn son after Riley.[31] Today, the popular impression is that youths are motivated by everything other than their families—media, music, money, sex, etc. But that's not true. A poll of 13- to 24-year-olds by Associated Press and MTV found out that they look a lot like Riley and Rose Mary's children. Approximately two out of three youths identified one or both of their parents as their heroes.[32]

The Simple Wisdom of Riley

Riley was certainly dedicated to his family and fulfilling his vow that none of his children would go to bed hungry. Furthermore, he was frugal to a fault, which was for him a sacrifice offered to better the life of his children. Nonetheless, I think that it is legitimate to ask how much difference does it make to buy chicken here, or skip a tollroad there? To illustrate the point, let's go out to dinner—of course!

In addition to steak, I love hamburger—specifically bacon cheeseburgers. I have handicapped bacon cheeseburgers all over Houston (as well as a few other cities)! I can tell you which ones are hickory smoked versus mesquite smoked versus chargrilled versus something altogether different. One of my favorite burgers in Houston is Pappas Burger (mesquite smoked with shoestring fries). It's not the most expensive burger in town, but it is considered a gourmet burger, so it's not cheap. I'd like to consider the cost of eating at Pappas Burger versus cooking the same meal at home.

For this example, let's assume that I'll have a bacon cheeseburger with fries. Shelly won't be caught dead with bacon (and its cholesterol) on her burger, so she will have a cheeseburger. She normally upgrades to a salad, but we'll assume fries. The kids will have a couple of kids' meals. Shelly and I will have water, but we will let the kids have a couple of sodas. When eating at home, we'll have the same basic meal, but we'll have lemonade all around and we'll definitely have a big salad.

With tax and tip, this meal costs $53.90 at Pappas Burger. I mentioned that this burger wasn't the cheapest in town, but note the meal does not include any alcohol or desserts. The same meal when cooked at home costs $13.48. You save $40.41 on that one meal. Not bad, but it's not going to make you rich. Now let's assume that you make the decision to skip one similar meal out each week and eat at home. That decision would save you $2,101.32 each year. Now let's assume that you make this decision for eighteen years, from the time your child is born until he or she goes off to college. This one decision would save you $37,823.76, which almost pays for a four-year in-state tuition at the University of Texas in Austin ($42,952 tuition).

Now, imagine that you made similar decisions not only about food and eating out, but about almost everything—like tollroads and cell phone packages and media in your home and clothes. Imagine the amount of money you would save, which means the amount of money you would have, because . . . "A dollar saved is a dollar earned." Welcome to the life of Riley!

Nonetheless, Riley's advice to "eat dinner together every night with your family" impacts much more than your pocketbook. Indeed, sociologists are beginning to understand that eating together as a family impacts in a positive way just about everything you would like to impact in a positive way. Let's just look at four areas comparing two groups of people—those who eat dinner together as a family at least five nights a week and those who eat dinner together as a family two nights a week or fewer.

First, let's look at the area of family relationships. Comparing those who eat dinner together at least five nights per week versus those who eat dinner together two nights a week or fewer, youth are

- twice as likely to spend at least 21 hours with their parents during the week,
- twice as likely to spend at least 30 minutes at dinner with their families,
- sixty percent less likely to have parents who argue a great deal, and
- thirty percent less likely to feel a great deal of stress in their lives.

Second, let's look specifically at the relationship between parents and their children comparing the same two groups. For those who eat dinner together on a regular basis, the youth are

- one and a half more times likely to say that their parents are proud of them,
- thirty percent more likely to have an excellent relationship with their mother,
- sixty percent more likely to have an excellent relationship with their father, and
- forty percent more likely to confide in their parents with a serious problem.

Third, let's consider a major issue for youth today, substance abuse. Compared to those who rarely eat together, youth who eat together at least five nights per week are

- one-third less likely to have tried alcohol,
- almost two-thirds less likely to use tobacco,
- sixty percent less likely to have tried marijuana, and
- seventy percent less likely to use illegal drugs or misuse prescription drugs.

Finally, let's consider education, which is critically important to a child's future well-being. Compared to those who rarely eat together, youth who eat together at least five nights per week are

- twenty-three percent more likely to receive mostly As and Bs in school,
- almost one-half less likely to receive mostly Cs or lower in school,
- twenty percent less likely to have friends who have tried drugs, and
- half as likely to have parents who do not know their children's friends well.

Who would have thought simply eating together with your family every night could make such a big impact? Riley Leggett. I can almost see the sparkle in his eye and the nudge he gave Rose Mary. He nailed it when he said, "Go home and eat dinner with your family every night." And Riley never needed to trudge through a bunch of studies and statistics!

The True Value of Money

Over time I came to see how differently Riley and I approached money. When we walked into that fancy restaurant, Riley and I were on totally opposite ends of the spectrum. I knew exactly what I was going to order, but had no idea how much it would cost. Riley had no idea what he was going to order, but knew exactly how much it would cost (cheapest on the menu). Hidden under these different approaches to money were different orientations in life. In my case, money was all about me and what it could do for me—like buy a great-tasting steak. For Riley, money was a tool to be used to improve the life of other people—beginning with his own family.

For all of his later success, Riley never forgot his beginnings in the Great Depression. Indeed, he would even say, "The Depression wasn't all bad. It taught you a lot of things. Like the value of money. Like the need for people to pull together for a common goal. Like the need to work hard and the ability to make sacrifices. Like the need to save for a rainy day." Sounds like the values of what we now call *the Greatest Generation*. The experience of the Depression was so severe that those lessons were burned into Riley's brain and he never forgot them.

But here is the amazing thing: Those same values are inside your brain as well. Your brain is wired to help you be charitable. The same reward circuitry we saw earlier that drives people to be successful at almost any cost also motivates people to be charitable. Neural activity in the ventral striatum, which includes the nucleus accumbens, increases when we give money away.[33] Indeed, we will see in Chapter 8 that our brain is wired to reward us whenever we are compassionate to another person. We are driven to be good to other people. When we are, we reap the rewards. When it comes to money, here's the goose that lays the golden eggs: When you use your money to benefit someone else, *you* reap a reward in terms of happiness, health, and (at least the feelings of) wealth.

This is not necessarily intuitive, but it has been very well documented. Consider happiness. Researchers gave a group of people a small sum of money and instructions to either spend it on themselves or on another person. At the end of the day, those who spent the money on someone else were happier than those who spent it on themselves.[34] This impact of charity on happiness has been measured in children as young as two![35] Furthermore, the impact of charity on happiness is as great as doubling the household income.[36]

Consider health. Not only do charitable individuals report better overall health,[37] but the decision to be charitable has been linked to lower levels of the stress hormone cortisol.[38] Over time, elevated levels of cortisol can lead to a host of physical issues.

Finally, consider the feelings of wealth. Charitable giving obviously does not increase wealth. However, it promotes the mindset of superabundance: "I have so much money, I can give some away." Controlling for other variables, individuals who give money away feel wealthier than those who don't.[39] It's really simple: Using money for other people is good for you.

Aunt Ethel and a College Education

On more than one occasion, I have had someone tell me, "Look, Steve, I admit I feel pretty good when I'm good to someone else, but I don't think I can ever measure up to Riley Leggett's standard!" Okay. Let's consider an elementary school teacher from a small town in Oklahoma.

Ethel Hill was my mother's cousin. However, since she was twenty-six years older than my mom and helped to take care of my mom when my grandmother passed away early, my mom referred to her as "Aunt Ethel" and that's the only way I knew her. She was born in 1914, one year earlier than Riley, to German immigrant farmers who came to Oklahoma to receive free farmland in the land run of 1889. She was also part of the Greatest Generation and shared their values.

She earned a college degree long before it was common for young ladies. She became a schoolteacher and taught elementary school in several small farming communities in Oklahoma. Places like Okarche and Piedmont. She never married, so she lived with her mother and cared for her after her father passed away. She was very active in church and had a wonderful singing voice.

Aunt Ethel is the only person I know who rivals Riley Leggett when it comes to being frugal. She drove in a basic Chevy Nova, and I mean basic. Power windows and doors? Haven't heard of them. Air conditioning? You can roll down the window. Carpeting? Just gets dirty and you have to clean it. Aunt Ethel fully embraced Riley's advice: "A dollar saved is a dollar earned." Aunt Ethel saved lots of dollars. I'm tempted to blame it on a hyperactive insula, which wouldn't allow her to part with hard-earned cash, but we will chalk it up to virtue.

How much money did Aunt Ethel save? When she purchased a modest home in the modest farming town of Okarche to live with her mother, she paid cash. During her forties, she had breast cancer and paid all of her medical bills in cash. Cancer returned during her mid-fifties, requiring additional treatments and live-in help at home. She paid for all of it in cash. When she passed away, all of her funeral arrangements had already been made and she had paid for them . . . in cash. Aunt Ethel did all of this on a teacher's salary from small farming communities in Oklahoma in the 1940s through the early 1970s. Aunt Ethel was frugal.

Nonetheless, Aunt Ethel had a warm heart and a soft spot for her "nieces and nephews." My mom had a twin sister and Aunt Ethel claimed the kids from both families as her nieces and nephews—nine in all. Every Christmas she had a gift for each child, typically . . . cash. When we came to visit, there was always a full carton of ice cream in the freezer, which was empty by the time we left. If you played your cards right, you could squeeze a quarter out of her to let her watch her afternoon soap opera in peace. Best of all, in the summer we could stay with her, which meant time out on a farm! Aunt Ethel was a wonderful person.

She died of recurrent cancer in 1973 when she was just fifty-eight years old. In her will she gave each of her nine "adopted nieces and nephews" enough money to pay the tuition for a four-year in-state college education. You can blame her for the studies and the stats! It is amazing the impact you can have in life when money isn't about you, but you use it as a tool to help other people!

Learning to Use Money for Others

I have found that many people have the desire to use their money for others, but it's not an easy thing to actually accomplish. Our brain chemistry is simultaneously driving us in competing directions: to be successful at all costs, and to be charitable to other people. We have to make a choice.

Unfortunately, a good portion of our popular culture reinforces the brain chemistry pushing us toward success at all costs. According to surveys by the United States government, charitable contributions account for only 1.4 percent of personal expenditures by Americans. At the same time, eating out accounts for 5.2 percent of personal expenditures and entertainment an additional 5.1 percent.[40]

If you wish to learn to use money like Riley Leggett and Aunt Ethel, I have seven practical steps to help you get started:

1. *Give the first fruits of your labor to God.* The first step to change your orientation toward money is to recognize that it is a gift you have received from God: "Every good . . . gift is from above, coming down from the Father of lights" (James 1:17). As such, we're asked to return 10 percent to him. When we do, He will bless it: "Honor the Lord with your substance and with the first fruits of all your produce; then your barns will be filled with plenty" (Proverbs 3:9).

2. *Keep $8 in your wallet that you must give away.* Scripture encourages us to be generous to those in need: "He who is kind to the poor lends to the Lord" (Proverbs 19:17). Every time you encounter a man, give him $1. When you encounter a woman, give her $5, since she might have children dependent upon her. In the course of a year, you'll probably give away less than $100, but it will change your orientation toward money and toward those in need.

3. *Moderate your consumption of the media.* The media frequently presents an image of "the good life" based upon the acquisition and consumption of expensive "things." As such, it places these things in your mind as "rewards" to be sought, and your brain will begin to drive you to acquire them.

4. *Live below your means.* Even if you reach the 99.9 percentile of wealth in the wealthiest country on Earth, you will still have financial constraints. Learn to live below your means—whatever they are.

5. *Cut up all credit cards until they are paid off.* Credit cards separate the pleasure of purchasing from the pain of paying. Reunite those two issues and your brain will make different decisions about spending money.

6. *Cut entertainment expense by eating meals together at home and enjoying nature as recreation.* Entertainment expenses are discretionary expenses that need to be under control. Eat together as a family because it is good for the life of the family. Eat at home because it is good for your pocketbook. It's the life of Riley.

7. *Begin saving and gradually increase the amount.* Scripture says, "A good man leaves an inheritance to his children's children" (Proverbs 13:22). Aunt Ethel was able to do so even on a public schoolteacher's salary from small Oklahoma farming communities.

Whew! That was a tough one, but we made it through. I promise to take my hand out of your wallet now. But I encourage you to put your own hand in it, take out some of your hard-earned cash, and use it for other people. When you do, it will transform you, your marriage, and your family. That's step two.

CHAPTER FOUR

STEP THREE:
Give God Some of Your Time

The third step to a superabundant marriage is to give God some of your time. I know, we keep going from bad to worse! We have gone from sex to money to religion. Well, at least you know we're not afraid to tackle the big issues. That's the point. These are difficult issues that trip up a significant portion of couples. That's why these three steps help to "divorceproof" your marriage. Get these three big rocks right, and it will substantially lower your probability of getting divorced and substantially increase the likelihood of a truly superabundant marriage.

Riley intuitively understood the value in giving time to God, which is why he told me, "Sit in church with your family every Sunday." We'll see that Riley nailed it once again. Going to church on a weekly basis will substantially lower your risk of divorce. Nonetheless, the third step—give God some of your time—involves more than checking a box that says "Pew Warmer" for an hour or more on Sunday. Riley understood this reality and he certainly gave God more than an hour on Sunday, but he did so in his own quiet way.

Not long after Shelly and I married, we were at Riley and Rose Mary's for a family holiday. Everyone was there. At the time, we could have fielded a baseball team with all the grandkids under five years old. Talk about mayhem! Talk about noise! Especially in the kitchen where the space was limited and the sound echoed off the tile floor and countertops. Shelly sent me on a quick trip to retrieve something from the car. To get back to the kitchen more quickly, I decided to cut through the formal living room— that is, the room that is off limits to anyone younger than Riley and Rose Mary, which included me! As I darted through the dark room, I tripped over Riley's feet! He was sitting there alone in the dark. I tried to politely excuse myself, "Sorry, Riley. I didn't see you sitting there in the dark." To which he responded, "No worries. I just couldn't take the noise. I mean a man can't even hear himself think in there."

I was now having another awkward moment with my father-in-law. I really wanted to rush back to the kitchen to faithfully fulfill the task Shelly entrusted to me, but . . . how can you leave your father-in-law sitting alone in the dark? So, I was stuck. Fulfill my wife's request, or chat with my father-in-law who is alone in the dark? I think I came up with something brilliant like, "Would you like me to turn on the light?"

After a brief pause, Riley responded, "No. Actually, I'm just sitting here saying my prayers."

Suddenly, I felt as if I had stumbled upon something I would like to call holy. The king of the castle didn't shout and demand peace and quiet. Indeed, he was happy to allow others to have a grand time. He simply slipped away unnoticed to give a little time to God!

This was Riley's way. He wasn't preachy. He didn't wear his faith or religion on his sleeve. Indeed, I don't think many people would have considered him religious. Nonetheless, faith was an important part of Riley's life. In this respect, Riley and Rose Mary were two peas in a pod.

Rose Mary was beautiful. She was filled with charm and grace, but had a wonderful sense of humor. Indeed, on more than one occasion she remarked, "If there aren't trees and champagne in heaven, I'm not going!"

But the lasting impression of Rose Mary was a woman alone in the dark in prayer. After she passed away, one of her daughters got up to share a few words at the funeral. She spoke about how on nights that she couldn't sleep or if she got up to go to the bathroom, she could see the light from the night-light in the hallway softly cast into Riley and Rose Mary's bedroom. There, she could catch a glimpse of Rose Mary kneeling alone in the dark beside the bed, saying her prayers.

Like Riley, Rose Mary understood the value of giving time to God. It changes you and it changes your marriage. In the midst of a very busy life, Riley and Rose Mary found a way to give time to God, and so can we.

"Sitting in Church" and the Probability of Divorce

In the previous chapter, we saw that Riley nailed it when it comes to the benefits of eating dinner together as a family. Well, I'm happy to let you know he nailed it once again. "Sitting in church with your family every Sunday" has a profound impact on your marriage and family life. Numerous studies have been published in the past couple of decades identifying a strong relationship between participating in formal worship services and marital stability.[1] Quite simply, "sitting in church with your family every Sunday" substantially lowers the probability that a couple will get divorced. Data from the General Social Survey indicates that couples attending weekly church services have a divorce rate 60 percent lower than those who never attend church services, 17.2 percent versus 41.3 percent.[2]

Given the almost shocking impact that attending weekly church services has on the probability of getting divorced, it is absolutely appropriate to ask why. To answer that question, we need to return to the study identifying the reasons people get divorced.

In the two previous chapters, we considered what are called the *proximate* reasons for getting divorced. In other words, if you asked someone why he or she got divorced, you will likely get an answer such as "My spouse cheated on me," or "My spouse spends money foolishly," or "My spouse has problems with alcohol or drugs." The proximate reasons for divorce are reproduced in Table 4.1.

In addition to these proximate reasons for getting divorced, the researchers also investigated more remote or "distal" reasons relating to divorce. These are factors that are not immediately related to the divorce, but that research has nonetheless definitively linked to an increased or decreased probability of divorce. A good example is the fact that children of divorced parents are more likely to get a divorce once they mature and enter into a marriage. The impact of the most important "distal" factors is presented in Table 4.2.

Behavior	Women	Men	Average
Infidelity	299%	363%	331%
Use Money Foolishly	187%	77%	132%
Drug/Alcohol Abuse	183%	216%	200%
Becomes Jealous	130%	101%	116%
Not Home Enough	105%	-NA-	52%
Critical Attitude	98%	93%	96%
Irritating Habits	92%	127%	110%

Table 4.1: Reasons for Divorce
Note: Table values are the percentage change in the odds of divorce. An increased probability of 100% indicates a doubling in the probability of divorce.
Source: Amato, P. R., and Rogers, S. J. "A Longitudinal Study of Marital Problems and Subsequent Divorce," *Journal of Marriage and Family* 59 (1997): 612–624.

Predictor	Impact*
Both Parents Divorced	137%
Second Marriage	31%
Wife Parents Divorced	29%
Prior Cohabitation	17%
Husband Parents Divorced	7%
Age at Marriage	(11%)
Church Attendance	(24%)

Table 4.2: Distal Reasons for Divorce
* Increased probability of divorce.
Source: Amato, P. R., and Rogers, S. J. "A Longitudinal Study of Marital Problems and Subsequent Divorce," *Journal of Marriage and Family* 59 (1997): 612–624.

A glance at the results brings to light two very important issues. First, the experience of the spouses in their family of origin is very important. If both sets of parents of the couple were divorced, it more than doubles the likelihood that the couple themselves will eventually divorce. Second, the single most important thing you can do to reduce the likelihood of getting divorced is to "sit in church with your family every Sunday." It is twice as important as delaying marriage to an older age.

Once again, I think it is appropriate to ask the question, "Why is 'sitting in church with your family every Sunday' so important?" Fortunately, our researchers helped answer the question. They investigated the impact of weekly church attendance on the immediate or proximate factors that lead to divorce—that is, infidelity, spending money foolishly, and so on. The results are presented in Table 4.3. A quick glance at the results reveals that the reason "sitting in church every Sunday" lowers the probability of divorce is that it changes the behaviors that lead to divorce.

Proximate Factor	Impact*
Infidelity	(33%)
Use Money Foolishly	(24%)
Drug/Alcohol Abuse	(27%)
Becomes Jealous	(18%)
Critical Attitude	(14%)
Irritating Habits	(20%)

Table 4.3: Church Attendance and Reasons for Divorce
* Increased probability of divorce.
Source: Amato, P. R., and Rogers, S. J. "A Longitudinal Study of Marital Problems and Subsequent Divorce," *Journal of Marriage and Family* 59 (1997): 612–624.

The little chuckle you hear right now is Riley. The little twinkle in his eye is a blinding beam, and he is smiling from ear to ear. He nailed it! "Eat dinner every night with your family, and sit in church with your family every Sunday. Do that, and everything will turn out just fine."

Prayer and Your Brain

We know more about the functioning of the brain than ever before in history. One thing we can say is that if a person's behavior is changed, then the functioning of the person's brain is changed. Specifically, if prayer changes a person's behavior, then prayer must also change the functioning of a person's brain.

Dr. Andrew Newberg[3] has spent more than two decades researching the impact of prayer and religiosity on the brain. He has written six books[4] and published numerous peer-reviewed articles for academic journals. The simple conclusion from Dr. Newberg's work is that prayer literally changes the functioning of your brain. Furthermore, what is truly amazing: The functioning of the brain is not only changed while a person is actually praying but also continues to be changed even after prayer is completed.

Some of the more significant findings include

- *Lower activity in the amygdala and limbic system.* This helps to reduce anger, fear, and anxiety.[5]
- *Increased activity in the anterior cingulate cortex.* This helps to make a person more empathetic and compassionate.[6]
- *Increased activity in the parietal lobe.* This helps to strengthen a person's sense of self.[7]

Since prayer changes the functioning of the brain, prayer changes the person. Research has confirmed a host of benefits of prayer, including greater overall well-being; a greater sense of purpose and meaning; increased hope and optimism; and greater self-esteem. Prayer also leads to lower levels of loneliness, depression, and anxiety; less substance abuse; lower levels of schizophrenia and other psychoses; and fewer suicides.[8] Prayer changes you, which changes your marriage.

Finding Time to Pray

That's the good news. The bad news is this change normally takes time, which is a major issue for Americans. According to the US government, the average American spends just 8.4 minutes per day in prayer.[9] I must admit that the number is a bit misleading. For the American who actually spends time in prayer, he or she prays for almost 1 hour and 35 minutes every day.[10] This certainly seems like ample time for prayer to work on the structures of the brain. The issue is that only 9 percent of Americans spend time in prayer on a daily basis.[11]

Given the fact that the vast majority of Americans profess a belief in God,[12] why do so few take time to pray on a daily basis? Not surprisingly, some of the most common answers relate to time. On one hand, many people see their lives as so busy that they simply do not have time to pray. On the other hand are people who intend to get around to prayer, but just not right now. Let's take a look at both of these reasons.

Every year the US government conducts a survey of how Americans spend their time. It is appropriately called the American Time Use Survey. The results for 2013 are presented in Figure 4.1. These results are for the average American, which include those who are working as well as those who are not. They include those who have children at home as well as those who don't. So obviously, the way a particular individual spends his or her time can vary a great deal from the results presented here. Nonetheless, these results indicate that the average American spends 5 hours and 22 minutes on leisure and sporting activities every day.[13] This includes 2 hours and 50 minutes watching television each day.[14]

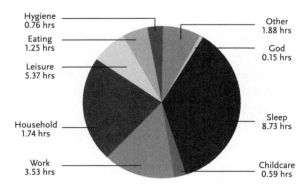

Figure 4.1: The Use of Time by Americans
Source: Bureau of Labor Statistics, U.S. Department of Labor, American Time Use Survey, 2012, Table 1.

No Time to Spare

I know that there are a lot of people right now saying, "I don't get close to five hours of leisure a day. Three hours of media? Forget it." Okay. Let's take the worst-case scenario in terms of being busy—a woman who works outside of the home and has children under the age of six at home. You know them when you see them. When you encounter them at the store, they give you a look that says, "Slow me down and I'll hand you your head!"

According to the US government these women certainly have less free time than anyone else. Their leisure activity time goes down to 3 hours and 5 minutes per day and they spend just over one and a half hours on television per day. Nonetheless, they are still able to get in 7 minutes of prayer per day, which is just under the overall average of 9 minutes per day. (It is amazing how young kids will drive a person to pray!)

It is certainly important to have a little downtime and we all know that exercise is good for you. (The average person spends just over 19 minutes per day on exercise and the average woman working outside the home who has children under the age of six at home spends just over 11 minutes per day in exercise.) Nonetheless, these numbers indicate that the vast majority of Americans have plenty of time to pray. They simply choose to spend it on other activities.

All the Time in the World

At the other end of the spectrum are those people who seem to have all the time in the world. They wouldn't disagree that prayer is a good thing and they'll get around to it—just not today! But do they really have all the time in the world? Who knows how much time he or she has left? The US government does its best to figure it out!

Every year the Social Security Administration publishes a Period Life Table, which is also known as an Actuarial Table or Longevity Chart. This chart provides an indication of the number of years a person can expect to live given his or her current age. The most recent chart is presented in Figure 4.2. This chart indicates that a 40-year-old person can expect to live another 42.32 years, while an 80-year-old person can expect to live another 9.61 years. In other words, as you age your life expectancy increases.

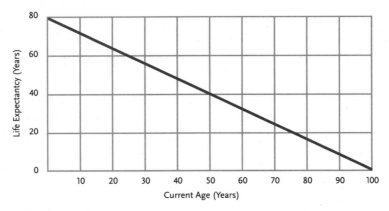

Figure 4.2: Life Expectancy for Americans
Source: Social Security Administration, Period Life Table, 2010.

Once again, this chart is for the average American. It lumps together men and women, smokers and nonsmokers, married and divorced, college graduates and those who did not finish high school. Nonetheless, all these factors have been shown to impact life expectancy. The best-case scenario is to be a married woman with an advanced college degree who has great health practices, which include not smoking, consuming alcohol with moderation, keeping your weight at an appropriate level, regular exercise, sufficient sleep, and a healthy diet! Whew! I guess I won't have that bacon cheeseburger for lunch.

I love presenting this data to a room full of men. The ears turn off. The analytical mind turns on. You can watch the wheels in the brain spinning: First comes the calculation of the number of years remaining, then comes the rationalization of how they are going to beat the odds. "Other guys are in much worse shape than I am. I actually do a better job taking care of myself than I give myself credit for. I'll cut back a bit on my drinking and you can add an extra five years!"

I remember the first time I presented this data to the men's ministry we founded in Houston. Several friends came up afterward. They had already finished the math and were now in the full-blown rationalization phase. "We're happily married. College graduates. Decent shape." These were smart men. I couldn't totally disagree with them. Then one of my best friends spoke up, "But guys, that's the point. The numbers are the numbers because everyone thinks he is going to beat the odds, but not everyone does."

The man was Robert Vaio. Several years earlier, we had been in a couples' Bible study together with our wives and some other friends. It was Robert's suggestion to found our men's ministry, That Man is You! He had been a partner in the consulting division of Arthur Andersen. When Enron came crashing down and brought Arthur Andersen with them, Robert lost everything. Suddenly the busy business executive had extra time on his hands.

Robert decided to use this time by engaging God and his faith more deeply. He had always been a man of faith, but family life and an executive position just didn't leave much time. Robert began attending a weekly men's Bible study that included several hundred men. He was amazed at the spiritual power involved when several hundred men publicly commit to live the Christian faith. Robert's faith life jumped to an entirely new level.

It was during this period that Robert and I were attending the couples' Bible study together. Robert really liked the things we were discussing and my ability to integrate the teachings of the faith with the findings of modern science. Before long, Robert was pushing me to found a men's ministry. I originally protested that I felt called to work with couples. Robert helped me with some pretty advanced math: "Men are half of the couple. Change the men and you'll change the couple." I finally agreed and That Man is You! was born. To Robert's and my delight, That Man is You! took off right away. Before long it was being hosted in parishes throughout the United States and impacting the lives of tens of thousands of men.

Soon thereafter, Robert accepted an executive position with an oil company in Houston. His time once more became a bit more scarce, but God used the time Robert gave him to transform lives and marriages. Indeed, a few years after the founding of That Man is You!, Robert, a few friends, and I stayed up into the wee hours of the morning after a big fiftieth birthday party Shelly threw for me. Truth be told, we were all a bit struck by the amazing things God can do if you are willing to just give him a little time.

About a week later, my family was just sitting down to breakfast on a Saturday morning. It was the Feast of Our Lady of Lourdes, which is my baptismal anniversary, so Shelly had prepared one of my favorite breakfasts.

The phone rang and we knew someone needed to talk to us because we just don't get many calls that early on a Saturday morning. It was my good friend Allan Klenke. In a second I could tell that Allan was very upset. He struggled to get out three words, "Robert is dead." Just as quickly, Shelly could tell something was wrong with me. Now it was my turn to struggle with three little words, "Robert is dead." I never ate that special breakfast.

Robert was 46. A week earlier he had seemed in perfect health. He and his wife had just completed construction on a beach house. His daughter had just enrolled at Notre Dame, Robert's alma mater. His older son was doing well in high school and his younger son was the apple of his eye. One of the last things Robert told me was how he loved to get on the floor with his four-year-old son and play with army men. Imagine a 6'3" business executive, accustomed to traveling first class throughout the world, playing army men with a four-year-old on the floor. That was Robert Vaio. I remember that after the birthday party, I told Shelly I had never seen Robert in a better place.

The chart says he had another thirty-seven years to live. Furthermore, he should have beaten the odds. He was happily married and engaged in his faith. He had a graduate degree and was an executive at a large corporation in Houston. As an executive for a large oil company, Robert had a medical evacuation plan in place. When he was found gasping for air from an undiagnosed embolism, the plan was activated and he was Life Flighted to a nearby hospital within minutes. But it was too late. The numbers are the numbers because not everyone beats the odds.

Robert didn't have as much time as he thought. Fortunately, he gave God a portion of the little time he had. God is so good; he takes our scraps and turns them into a feast. Men all over this country, and indeed the world, are still being impacted by Robert's decision to engage God and his faith more seriously by giving God a little extra time.

Climbing the Staircase to Jump out the Window

I'll be honest; a good number of people readily embrace the need to give God some of their time. Many have a predisposition to prayer and once they see the research regarding the benefits, it becomes a no-brainer. Nonetheless, there remains a question suspended in midair: How much time? Most people approach this question from a negotiating posture.

"Okay. Eight minutes isn't enough. What can I get for fifteen? What's it take to get 80 or 90 percent of the total benefit?"

Of course, it's never so simple.

The best analogy is probably to a physical workout plan. Some people need more while others can get by on less. Some can miss a workout with little consequences while others miss one day and they are done.

In my own life, it's kind of like an old trader's saying: "We climb a staircase so we can jump out the window!" Every day, I'm trudging, trudging, trudging. It takes me forever to get to the top of the staircase. But take one day off and it is like I jumped out the window. It is amazing how far and how fast I can fall.

Nonetheless, I would say that many people experience a certain pattern. A little inconsistent work does basically no good. They don't even make it up a couple of stairs. Those who work harder for a longer period of time make some respectable progress. They normally make it to the top of the stairs. Unfortunately, they take a day off and it's like they jumped out the window. They hit bottom really hard, really fast. Finally, there are the workout animals. They put in tons of time working really hard. They're the ones jumping rope at the top of the stairs! If they fall out the window, they simply catch themselves—with one arm—and pull themselves back in the window.

Think of prayer as a spiritual workout for your mind. A little prayer—such as 8.4 minutes per day—isn't really going to be able to transform your life. You won't really reap many of the benefits that prayer offers. A little additional time spent in prayer more consistently over a longer period of time will certainly begin to make a difference. Your problems will be put into perspective. Your relationships will improve. The future will look brighter. Nonetheless, your mind can quickly go back to its old way of thinking if you get off track just a bit. Finally, if you're willing to roll up your sleeves and put in some real effort up front, then you will be truly transformed. Indeed, you will receive the gift of a peace "not of this world" (cf. John 14:27) and become unmovable, even in the midst of all the challenges of modern society.

Uniting Heaven and Earth

Fortunately, God has provided us with a blueprint for building an effective prayer life. Contained within the first five books of the Bible (known as the Pentateuch or Books of Moses) are God's instructions to Israel on the means they are to use to worship him. We will discover in these instructions the foundation for an effective prayer life. Furthermore, when we look carefully, we will be able to see hidden within this blueprint all of the benefits of prayer discovered by modern science.

The concept behind this blueprint is very simple. Israel was to give God a portion of every major division of time—day, week, month, year, and lifetime. The significance behind this simple concept may not be apparent to the average person today, but it goes something like this. Each major division of time has a basis in some natural phenomenon. For instance, the day is the amount of time it takes for Earth to rotate one time on its axis. By uniting each major division of time to God through prayer, humanity was called to unite heaven and earth.

The major divisions of time and their basis in the natural world are presented in Table 4.4. Also presented are the means for transitioning these divisions of time into a well-structured prayer life.

Unit of Time	Natural Basis	Scripture	Christian Prayer
Day	Rotation of Earth on its axis	Morning and evening sacrifice. (Exodus 29:38–39)	Morning and night prayers
Week	Seven planets in the ancient world	Keep holy the Sabbath. (Deuteronomy 4:12)	Sunday church service
Month	Moon cycle	Feast of the new moon. (Numbers 28:11)	Feast Days
Year	Revolution of Earth around Sun	Jewish liturgical calendar. (Leviticus 23:1–36)	Liturgical calendar
Lifetime	Human Life	The Jubilee. (Leviticus 25:8–17)	Pilgrimage

Table 4.4: The Foundation of Prayer

The Day

In Scripture, God asked the Jews to begin and end their day by uniting it to him: "This is what you shall offer upon the altar; two lambs a year old day by day continually. One lamb you shall offer in the morning, and the other lamb you shall offer in the evening" (Exodus 29:38–39). Now we are asked to offer the sacrifice of our time instead of a lamb. We should begin and end the day in prayer. This is the basis for the morning and night prayers many of us were taught as children.

God attached a promise to this morning and evening sacrifice: "I will meet with you, to speak there to you" (Exodus 29:42). This does not imply some kind of vision or mystical experience. Rather, it simply means that the individual would become aware of God's presence in his or her life: "With the Lord on my side I do not fear" (Psalm 118:6). Prayer increases our awareness of God's presence in our life and decreases fear. Modern science has shown that prayer reduces activity in the amygdala and limbic system,[15] where fear and anxiety are processed in the mind.

Reading Scripture is perfectly suited to daily prayer. Indeed, when we read Scripture we are able to "hear" God speaking to us, which was the promise of daily prayer: "We speak to God when we pray; we listen to him when we read the divine oracles."[16] Reading Scripture can take many forms, from simply reading the Bible[17] to reading a good daily meditations book,[18] from praying the Divine Office[19] to reciting the Rosary.[20] Simply find the means that suit you best, which may change over time.

The Week

The week has its basis in the seven nonfixed objects in the sky of antiquity—called *planets*—sun, moon, Mercury, Venus, Mars, Jupiter, and Saturn.[21] The names for the days of the week were derived from the names of these seven "planets."[22] In Scripture, God asked the Jews to dedicate one day a week to him: "Observe the Sabbath day, to keep it holy" (Deuteronomy 5:12). It is interesting that Scripture tied the Sabbath rest to freedom from slavery: "You shall remember that you were a servant in the land of Egypt, and the Lord your God brought you thence with a mighty hand and an out-stretched arm" (Deuteronomy 5:15). God wants us to have freedom, which entails rest from our labors.

This is very important in a 24/7 world, where we are able to remain continually plugged in. Indeed, in the previous chapter we saw that many people are expected by their employers and customers to be always accessible. As such, many people today are beginning to feel a type of enslavement to their jobs. They desire rest from their labors. Nonetheless, we can go further. Today, many people are enslaved by a whole host of issues: debt, alcohol or other substances, pornography. We have seen how this enslavement is striking at the heart of marriages.

God wanted his Chosen People to experience freedom and rest 3,500 years ago[23] and he wants the same thing for you today. One of the best ways to experience this is to follow Riley Leggett's advice: "Sit in church with your family every Sunday." This is the day when Christians celebrate the "Christian Sabbath" or the "day of the Lord's Resurrection." This simple act can have a profound influence on your life. Indeed, social science reveals that individuals who go to church on a weekly basis have lower levels of substance abuse.[24] As such, going to church once a week helps them to experience freedom from those addictions.

The Month

The month is roughly equal to the amount of time it takes for the moon to orbit Earth—27 days, 7 hours, 43 minutes, 11.6 seconds, to be exact. In Scripture, God asked the Jews to celebrate the Feast of the New Moon by taking a break from their labors and sacrificing "as a holocaust to the Lord two bullocks, one ram, and seven unblemished yearling lambs" (Numbers 28:11). God understands that all work and no play makes all of us unhappy campers. He wants us to experience superabundant joy.

For centuries this found an expression in the feast days in the liturgical calendar. Long before public holidays, workers were given a day off on major feast days as towns and cities had festivals celebrating their favorite saints.[25] These were days of great joy that the whole community looked forward to with great anticipation. Modern studies indicate that individuals more active in their faith have better overall emotional well-being, including greater hope and optimism.[26]

Catholics, Orthodox, and many Protestant denominations have developed a liturgical calendar to help Christians recall and celebrate the most significant moments in Christ's life. The major feast days in the Catholic Church are given in Table 4.5. In our own home, Shelly allows each person to select his or her favorite feast day and then turns it into a special day. The person gets to select his or her favorite meal and dessert, and there's normally a little more time for fun. There's not a month that goes by that we don't find a reason to celebrate. Some months we sneak in two. God doesn't want your marriages and families to just survive. He wants them to thrive. He wants them to be superabundant.

Month	Feast Day	Marian Feast Day
January	6th: Epiphany	1st: Mary, Mother of God
February	2nd: Presentation	11th: Our Lady of Lourdes
March	19th: St. Joseph	25th: Annunciation
April	Easter (varies)	
May	Pentecost (varies)	31st: Visitation
June	Sacred Heart (varies)	Immaculate Heart (varies)
July		16th: Our Lady of Mt. Carmel
August	6th: Transfiguration	15th: Assumption of Our Lady
September	14th: Triumph of Cross	8th: Nativity of Mary
October	2nd: Guardian Angels	7th: Our Lady of Rosary
November	1st: All Saints Day	21st: Presentation of Mary
December	25th: Christmas	8th: Immaculate Conception

Table 4.5: Major Feast Days

The Year

The year is the amount of time it takes for Earth to go around the sun and is the source of our seasons. In the book of Leviticus, chapter 23, God establishes a liturgical calendar for the Jews by defining their major feasts:

Passover, Shavuot, Yom Kippur, Rosh Hashanah, Sukkoth. These feasts recalled God's action in the life of his Chosen People, from their liberation from Egyptian slavery to their journey to the Promised Land to the giving of the Covenant to Moses. Recalling God's actions in the life of the Chosen People, these feasts were indispensable in helping to forge a national identity for Israel.

The liturgical calendar helps Christians recall and celebrate the most significant moments in Christ's life. The basis of this calendar is the two great feasts of Christmas and Easter. At Christmas, we recall the birth of Christ and celebrate the reality that God loved us so much that he entered human history by taking on a human nature. At Easter, we celebrate the Passion, death, and Resurrection of Christ and celebrate a truly unfathomable love. God's love for humanity is so superabundant that he was willing to descend to the very depths of humanity's brokenness. Furthermore, he overcame this brokenness and offers us the opportunity to share in his victory. Ultimately, it is the love of God that gives meaning to our lives. God loves us. He walks with us on our worst days. He helps us to get up and begin again whenever we've fallen. Modern science reveals that an authentic prayer life increases activity in the parietal lobe, which helps an individual experience a greater sense of self.[27]

The Lifetime

The final division of time is the lifetime of a person. During the time of the Kings of Judah, the life expectancy for men who survived infancy was approximately fifty-two years.[28] Interestingly, God asked Israel to celebrate a Jubilee once every fifty years: "You shall hallow the fiftieth year, and proclaim liberty throughout the land to all its inhabitants; it shall be a jubilee for you, when each of you shall return to his property and each of you shall return to his family" (Leviticus 25:10). More than anything else, the Jubilee was a time of superabundant mercy. Debts were forgiven. Land was restored to its original owner. There was reconciliation among family members. Modern science reveals that an authentic prayer life increases activity in the anterior cingulate cortex, which helps to make a person more empathetic and compassionate.[29]

At least once in your life, you too should experience the absolute super-abundance of God. For many Christians, this has been fulfilled in the form of a pilgrimage—a journey to a special place where heaven and earth seem to touch in a special way. In the Middle Ages, the three most significant pilgrimage destinations were the Holy Land;[30] Rome;[31] and Santiago de Compostela, Spain.[32] In more recent years, Lourdes, France;[33] and Fatima, Portugal,[34] have been added to this list. Each year, millions of pilgrims flock to these sites, bringing with them their burdens and sorrows. Countless men and women experience an encounter with God and find rest for their souls.

Whew! That's it! Being transformed through prayer takes work, a lot of work. But the benefits are worth it. Who doesn't want reduced fear and anxiety; increased peace, compassion, and empathy; greater hope and a sense of purpose? It sure beats jumping out a window!

A Bolt of Lightning from the Sky

Okay. You're one of those special people. You do the 30-minute boot camp and can kick holes in the wall to make windows. You're looking for the equivalent in the spiritual life. How about a bolt of lightning from the sky? It's happened before:

> As Paul journeyed he approached Damascus, and suddenly a light from heaven flashed about him. And he fell to the ground and heard a voice saying to him . . . Rise and enter the city, and you will be told what you are to do (Acts 9:3–6).

Such was the conversion of St. Paul. Believe it or not, God still touches people with a flash of lightning and he does so much more frequently then many people realize. According to data in the General Social Survey, approximately 40 percent of American adults claim to have had a religious experience so profound that it changed their life.[35] Women are slightly more likely than men, 43 percent versus 37 percent.[36]

Unfortunately, there's more to the story regarding bolt-of-lightning conversions. The flash of light is just the beginning of the process. After being knocked from his horse, St. Paul went into the desert for three years and then went to Jerusalem to speak with the other apostles (cf. Galatians 1:16–19). Such is normally the case for us as well. The flash of light turns into a process that takes years. For Alexis Carrel it took more than thirty years![37]

Alexis Carrel was born into a devout Catholic family in Lyon, France, in 1873. He was brilliant from his youth, eventually earning his bachelor of letters, bachelor of science, and doctor of medicine degrees from Lyon University. He went on to become one of the "fathers of modern medicine." In 1902, he published work on his new technique of suturing blood vessels, which was the necessary advance that made modern surgery possible. For this work he was awarded the Nobel Prize in Medicine in 1912. He came to the United States and taught in our leading university medical hospitals for almost three decades before returning to France shortly before his death in 1944.

During his academic studies, Alexis Carrel was carried away by the dominant thinking of his day. He rejected faith in God as incompatible with a scientific understanding of man and the world. Alexis Carrel became an atheist. But God had other plans for him.

Shortly after publishing the work that would lead to his Nobel Prize, Alexis Carrel was offered the opportunity by a colleague to make a trip to Lourdes aboard one of the "sick trains" packed with pilgrims going to Lourdes seeking a cure for their ailments. Dr. Carrel was shocked that his colleague could retain his faith while being a man of science. Dr. Carrel accepted the opportunity—determined to expose Lourdes as a hoax or to scientifically investigate the medicinal properties of the miraculous spring of water. He boarded the train on May 25, 1902.[38]

A young lady by the name of Marie Bailly was secretly placed on the same train because she was already at the point of death from tubercular peritonitis—tuberculosis of the stomach. En route to Lourdes, a nurse discovered Marie Bailly and summoned Dr. Carrel. He immediately and correctly diagnosed her as being at the point of death from tubercular peritonitis. He stated that she would not arrive alive in Lourdes and gave the nurse a bottle of morphine with the instructions to administer it to Marie Bailly as needed to moderate pain.

Of course the story wouldn't be any good if she died en route. When they arrived in Lourdes, Marie Bailly was taken to one of the hospices while Alexis Carrel went—as a man of science—to the baths to observe the other pilgrims. Nonetheless, Marie Bailly was able to summon just enough strength to convince a nurse to take her to the baths. She was placed on a stretcher and taken to the baths.

Dr. Carrel arrived on the scene just as they were placing Marie Bailly next to the baths. Dr. Carrel then had one of those "doctor moments" we wish didn't happen. He argued with the nurse about why she didn't follow his instructions to leave Marie Bailly in the hospice to die! I said Dr. Carrel was brilliant. I didn't say he was warm!

While they were arguing, a different nurse gave Marie Bailly a small drink of Lourdes water. Instantaneously there was a change. Her heart rate slowed and returned to normal. Her profuse sweating eased. She gained enough strength to ask the nurse to pour some Lourdes water on her stomach. Instantaneously her distended stomach returned to normal. A few hours later Marie Bailly returned to the hospice totally out of danger. Indeed, a few days later, Marie Bailly returned home and fulfilled the promise she made to her family when she left: "Either I will die in Lourdes or I will walk through that door under my own power."

Dr. Carrel witnessed the entire miraculous cure of Marie Bailly. He did so as a man of science. He took notes so feverishly that when he ran out of paper in his notebook, he wrote on his shirtsleeve. As Marie Bailly returned to the hospice, Dr. Carrel's mind raced in disbelief of the miracle he had witnessed with his own eyes. He knew his diagnosis was correct. He knew science could not explain what had happened before his eyes. He wandered aimlessly for hours. Finally, in the wee hours of the morning, as he walked along the stream with the grotto of Lourdes as a backdrop and the flames of the candles flickering in the night, Dr. Carrel found himself saying this prayer:

Gentle Virgin, who bringeth help to the unfortunate who humbly implore thee. Keep me with thee. I believe in thee. Thou didst answer my prayers by a blazing miracle. I am still blind to it. I still doubt. But the greatest desire of my life, my highest aspiration, is to believe, to believe passionately, implicitly, and never more to analyze and doubt. Thy name is more gracious than the morning sun. Take unto thyself this uneasy sinner with the anxious frown and troubled heart who has exhausted himself in the vain pursuit of fantasies. Beneath the deep, harsh warnings of my intellectual pride a smothered dream persists. Alas, it is still only a dream, but the most enchanting of them all. It is the dream of believing in thee and of loving thee with the shining spirit of the men of God.[39]

I'm always humbled by the beauty of this prayer. I think it impossible for God to allow this prayer to go unanswered. Nonetheless, the key words were: "I am still blind to it. I still doubt . . . harsh warnings of my intellectual pride." God did indeed answer this prayer, but it took Alexis Carrel over thirty years to accept the answer.

Dr. Carrel returned to Paris and reported what he termed "an inexplicable cure." He was rejected by the French intellectual establishment, which motivated his move to the United States. In 1910, he returned to Lourdes and witnessed a second instantaneous miracle, this time of an 18-month-old child who had been born blind. Dr. Carrel married the nurse holding that little child. Nonetheless, Dr. Carrel would continue to struggle with his faith.

He was once again swept away by the intellectual climate in vogue in the United States and Europe. He embraced the concept of eugenics[40] and wrote a best-selling book entitled *Man, the Unknown*. Although taken out of context, portions of this book were used by the Nazis to justify their T-4 euthanasia program.[41] Dr. Carrel had a long and winding road.

Finally, as Dr. Carrel began to see the end of his life approaching, he decided to visit a Catholic monk. In 1938, Alexis Carrel met his intellectual match in Dom Alexis Presse, who could answer all of his spiritual questions. It took another four years, but Alexis Carrel rediscovered the faith of his youth:

I believe in the existence of God, in the immortality of the soul, in Revelation and in all that the Catholic Church teaches"[42]

Finally, shortly before his death, Alexis Carrel, Nobel laureate in medicine, rediscovered the simplicity of a child:

> When one approaches one's own death, one grasps the nothingness of all things. I have gained fame. The world speaks of me and of my works, yet I am a mere child before God, and a poor child at that.[43]

So, how much time should you give God? The simple answer is *more*. No prayer uttered in sincerity goes unanswered. The road may be long, and it may be winding, but every prayer is answered. Give God some of your time. It will change you, your marriage, and your family.

CHAPTER FIVE

STEP FOUR:
Set Your Mind on the Things Above

Now it gets interesting!

To this point we've simply been doing damage control. We've been trying to protect your heart and guard your pocketbook. By radically lowering
your probability of getting divorced, we radically increase the probability
that you be will be happier, healthier, and wealthier. That's why we begin
with the three steps that help to "divorceproof" your marriage.

But, as we stated at the outset, God doesn't want you to simply struggle
through twenty, thirty, forty, or fifty years of a bad marriage. He wants you to
have superabundant joy. He wants you to taste the Choice Wine. That's where
we're headed! The next three steps are about experiencing superabundant joy.

To experience this superabundant joy, we have a major challenge—and
it's not your spouse! We need the ability to see beyond the external and the
superficial. We need to stretch your mind until we discover the extraordinary hidden behind the mundane. I would even say to find the supernatural
hidden behind the natural. There is so much more going on in marriage than
meets the eye—and I'm not talking about caustic comments, subtle digs,
and manipulation.

To stretch the mind, we'll go places that, quite frankly, Riley and Rose
Mary would never go. Being part of the Greatest Generation, they felt no
need to prove what "just makes sense." We, however, are part of a different

generation, one that needs objective, preferably scientific, validation of almost every facet of life. For this, engineering degrees and even MBAs are quite handy.

In this chapter, I would like to use everything at our disposal to stretch our minds beyond the limits of this material world. We will use some of the latest findings from some of the best minds in modern science. We will consider teachings dating to the earliest days of Christianity from some of the true giants from the past two thousand years. We will even consider the reality of supernatural experience. To some people, the thought of combining science and religion may seem a bit surprising, if not downright troubling. Don't worry. We allow each field its appropriate autonomy, but as Werner Heisenberg, Nobel laureate in physics in 1932, stated,

> The first swallow from the cup of natural sciences makes atheists, but at the bottom of the cup God is waiting.[1]

That's our goal: stretch our minds far enough and drink deeply enough that we are able to glimpse something of the supernatural in this seemingly natural institution we call marriage. It is really simple: If we want our marriages to be truly different, then we need to see them in a new and different light. To do this I will attempt to stretch your mind regarding the three significant moments leading to the establishment of marriage. If we are able to find God in each of these three moments, we will be able to find God in our marriages:

1. the creation of the universe
2. the creation of the human person
3. the formation of the spousal bond

The light you just saw turn off was the twinkle in Riley's eye. He just doesn't believe we need to spend all this time proving what he already knows. But I promise you that by the time we get to the end, the smile will be back on Riley's face. Now it gets interesting.

Mind Stretch #1: The Creation of the Universe

Modern cosmology has certainly been one of the most fascinating developments of the past generation. Findings from quantum physics to antimatter to dark matter to dark energy are as mysterious as they are amazing. Nonetheless, thanks to the Hubble Telescope we have all seen pictures of the birth of a star, the death of a star, the Milky Way galaxy, and the edges of the observable universe.

Don't worry. You won't need a PhD in physics to follow the discussion, but we will see some pretty amazing concepts. But first, the boring stuff. I'm going to begin with a 100,000-foot flyby on modern cosmology's understanding of the formation of the universe. According to modern cosmology, the universe began with a big bang approximately 13.8 billion years ago in which all of the energy and matter in existence were released. The formation of the first stars began within about 200 million years. Our own Milky Way galaxy formed over the course of billions of years. The oldest stars date to approximately 13.2 billion years ago. The thin disk containing most of the stars in the Milky Way began forming about 8.8 billion years ago. Our own sun formed about 4.6 billion years ago.

Moving closer to home, Earth formed about 4.5 billion years ago, "just" 100 million years after the sun. Earth cooled over the course of 700 million years until liquid water could form, approximately 3.8 billion years ago. Just 200 million years later, we see the first life on Earth, single cell algae and bacteria. The algae began the process of photosynthesis—breathing in carbon dioxide and exhaling oxygen. Over the course of the next 1.5 billion years, Earth's atmosphere became oxygen rich and transformed from a murky brownish color to a beautiful translucent blue. For the first time the sun and moon become clearly visible from Earth. About 500 million years ago, the Cambrian explosion of life occurred during which most of the animal phyla existing to this day appeared with geographic suddenness. Finally, conscious living beings—humans—appeared on the scene to actually think and talk about such things. This very abbreviated timeline of creation is presented in Figure 5.1[2]

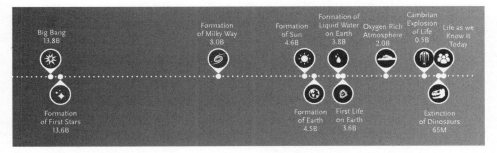

Figure 5.1: Timeline of the Universe

I warned you that it would be a bit dry, but that is the current snapshot of the development of our universe according to modern cosmology. Of course, this understanding will be refined throughout the years, but I accept that this story paints a reasonable picture. As such, this is our first sip from the cup of natural science and it is easy to see how a superficial understanding of this story could lead to atheism. There doesn't seem to be a need for a Creator. The story of the universe simply unfolds according to the laws of nature. Furthermore, let's be honest, 13.8 billion years just doesn't seem to fit within the Biblical story of creation.

Most people have heard something of the Genesis creation story, at least in their childhood. In this Biblical account, God created the entire universe in a mere six days:

> In the beginning . . . God said, "Let there be light. . . . Let there be a firmament. . . . Let the waters under the heavens be gathered together into one place, and let the dry land appear. . . . Let the earth bring forth vegetation. . . . Let there be lights in the firmament of heavens to separate the day from the night. . . . Let the waters bring forth swarms of living creatures, and let birds fly above the earth. . . . Let the earth bring forth living creatures. . . . Let us make man in our image, after our likeness" (Genesis 1:1–26).

On the surface, these two stories certainly seem to have little or nothing in common. Indeed, they appear to be irreconcilable. Nonetheless, if we are willing to follow Werner Heisenberg's advice and enter more deeply into the science, we will be able to find God. But, I must warn you, it will take some of the most brilliant minds from the past sixteen hundred years to do it.

In Judeo-Christian theology, the understanding of the six days of creation is not nearly as simple as many would be led to believe. Indeed, a literalist, superficial reading has been excluded for centuries, long before the advent of modern cosmology. It was noted that Earth does not appear until Day Three and the sun and moon, which were specifically given to mark the passage of time (cf. Genesis 1:14), don't appear on the scene until Day Four. As such, almost sixteen hundred years ago, St. Augustine, one of the most important and influential thinkers in Christian history, could write: "As for these 'days,' it is difficult, perhaps impossible to think—let alone to explain in words—what they mean . . . [since] the first three 'days' of creation passed without benefit of sun, since, according to Scripture, the sun was made on the fourth day."[3,4] St. Augustine recognized that without an Earth, sun, or moon, the perspective of time given in the "days" of creation must be different from our common perspective of time[5]—and that's the key word: *perspective.*

Now it's time to stretch the mind. Time is not constant. The little shuffle you heard was Riley leaving to get a cup of coffee. As he left, I heard him mumble something about, "I always worried about him!" Nonetheless, it's true. Time is not constant. The flow of time is absolutely dependent upon where you are standing in the universe. Indeed, one year on the sun is actually 67 seconds shorter than one year on Earth![6] I'll be honest. I don't get it. I've only experienced the flow of time on Earth. Nothing seems more certain than the flow of time. The same is true for everyone else.

That's why it took the genius of Albert Einstein to discover this property of nature. The "dilation of time" was implied in his theory of relativity.[7] Furthermore, this theory implied the Big Bang, the expanding universe, black holes, and a host of other things never before imagined. In the past century, the insights of Einstein have been scientifically verified. For his work, Einstein received the Nobel Prize in Physics in 1921 and rightly earned recognition as one of the most brilliant men to have ever lived. Of particular interest to us is the expansion of the universe and its impact on the flow of time.

While Riley is still in the kitchen, let me sneak in another brilliant scientist and concept. During the 1920s, Edwin Hubble made a series of observations leading to the publication of several papers indicating that the universe was much larger than the Milky Way galaxy—a novel thought at the time—and that the universe was expanding in all directions. Furthermore, this expansion occurred not by "lengthening the edges of the universe," but by stretching the entire universe. Our universe is literally stretching in all directions! For his work, a scientific law was named after him, Hubble's law, and his original estimate for the expansion of the universe was named Hubble's constant.

The discovery that the universe is expanding is absolutely critical to our understanding of the flow of time. As the universe expands, the flow of time proportionally slows. Let me give you an example. Let us assume that a star exploded seven billion years ago. The light from this explosion would begin traveling to Earth. Let's assume a second star exploded one year later in essentially the same location and its light began traveling to Earth. At the point of origin, these two explosions of light would be separated by the distance that light travels in one year, a light year. However, as these two explosions of light make their seven-billion-year journey to Earth, the entire universe is stretching—including the distance between these two explosions. In the past seven billion years, the universe has roughly doubled in size, which means that the distance between these two explosions of light has also roughly doubled in size. When the two beams of light finally reach Earth, it appears that they occurred two years apart!

I see Riley heading back from the kitchen, so we had better pull all this together quickly. To do so, we need to introduce one more brilliant mind. Gerald Schroeder received his PhD in nuclear physics from MIT. He is well published in academic journals and holds a patent or two. He also has the distinction of being one of the few men who have been present at the detonation of six atomic bombs and lived to tell about it! Indeed, it was the detonation of one of those bombs that changed Schroeder's life. As he says, "When I saw half a mountain disappear before my eyes, I decided I needed to start thinking about the work I was doing. My degree is a doctor of philosophy in nuclear physics. I decided to be more philosophical about my work."

Schroeder now lives in Jerusalem and spends all his time integrating a deep understanding of modern science with the timeless teachings of faith. He has the amazing ability to allow each realm (science and faith) its own autonomy while finding a pathway to integrate them together. He has written several best-selling books.[8] For our purposes we will be guided by his work in *The Science of God*.

Recognizing the implications of the stretching of space on the perception of time, Schroeder asked himself the very reasonable question, "What would happen if instead of standing on Earth and looking back to the moment of the Big Bang, which occurred 13.8 billion years ago, I stood at the moment of the Big Bang and looked forward to today?" So he placed himself at the instant of proton–antiproton formation (intellectually of course, otherwise there would be no more Schroeder!). This moment occurred 1/100,000th of a second after the Big Bang. Following that moment the universe has stretched approximately a million million times.

Here is Schroeder's truly amazing insight: If you placed six 24-hour Earth days at the moment of proton–antiproton formation and stretched them a million million times, do you know how much time would have passed? Approximately 13.6 billion years[9]—almost the exact number indicated by modern science. As hard as it is to believe, the 13.8 billion years of modern cosmology and the six days of creation in Genesis are actually the same amount of time! It just depends on your perspective. Cosmology stands on Earth today and looks back to the moment of the Big Bang. The creation story in Genesis stands at the moment of the Big Bang and looks forward to today.

Amazingly, Schroeder was able to go even further. He calculated the time of each of the six days beginning at the moment of the Big Bang. The time for each day changes because the relative stretching of space changes. He then compared the story of creation in Genesis to the findings of modern cosmology. A summary of his results is given in Table 5.1.

Biblical Account	Time (billions of years before present)	Modern Cosmology
Day 1: "Let there be light"	13.9–6.9	Big Bang, light, galaxies form
Day 2: "Let there be a firmament"	6.9–3.4	Milky Way galaxy and sun form
Day 3: "Let dry land appear"	3.4–1.6	Formation of water, bacteria, algae
Day 4: "Let there be lights in heaven"	1.6–0.7	Photosynthesis, transparent atmosphere
Day 5: "Let water have life/birds"	0.7–0.2	Cambrian explosion of life, winged insects
Day 6: "Let land have life/humanity"	0.2–Now	Land animals, humans

Table 5.1: Creation: Genesis and Cosmology
Source: Schroeder, Gerald L. *The Science of God—The Convergence of Science and Biblical Wisdom* (New York: The Free Press, 1997) p. 67 and Schroeder, Gerald, L., "The Age of the Universe," October (2013) at www.geraldschroeder.com.

A quick glance at the table indicates an amazing harmony between the two stories of creation. On the first day of Genesis, God said, "Let there be light" (Genesis 1:3). This day lasted from the Big Bang until 6.9 billion years ago and includes not only the Big Bang, but also the formation of the first stars. It includes light.

On the second day of Genesis, God said, "Let there be a firmament" (Genesis 1:6), which are stars. The second day lasted from 6.9 billion years ago to 3.4 billion years ago. During this period a good portion of the Milky Way's thin disk formed, which are the stars (firmament) we see at night.

On the third day of Genesis, God said, "Let the waters under the heavens be gathered together into one place . . . [and] let the earth put forth vegetation" (Genesis 1:9–11). The third day lasted from 3.4 billion years ago to 1.6 billion years ago. The formation of liquid water and appearance of algae only slightly preceded this date.

On the fourth day of Genesis, God said, "Let there be lights in the firmament . . . And God made two great lights, the greater light to rule the day [i.e., the sun], and the lesser light to rule the night [i.e., the moon]" (Genesis 1:14–16). This day lasted from approximately 1.6 billion years ago to 700 million years ago. Although both the sun and moon formed much earlier, it was only during this period that Earth's atmosphere turned a beautiful translucent blue so that the sun and moon became visible for the first time.

On the fifth day of Genesis, God said, "Let the waters bring forth swarms of living creatures . . . and every winged bird according to its kind" (Genesis 1:20–21). This day lasted from approximately 700 million years ago to approximately 200 million years ago. During this period, Earth experienced the Cambrian explosion of life when almost all the animal phyla existing to this day appeared with geographic suddenness. Note that this life first appeared in the ocean. Also, this period witnessed the first appearance of winged creatures—insects.

Finally, on the sixth day of Genesis, God said, "Let the earth bring forth living creatures . . . [and] let us make man in our image, after our likeness" (Genesis 1:24–26). This day lasted from about 200 million years ago until today. During this period life became ever more complex upon the earth, especially the land, until finally we see the appearance of humans.

Given the fact that the creation story in Genesis was written thousands of years ago and used just thirty-one verses to tell the entire history of the universe, the parallels are amazing. Schroeder concludes, "Genesis and science are both correct."[10] It just depends on perspective—and what is the perspective of the creation story in Genesis? It begins when "the earth was without form and void" (Genesis 1:2). As such, it stands at the moment of creation and watches the creative work of God unfold. Amazing.

If you look carefully, you will see Riley peeking around the corner. He wants to come back, but is a bit nervous. We're not done stretching the mind. We still need to consider the mystery of the human person and the beauty of the spousal union. The good news—they are not nearly as difficult, but even more amazing.

Mind Stretch #2: The Creation of the Human Person

One of the most influential books of the modern era—if not all history—is Charles Darwin's *On the Origin of Species*, published in 1859. Although not the first person to discuss evolution—or the *theory of transmutation* as it was then called[11]—Darwin introduced this topic to the general public. The idea that would revolutionize modern culture in many ways was put forth at the very outset of the book:

In considering the origin of species, it is quite conceivable that a naturalist . . . might come to the conclusion that species had not been independently created, but had descended, like varieties from other species.[12]

One of the reasons the theory of evolution is associated with Charles Darwin versus others who previously discussed the idea is that he put forth a very reasonable and compelling explanation for the mechanism driving evolution. This mechanism was based on four principles:

1. Super fecundity: "More individuals of each species are born than can possibly survive."
2. Fitness: "There is a frequently recurring struggle for existence . . . if any being vary however slightly in any manner profitable to itself."
3. Natural selection (i.e., the survival of the fittest): "It will have a better chance of surviving, and thus be *naturally selected.*"
4. Evolution: "Based on the principle of inheritance, any selected variety will tend to propagate its new and modified form."[13]

Evolution has been used to explain the development of life on Earth in general and, specifically, the development of humans. Schoolchildren for several generations have learned the evolutionary tree, *Homo habilis*, *Homo erectus*, Neanderthals, Peking Man, and more. As such, we've all become accustomed to seeing a picture that shows a progression from an ape to a human.

Once again, it is easy to see how this "sip from the cup of natural science" could lead to atheism. Similar to a cursory consideration of the story of creation in modern cosmology, there doesn't seem to be a need or even a place for God. The evolution of species just seems to unfold across millions of years according to the laws of nature. Indeed, if we accept Darwin's own words at face value, it appears that Darwin himself followed this path:

Thus disbelief crept over me at a very slow rate, but at last was complete. The rate was so slow that I felt no distress, and have never since doubted even for a single second that my conclusion was correct. I can indeed hardly see how anyone ought to wish Christianity to be true.[14]

The story of the creation of humanity contained in Scripture seems to be at odds with this understanding from science. Nonetheless, the text of Scripture once again provides us an indication that a deeper understanding lies hidden beneath the surface. The creation story in the first chapter of Genesis records the creation of humans as follows:

Then God said, "Let us make man in our image, after our likeness. Let him have dominion over the fish of the sea, the birds of the air, the tame animals, all the wild animals, and all the creatures that crawl on the earth." God created man in his image; in the image of God he created them; male and female he created them (Genesis 1:26–27).

This text includes a very significant distinction not recorded in the creation of anything else. The text of Genesis chapter 1 indicates that God both "makes" and "creates" man. We commonly use these terms interchangeably, but, in fact, they are very different. To "make" something is to transform something that already exists into something else. I can take a tree and use it to "make" a table and chairs—and then sit down to a tasty dinner. To "create" something is to bring it into existence from nothing. The creation story of Genesis 1 indicates that God both "made" and "created" humanity. This theme returns in the story of the Garden of Eden where we read,

The Lord God formed the man out of the dust of the ground and blew into his nostrils the breath of life, and the man became a living being (Genesis 2:7).

As such, Scripture indicates something very unique about the human person. There is something in him that is made "from the ground" that would obey the laws of nature. At the same time, he is animated by the "breath of God." There is in him something of a spark of the divine. Over sixteen hundred years ago, St. John Chrysostom, one of the most important personages from Orthodox Christianity, could write

> Let us notice instead what it says in the case of the creation of human beings. "God formed the human being" . . . he changed the dust from soil into body . . . [and] "He breathed into him the breath of life." . . . You see, this body created in the Lord's design was like an instrument needing someone to activate it, rather like a lyre that needs someone who can by his own skill and artistry raise a fitting hymn.[15]

Science and Scripture present two seemingly very different explanations for the creation of the human person. If we allow another Nobel laureate to help us enter more deeply into the science, we will find God waiting. That deep guttural groan you just heard was Riley. I think that he was willing to forgive me for the first mind stretch, but he's not yet willing to trust me with the next. I'm not sure which is more difficult—stretching the mind or convincing Riley to keep me in the family!

Dr. John C. Eccles had one of those incredibly brilliant minds that just couldn't get enough. Originally from Australia, he received his medical degree from the University of Melbourne in 1925. He then moved to England to study as a Rhodes Scholar at Oxford where he received a PhD in 1929. During the 1950s he made a series of pioneering experiments on the working of the human brain. These experiments led to the discovery of the synapse—the small gaps between neurons—for which Dr. Eccles would receive the Nobel Prize in Medicine in 1963.

Based upon the work of Dr. Eccles, our current understanding of the working of a synapse goes something like this: A thought travels down a neuron as an electrical current. When it reaches a synapse, there is an increase in the calcium concentration on the membrane of the presynaptic neuron. Vesicles then release a chemical neurotransmitter, which travels across the synapse and is received by receptor cells on the postsynaptic neuron. It is reconverted into an electrical current and races down a new neuron. Finally, the synapse is cleared of all chemicals so that it is ready to respond to a new electrochemical stimulus once a new thought arrives. This process is shown in Figure 5.2.

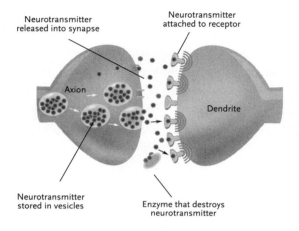

Figure 5.2: The Neuron
Source: Lodish, H. et al., *Molecular Cell Biology*, 4th Edition, New York, W.H. Freeman, 2000.

To many people this will seem like incredibly complicated technical language. They are desperately longing to join Riley in the kitchen for a cup of coffee! Nonetheless, let's not get overwhelmed or bogged down in the scientific language. Instead, let's ask ourselves a very important question implied by this scientific understanding of the working of the brain. "Is it possible that a thought could ever transform itself into calcium or an inert chemical that is used as a neurotransmitter?"

When I'm giving a live presentation on this topic, I hold up two vials: one containing calcium and the other the neurotransmitter oxytocin. Everyone is familiar with calcium. It is a white chalky material contained in milk that the body uses to make bones. Oxytocin looks like water and is called the "cuddle hormone" since it works on the attachment and trust centers in the brain. I then challenge the audience to find a thought in one of the vials. Not surprisingly, a little chuckle goes around the room. It is obvious that there is no thought in the vial of calcium. Likewise, it is obvious that there is no thought—or hug—in the vial of oxytocin. Nonetheless, our scientific understanding of the working of the synapse indicates that there is a fleeting moment in time when a thought exists solely as an increased calcium concentration on the presynaptic neuron and the release of a chemical neurotransmitter, which travels across the synaptic gap.

Dr. Eccles had the wonderful ability to be philosophical about his own work and he clearly understood the implications of the scientific understanding of the working of the brain. At the age of seventy-two—while still in perfect health—he retired to work on the "mind–brain problem." Indeed, he considered solving this mystery to be "the romance of my life."[16] To understand Dr. Eccles's solution, we need to once more be very precise about a couple of terms that we frequently use interchangeably. The "brain" is a physical bodily organ that sits inside your skull. The "mind" is the part of the human person that thinks and has an awareness or self-consciousness. Although we frequently use the terms synonymously, they are in fact very different. The genius of Dr. Eccles was to clearly solve the distinction and interactions between the "mind" and the "brain":

> The essential feature . . . is that the mind and brain are independent entities . . . and that they interact by quantum physics. . . . There is a frontier, and across this frontier there is interaction in both directions, which can be conceived as a flow of information, not of energy. Thus we have the extraordinary doctrine that the world of matter-energy is not completely sealed.[17]

Oh, am I in trouble! Before Riley does me bodily harm, let me call Schroeder to the rescue! I once heard him use the following analogy. In a crowded auditorium, there are hundreds of cell phones, which are visible—usually strapped to a man's belt or tucked away in a woman's purse. At the same time, there are thousands of cell phone waves, which are not seen. The invisible waves activate the visible phone. Furthermore, specific phones are tuned to specific waves. A phone will only ring when activated by its specific wave. The mind and the brain work in an analogous manner. The brain is like the phone and the mind is like the invisible waves. The brain is activated by the mind to which it is specifically tuned.

There are some obvious limitations of this analogy, but it really helps to illustrate the relationship between the mind and the brain.[18] However, it is truly amazing that this analogy—which helps us to understand the modern scientific understanding of the working of the brain—sounds incredibly similar to that statement St. John Chrysostom made sixteen hundred years ago, "You see, this body created in the Lord's design was like an instrument needing someone to activate it."[19]

Beyond the Limits of the Material World

We should learn from Dr. Eccles to take a moment to ponder the implications of a spiritual mind. If we take just a moment to ask ourselves a couple of very important questions, we will see the human person in a new and amazingly beautiful way.

The first critical question is, "Since your mind is spiritual, where did it come from?" The spiritual mind is not made of matter. As such, it is impossible for the spiritual mind to have come from the material world. A spiritual mind must come from something else that is spiritual. The answer to this question lies beyond the realm of science, which deals specifically with the material world. Scripture says that the spiritual mind comes from a spiritual Being—God: "The Lord God . . . blew into his nostrils the breath of life" (Genesis 2:7). It is possible that man's material body evolved through the course of time according to the laws of nature, but the spiritual dimension of the human person comes directly from God.[20] Furthermore, when God creates the spiritual dimension of the human person, he does so in a very personal way, "I have called you by name" (Isaiah 43:1), which will become very important when considering the marriage covenant.

A second critical question is, "If your mind is spiritual, where does it exist?" The "easy" answer is that it exists with you. While Riley is looking the other way, I'll slip in a very difficult theological term. Theologians call the mind an "embodied consciousness," which means that the spiritual dimension of the human person is not separate from the material dimension. Nonetheless, the spiritual dimension of the human person transcends the limits of the visible world of created things. Amazingly, that statement mirrors in many ways our understanding of God. He certainly transcends the limits of the created world, while at the same time he is present to it.

I know that Riley is already on the phone trying to get me a ticket out of Texas as fast as possible, but this is amazing stuff. Your mind and God both exist in a spiritual realm. As such, it is absolutely natural for you to talk with God. Indeed, it is unnatural for the human person to not talk with God. As such, it just doesn't work when you try to function in a way that is not natural to the human person, which probably helps to explain the link between spiritual practices and health that we have already noted on several occasions. Furthermore, since you and God both exist in a spiritual dimension, your communication with God is not limited to your sensible perceptions of the eyes and ears. You have been perfectly made to communicate with another spiritual being—God.

A final critical question is, "What happens to your mind when you die?" To answer this question, let's go back and consider those table and chairs I made from a tree. After I finish my tasty—homemade—bacon cheeseburger cooked on the grill, let's assume I allow my wooden picnic table to remain outside exposed to the elements. After a few years of sun and rain, it begins to look really bad—even worse than it does today. If I wait long enough, it falls apart. It returns to its fundamental elements—primarily hydrogen, oxygen, and carbon. Indeed, that's the life cycle of a tree. It grows by absorbing water (H_2O) from the ground and breathing in carbon dioxide (CO_2). It breaks apart these elements and uses them to form the structures of the tree. When the tree dies, these elements simply break apart and fall back into the earth.

This is exactly what happens to the human body. Approximately 93 percent of the human body is composed of these same three basic elements, oxygen, carbon, and hydrogen.[21] When a person dies, these elements in the human body break apart and go back into the ground. Scripture says, "Out of the ground you were taken. You are dust, and to dust you shall return" (Genesis 2:19). This is literally true. Death marks the decomposition or breaking apart of an organism into its most elemental pieces.

But what about the mind? It is spiritual. It is not material. As such, it cannot be broken down into smaller parts. Furthermore, since it cannot be broken apart, it survives the death of the body. In the words of Schroeder, "Smash the cell phone and the waves continue to exist." This is pretty monumental! Science itself leads us to the conclusion that there is something in the human person that transcends this material world—the mind—and that this mind survives death. Amazing. Nonetheless, we need to ask ourselves, "Can science take us any further?" Actually, yes.

Thanks to the advances in modern medicine, we live in an amazing age when on a daily basis there are numerous people who die and then are brought back to life. It is called a *near-death experience* (NDE), although it is actually a *real* death experience. What was once the realm of science fiction now occurs on a regular basis in America's leading hospitals. Furthermore, the sheer number of these occurrences has transformed them from fodder for the *National Enquirer* to an accepted field of academic study.

Studies indicate that approximately 18 percent of cardiac arrest patients who are resuscitated have an NDE. The most common experiences of these patients are given in Table 5.2. A quick look at this list reveals many of the points we have just discussed. Many experience an existence that transcends the material body. They meet others who have "passed through death" and are able to communicate without being bound to spoken words. And, yes, many meet another spiritual being.

The experience of these patients while they are "dead" transforms their lives once they are brought back to life (see Table 5.3). Not surprisingly, they have a strong belief in the afterlife and many lose the fear of death. Perhaps more surprisingly, their values change. Many lose a desire for the superficial things in life—all the things we discussed in Chapters 2, 3, and 4, which frequently lead to divorce. Instead, they have an appreciation for the more ordinary things in life and become more involved in their families.

One man who personally experienced a very real death experience was Don Piper. He was driving across the two-lane Lake Houston bridge during one of those torrential Houston downpours. An oncoming truck pulled out of its lane to attempt to pass a car and hit Piper's car head on. He was instantaneously killed. The impact from the collision was so great that a four-inch section of his leg was ejected from the car. His arm was

Near-Death Experience*	
Positive emotions	56%
Awareness of being dead	50%
Meet deceased relatives/friends	32%
Move through a tunnel	31%
Perception of celestial landscape	29%
Out-of-body experience	24%
Perception of colors	23%
Communicate with "the light"	23%

Table 5.2: Near-Death Experience
* Eighty-two percent of resuscitation patients report no NDE.
Source: van Lommel, P. et al., "Near-Death Experiences in Survivors of Cardiac Arrest: A Prospective Study in the Netherlands," *Lancet* 358 (2001): 2039–2045.

Near-Death Experience Impact on Life	
Belief in afterlife	+162%
Sense meaning in life	+128%
Increased acceptance of others	+90%
Appreciate ordinary things	+68%
Lose fear of death	+54%
More empathetic	+36%
More involved in family	+34%
Increased interest in spirituality	~

Table 5.3: Near-Death Experience Impact on Life
Source: van Lommel, P. et al., *Consciousness Beyond Life: The Science of Near Death Experience* (New York: HarperOne, 2007) p. 52.

almost ripped from his body. He had massive internal injuries from being impaled by the steering wheel.

When the police and medical personnel arrived on the scene, Don Piper was pronounced dead. Since state law mandated certification by the county coroner's office before the body could be removed, his body was covered with a tarp while emergency personnel treated other casualties. Traffic on the two-lane bridge backed up for miles and the county coroner was unable to get to the scene of the accident. Furthermore, since the thunderstorm was just short of a deluge, helicopters could not fly. Don Piper remained under the tarp, trapped in his mangled car, for ninety minutes.

During the time that his body remained dead on the Lake Houston bridge, Don Piper's spirit was somewhere else. He met deceased family and friends. He experienced communication that did not need words or sound. He heard incredibly beautiful music and even saw God.

During these ninety minutes, a Baptist minister came upon the scene of the accident. He placed his hand on Don Piper's back under the tarp. He prayed for him and began singing old church hymns. At length, the minister felt movement in Don Piper's mangled body and raced for help. It took hours, but an ambulance arrived and transported him to a succession of hospitals until he arrived at the only hospital in Houston capable of addressing his injuries. Don Piper survived, but had a very, very long and hard road to recovery. He recounted his story in *90 Minutes in Heaven*, and today he travels the world helping people understand that there is something in the human person that survives death and is capable of experiencing a beauty that transcends this material world. Science understands the experience of Don Piper. So does faith.

Mind Stretch #3: The Spousal Union

Now it gets interesting. I only have one shot left to get back in Riley's good graces! Although we will see some pretty amazing science in this last mind stretch, I promise no more Nobel laureates. As ironic as it may seem, we are going to talk about a little rodent to help us better understand the spousal union between man and woman. Nonetheless, it is precisely this irony that gives me hope. Riley grew up on a farm in East Texas. He knows a lot about rodents!

In Judeo-Christian history, the concept of the spousal union between man and woman holds a very unique place. Its definition goes all the way back to the second chapter of the Scripture when man and woman are still enjoying the good life in the Garden of Eden:

Therefore a man leaves his father and his mother and cleaves to his wife and they become one flesh (Genesis 2:24).

To the nonreligious person, this may simply seem like poetic or romantic language. To the skeptic, it may seem like the Bible's way of avoiding the word S-E-X. Nonetheless, for people of faith it is much, much more. Indeed, Christ said that he expected his followers to live their marriages as had been intended for man and woman in the Garden of Eden (see Matthew 19:3–9). As such, the blessing given to Catholic couples during the marriage ceremony proclaims marriage to be "the one blessing that was not forfeited by original sin or washed away in the flood."[22]

One of the strongest statements made by a Christian thinker on marriage in the past two thousand years was made by Pope John Paul II near the end of his life: "One flesh! How can we not see the power of this expression? . . . What the spouses achieve is not only a joining of bodies, but a true union of their persons."[23]

You will never find such language in a scientific journal discussing the relationship between men and women. Notwithstanding our previous discussion, the vast majority of scientists do not consider the spiritual dimension of the human person, which is not too surprising since science deals with the material world. Considering only the material dimension of the human person, humans are placed on par with every other species of living animals. Therefore, the relationship between male and female animals becomes the surrogate for understanding the relationship between men and women.

In the animal kingdom, the relationship between males and females is largely determined by the possibility of reproduction. By and large, male and female animals come together for a close encounter when the female enters the fertile period of her cycle. Once the close encounter is accomplished, the male animal goes on his way and the female animal bears and raises the new offspring. In the animal kingdom, it's pretty much that simple.

During a presentation, a farmer once replied, "I could have told you that. Put a bull in a pasture with a whole herd of cows and he couldn't care less. But let one cow come into heat a mile away, and he will go through three barbed-wire fences to get to her!"

Farmers get it. There's hope for me with Riley.

I certainly agree that reproduction is an important aspect of the relationship between men and women. Furthermore, since we have a material body, it obeys the laws of the material world. Therefore, I readily embrace some pretty amazing science regarding the attraction between men and women, which is explicitly tied to the possibility of reproductive success.

From a distance, men and women are checking for visual clues regarding fertility and overall health. Men are checking for overall body symmetry, complexion, and a magical hip-to-waist ratio. Women are checking for overall body symmetry, complexion, a rugged jaw line, and signs of success. When men and women move in a little closer, they are able to subconsciously get a sense of the compatibility of their immune systems in the pheromones emitted by the body. Sensing the possibility of success, they move in for a close encounter of a human kind, a kiss. In the exchange of saliva, the brain is able to subconsciously determine genetic information and compatibility of a potential mate.[24]

The most important sexual organ of all—the brain—has been following this journey with keen interest. Convinced that a suitable partner is within reach, the brain's reward circuitry kicks into high gear. The caudate nucleus activates, helping the person to identify a "reward," and motivates them to attain the "reward." Dopamine, that cocaine-like, addictive substance we encountered in Chapters 2 and 3, is secreted in the ventral tegmental area and released in the nucleus accumbens. Throw in a little testosterone, epinephrine, and norepinephrine and the person experiences an exhilaration and unwavering motivation to attain a close encounter of a very personal kind.[25] Let the pursuit begin. He may not need to go through three barbed-wire fences, but flowers, chocolates, romantic dinners, walks in nature? No problem!

Such is the science of "animal attraction." By the way, Riley is back from the kitchen. He's in the front row with a big smile.

All of this is fine and good for as far as it goes. But for humans, men and women have more than a brief encounter. They form attachments, very deep attachments. Even in a culture where 40 percent of marriages end in divorce, humans form attachments between males and females that are rare in the animal kingdom. One such monogamous animal is a very interesting little rodent. Once prairie voles mate, they form pair bonds that generally last until one of the partners dies. This distinction has led to incredible interest in the prairie vole and has made it subject to an endless array of testing.

Researchers have discovered that prairie voles have an extra piece of DNA on the gene that controls the distribution of vasopressin receptors. Vasopressin is very important in forming attachments, especially for males. Take this little piece of DNA out of the prairie vole and he becomes just as promiscuous as other animals. Insert this piece of DNA into a normally promiscuous mouse and he suddenly becomes monogamous.[26] Interestingly enough, humans have this same piece of DNA on the gene that codes for vasopressin expression in humans. It seems as if we have been "made" with the biology to enable us to form substantial, permanent bonds.

Furthermore, scientists have meticulously studied the process by which two prairie voles from a pair bond.[27] After selecting a partner, prairie voles mate *a lot* over a 24-hour period, releasing copious amounts of dopamine, oxytocin, and vasopressin. Under the influence of these neurotransmitters, the brain is restructured. Dopamine works to restructure the nucleus accumbens where it is released. Oxytocin and vasopressin are hormones related to attachment. They work to restructure the lateral septum, which is important in mood and stress regulation. This makes perfect sense. If you are going to have a preferential option for one mate over another, you must "feel" comfortable in his or her presence, which implies a reduction of stress—the ultimate killer of physical intimacy—and you must be neurochemically rewarded for your choice.

I know that it's not very romantic, but this sounds a lot like the honeymoon period for a young couple. Right after a couple is married, they normally have lots of physical intimacy. During this period, the brain receives a little dopamine reward for each intimate encounter, which reinforces the behavior ensuring that it will be repeated. At the same time, the lateral septum is being rewired so that the couple experiences peace and joy in each other's presence, which creates a preferential option for the couple to spend more time together.

More amazingly, research indicates a long-term romantic partner impacts regions of the brain that are crucial to a person's awareness of self, specifically the middle insula and anterior cingulate.[28] Furthermore, studies indicate that the brain's response to hearing the name of a loved one is similar to hearing one's own name.[29] Researchers talk about the neural reality that a loved one becomes "part of the self . . . such that the self includes the other in its very makeup."[30]

Oh no! The smile is gone from Riley's face, but I think I can help him pretty easily. Science indicates that the union Shelly and I experience is so intimate that I truly begin to see Shelly as part of my very self—so much so that I will carry Shelly's name in the same place that I carry my own name! Wow! That's pretty monumental. Science has taken us to the very cusp of the statement from Pope John Paul II: "What the spouses achieve is not only a joining of bodies, but a true union of their persons."[31]

Let's try to better understand this moment when the two become one. To do so, we will need to introduce two brain structures and two bodily systems, but it's not too bad considering everything we've already covered. I think Riley will be just fine.

You have an area in your brain that helps you to define yourself relative to everything else. It's called the *posterior superior parietal lobe*. Think of it as the mental on–off switch. It allows you to distinguish between "this is me" and "that's not me." This structure is not fully developed in newborns, so they have trouble determining the boundary between themselves and their mother. But in the vast majority of individuals it functions so effortlessly that we are not aware it even exists.

As spouses enter into physical intimacy there are two key systems that influence activities throughout the body. The sympathetic or arousal system is located in the middle spinal cord and it helps the body to enter into an aroused state. Adrenaline and testosterone are released into the blood stream. Pupils dilate. Blood vessels constrict. Sweat glands turn on. Heart rate accelerates. The body is prepared to act.

At the same time, the parasympathetic or quiescent system kind of takes a break. This system is located in the brain stem and exerts a calming influence on the body. When the quiescent system dominates, the heart rate slows. Salivary glands turn on. The stomach prepares to sit down and enjoy that bacon cheeseburger I just cooked.

Under normal conditions the arousal and quiescent systems work in tandem. One dominates while the other takes a bit of a break. However, as spouses approach the moment of climax, something interesting happens. The arousal system attains such a heightened state that it robs the quiescent system of the input it needs to operate. The quiescent system does what most systems in the body do when they are deprived of input. It fights for its life by kicking into overdrive. Suddenly, two systems that are called to work in tandem are both operating at maximum capacity. The body is in a simultaneous state of arousal and blissful peace. This is the ecstatic bliss of orgasm.

At this moment, a new structure in the brain turns on. The prefrontal cortex has the job of sorting out all the relevant data that the body sends to it. Suddenly, it is flooded with an overload of information from both the arousal and quiescent systems. To handle the flood of information from both systems, the prefrontal cortex deprives the posterior superior parietal lobe of the input it needs to function. Deprived of input, the posterior superior parietal lobe is unable to clearly determine the boundaries between the self and the beloved. The two become one in a union that originates in the body, but transcends it.

Since we're almost to the end of our chapter on stretching the mind, I would like to stretch it almost to the breaking point. In the previous mind stretch relating to the human person, we came to understand that the mind, which includes an awareness of self or a self-consciousness, is a spiritual reality that comes from a spiritual being—God. We even saw that God has "called us by name" (cf. Isaiah 43:1). Now we have come to understand that the boundaries between spouses blur in the mind so that the awareness of self may contain two names—the individual and the spouse. Is it possible to believe that when God spoke you into existence he already had the image of your spouse in his mind? Scripture seems to hint at this mystery. It says that the spousal union is a work of God: "They are no longer two, but one. What therefore God has joined together, let no man put asunder" (Matthew 19:6).

If you look closely, you will see a tear in Riley's eye. He gets it. He knows that Rose Mary was God's great gift to him. They have been one for almost fifty years. He can't imagine his life any other way.

So—that's Step #4. If we're willing to do a little work, read science and Scripture with an open mind, be patient, and pray, we'll be amazed. We'll discover a depth and beauty unimagined. We might even be able to catch a fleeting glimpse of God. That's where we're headed.

CHAPTER SIX

STEP FIVE:
Find God in Yourself

The fifth step to a superabundant marriage is to find God in yourself. I know. I can already hear it. "Find God in myself? No way. My life is a total disaster! Rushing to the soccer game. Forgot to pick up the snack. Forgot to put out the dog. The dog eats the snack—then gets sick. Kid can't live without his brownie goldfish snack. Melts down. Screams at me. I scream at my husband. He goes out to the doghouse. Everyone goes to bed hungry and upset—except the dog. He loves soccer game days, but is a bit disappointed in me. I really need to stick to it when I say no more chocolate snacks for the kids."

The biggest issue most people have with the fifth step is the life they live. Nothing could seem further from the divine. I am confident that Riley and Rose Mary would have said the same thing. Furthermore, being part of the Greatest Generation, their feet were planted so firmly on the ground that they would never speak in such lofty terms about their own life, nor would they appreciate it if I did. You think Riley had problems with me in the previous chapter? He never sold that express ticket out of Texas! Nonetheless, one of the reasons we waded through all the science in the previous chapter was to discover how the extraordinary lies just on the other side of the ordinary.

For just a moment think about the life that the Greatest Generation lived. Riley was born in 1915. Although the car had been invented, the most common means of transportation by far was the foot—either your own or that of a horse. By the end of his life, international air travel was common and a select group of individuals had been to the moon and back. In his lifetime he saw the advent of radio, telephones, television, computers, cell phones, the Internet, and countless other technological breakthroughs. He faced monumental challenges: World War I, the Great Depression, World War II, Communism and the Cold War, the resignation of a president in disgrace, oil embargoes, runaway inflation, and stock market booms and busts.

In the midst of these monumental events Riley and Rose Mary lived pretty ordinary lives. They fell in love and got married. They had children and worked hard to put food on the table. They did their best to instill solid values in their children and place their feet on the road to happiness.

Nonetheless, if we are willing to stretch our spiritual legs, we will discover the divine hidden behind the mundane details of Riley's and Rose Mary's lives. We will be able to glimpse a hint of the mystery in their unquestioned moral and ethical code that is founded in an unquestioned belief in God. We will see it in their willingness to believe in the power of love when the world is enveloped in darkness and races toward its own destruction. We will see it in their willingness to bring new life into this world when they were not sure if the world had a future or what it would hold. Yes, the divine was very much a part of Riley's and Rose Mary's lives, but in a subtle and hidden way.

Every generation faces social upheaval, fiscal uncertainty, and technological innovation. Our challenge is to learn from Riley and Rose Mary the art of keeping our feet planted firmly on the ground during tumultuous times and embracing a normal everyday life as the pathway to union with God.

To Be a Person of Integrity

I think that the unquestioned moral and ethical code that Riley, Rose Mary, and the Greatest Generation embraced is most easily recognized in action. In his book, *Wisdom of Our Fathers*, the late Tim Russert tells the story of Grady Donaldson.[1] Grady and his twin brother, Frank, were born in 1922 in the small town of Adamsville, Tennessee. Born prematurely, no one expected them to survive, but they did. Grady had one of those magnetic personalities. Greatness was written across his face and everyone knew that an impressive future was in store.

Then came World War II. Grady and Frank served under General George S. Patton. They were both captured during the Battle of the Bulge and sent to a German prisoner of war camp. Life in the prison camps was hell. Grady dropped to 95 pounds and Frank became deathly ill. He seemed destined to die a forgotten death in a German prison camp like so many other American soldiers. Grady knelt beside Frank's bed and offered a prayer to God: "If you allow Frank and me to survive and go back to Adamsville alive, I will never ask for anything again. I will accept whatever you send me."

Frank recovered. He and Grady returned to Adamsville. Grady kept his promise to God. He accepted the first job that was offered him—minimum wage at a local garment factory. He never moved on. He stayed at that same garment factory for over forty years. Nonetheless, he had a beautiful life. He was happily married and had more friends than anyone could count. He remained deeply religious and had a joy that could not be shaken. Furthermore, he had the respect of every man in that town. They knew that he had made a deal with the "man upstairs." Grady was a man of integrity. He gave his word and he kept it.

Grady lived in a time where you were expected to be "a man of your word." In some ways, things haven't changed much. People still value the truth. In surveys of American high school students, 98 percent say that it is important to be honest in your interpersonal relationships and 95 percent say that it is important to be honest in your business dealings.[2] Nonetheless, as seen in Figure 6.1, the same group of high school students has significant difficulty living the values they espouse. Over 80 percent have lied on *an important matter* in their most important relationship (with their parents) and over 80 percent have been dishonest in their "job." They copied someone else's homework. Furthermore, almost 50 percent have violated their personal moral principles and, amazingly, one in four student admits to having lied on the survey about honesty—although I'm not sure we can believe them!

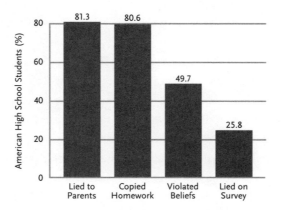

Figure 6.1: Honesty Among High School Students
Source: Josephson Institute, Center for Youth Ethics, *2010 Report Card on the Ethics of American Youth* (2011). Data Tables.

How do we explain this incredible gap between the values the students espouse and the life they live? Obviously, there is no one single answer, but a good place to start is pressure. It is amazing what a little pressure from the right people can do to alter behavior. Surveys indicate that approximately 79 percent of college students were introduced to alcohol by their friends[3] and 94 percent were introduced to drugs by their friends.[4] Furthermore, almost one-third of college students use alcohol and/or drugs as their primary means for handling stress.[5] Unfortunately, this leads many down a path to further problems. Seventy percent of college students admit to engaging in sexual activities primarily as a result of drinking and 60 percent of college women infected with sexually transmitted diseases (STDs) report that they were under the influence of alcohol at the time they had intercourse with the infected person.[6]

Introduce God into this equation and it is amazing how things change. A survey of high school students indicates that students attending weekly religious services were about one-half as likely to have substance abuse issues. As shown in Figure 6.2, alcohol usage drops from 27 percent to 15 percent and marijuana usage from 16 percent to 6 percent. Behind these statistics is a certain value system. But as we have seen relating to honesty, many people espouse a certain value system, but struggle to live it. As such, there is more involved than a set of intellectual beliefs.

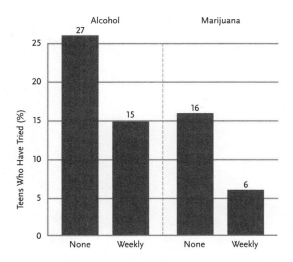

Figure 6.2: Religious Attendance and Substance Abuse
Source: The National Center on Addiction and Substance Abuse at Columbia
University, "The Importance of Family Dinners VI," (September 2010): 14

On the one hand, God strengthens the person from within to withstand the pressure from without: "God may grant you to be strengthened with might through his Spirit in the inner man" (Ephesians 3:16). But we must go much further. If God dwells within us, then we "are God's temple" (1 Corinthians 3:16). This gives an entirely new dignity to the body. It is holy and should be treated as such. Substance abuse? Not consistent with the dignity of the body. Poor diet? Oops—I guess supersizing the fries and soda at lunch was a bad idea! Exercise? Does watching football count?

The realization of the dignity of the body impacts much more than eating, drinking, and—thankfully—exercise. It has a direct relationship to sexual beliefs and practices. "Do you not know that your bodies are members of Christ? . . . He who joins himself to a prostitute becomes one body with her. . . . The immoral man sins against his own body" (1 Corinthians 6:15–18). As such, it is not surprising to find a direct link between religious practice and sexual activity. As seen in Figure 6.3, never-married individuals who go to church on a weekly basis are twice as likely as those who never go to church to refrain from sexual activity. On the other hand, married individuals who never go to church are almost twice as likely to cheat on their spouse versus those who go to church on a weekly basis.

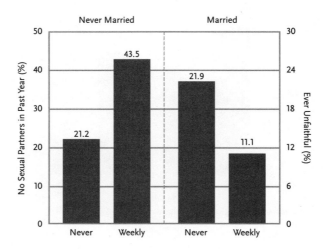

Figure 6.3: Church Attendance and Sexual Activity
Source: General Social Survey 1972–2012.

There are some very practical implications related to this sexual ethics or moral code. The number one risk factor for an STD is the number of sexual partners.[7] Religious practice is tied to a reduction in the number of sexual partners, which ties to a reduced risk of sexual disease. The sexual moral code makes "good health sense"—as did the reduced substance abuse, improved diet, and exercise.

Furthermore, we just addressed two of the top three reasons leading to divorce—infidelity and substance abuse. They tie right back to the moral or ethical code, which ties to a relationship to God. Riley is already smiling, but watch this . . . so do money issues. Believe it or not, religious practice changes a person's "relationship" with money. People more involved in their faith life are better able to forego immediate material gratification.[8] Translated into everyday language—they are better able to leave the credit card in its place when the blue light special rings! Spending money foolishly was the third big issue leading to divorce. A strong moral or ethical code built upon a relationship with God is really good for your marriage.

The Ultimate Love Affair

Riley loved the last section, but here comes the tricky part. If you consider Judeo-Christian revelation, the ultimate point is not the revelation or institution of a moral or ethical code. It is the revelation of a relationship—the relationship between God and humanity. This relationship is not ultimately revealed to be between the Creator and creature or even Savior and sinner. These are certainly true, but the relationship between God and humanity is much more intimate. Scripture reveals it in terms of the lover and beloved. It even uses terms expressing spousal intimacy:

> As a young man marries a virgin, your Builder shall marry you; And as a bridegroom rejoices in his bride so shall your God rejoice in you (Isaiah 62:5).

Just as spouses become "one," we are called to become "one" with God. St. Paul, the great apostle to the gentiles, would boldly proclaim: "It is no longer I who live, but Christ who lives in me" (Galatians 2:20). Since we live in such intimate union with God, we are called to live something of the divine life of God. More accurately, we are called to allow God to live his divine life in and through us.

Interestingly enough, the divine life of God has been revealed to us in explicitly familial terms. We no longer speak of God as simply the Creator. We call him Father: "When you pray, say: 'Father, hallowed be thy name'" (Luke 11:2). Furthermore, we also understand God to be the divine bridegroom: "The marriage of the Lamb [i.e., Jesus] has come, and his Bride has made herself ready" (Revelation 19:7). Suddenly, my normal, everyday life takes on an entirely new light. My life as a parent or as a spouse has been caught up into the divine life. The extraordinary lies just on the other side of the ordinary. This is the life that Riley and Rose Mary lived.

Finding God in Your Life as a Parent

Anyone who has been a parent knows that the biggest part of parenting is filled with the mundane: putting food on the table, washing clothes, helping kids with their homework, trying to keep the dog from eating the homework—and the chocolate! Nonetheless, behind the ordinary lies the extraordinary. To help us glimpse this mystery, let's take a look at the fatherhood of God, which we first encounter in the Garden of Eden. There we can identify four specific aspects of God's fatherhood:

- God begets life by taking preexisting matter and animating it with the breath of God (cf. Genesis 2:7).
- God provides superabundantly for His children (cf. Genesis 2:9).
- God places the person in a face-to-face relationship so that the isolation of self is shattered and speech bursts forth (cf. Genesis 2:22–24).
- God provides a moral code, which will help humanity live forever. He expects this moral code to be shared from person to person (cf. Genesis 2:16–17).

If we carefully consider our life as a parent, we will see that these same four aspects are involved. Indeed, we will see that our parenting is actually a cooperation with the fatherhood of God.

The Miracle of Life

For many people the greatest experience they have of something transcendental in their lives is the birth of their first child. I remember the moment the nurse placed our first daughter in my arms. I looked at our daughter. Then I looked at Shelly. I looked back at our daughter and then back at Shelly.

Finally, in a moment of pure awe, I blurted out, "Honey, I can't believe what you did!"

Of course, Shelly replied, "I didn't do it!"

Even if couples don't place an explicitly religious label on the birth of their child, many sense that "something beyond them" was involved. Our discussion in the previous chapter certainly led us to the same conclusion. We saw that science is beginning to grasp the spiritual reality of the mind. Furthermore, we saw that this spiritual dimension of the human person must come from another spiritual being—God. We explicitly related it to the "breath of God" or soul that animates a human person. As such, it is easy to see that the conception and birth of a new child is a cooperation between the couple and God.

However, let's go a little further. When we consider the human person from a purely biological perspective, science seems to have an opening for God's cooperation. I certainly understand the "birds and the bees," but let us begin by noting that identical twins aren't truly identical. They're close enough to have a little fun with some harmless mischief, but, in fact, family and friends can easily tell identical twins apart.[9] Let's think about this for a moment. Identical twins have the same father, the same mother, the same egg, and the same sperm. Why aren't identical twins absolutely identical?

One potential answer is epigenetics, which are inheritable changes that are not encoded on the DNA.[10] In epigenetics, certain behaviors and foods can impact gene expression through the process of DNA methylation. This change in gene expression can be passed on to the offspring and in some cases passed on to the third generation. Nonetheless, we can simply alter our previous question slightly, "Since the identical twins have the same mother and father who had the same behaviors and ate the same foods, why would there be a different gene expression?"

Undoubtedly, science will continue to investigate this question and make progress. Nonetheless, I personally think we will discover a degree of randomness or freedom that allows for God's action within the laws of nature. Amazingly, this would take us very close to the story of creation in Genesis where God took preexisting matter and formed it into a human body into which he breathed the "breath of life." Just as God took flesh from Adam to form Eve, he could take flesh from the husband and wife to form into a baby: "You formed my inmost being; you knit me in my mother's womb" (Psalm 139:13).

If such is the case, let us ask ourselves why he chooses to use the flesh of husband and wife to create a new child. God could form humans from the dust as he did for Adam. God chooses to allow us to cooperate in the birth of a child because he wants us to share in his own fatherhood "from whom every father in heaven and earth is named" (Ephesians 3:15).[11]

The Birth of a Parent

Amazingly, as soon as parents gaze into the eyes of their newborn infants, their brains are transformed. Indeed, the same mechanisms that we saw in the previous chapter regarding the love between man and woman are active again. The nucleus accumbens starts pumping out dopamine and the brain is bathed in vasopressin and oxytocin, the bonding hormones.[12] The parents' brains are primed to fall in love with the little tyke. Furthermore, the prefrontal cortex activates, which is the area of the brain used for thinking and predicting consequences.[13] Suddenly, the formerly carefree couple who enjoyed vacationing around the globe is worried about providing for their child, including saving money for college, which is almost two decades into the future.

The need to provide for your children is certainly a big deal and I know that parents work very hard to do so. At times it is very easy to lose sight of the supernatural aspect of work and focus solely on our own efforts. But, I already see Riley shaking his head. "Go to bed hungry just once in your life and it will change you forever." He lived through the Great Depression. He saw that hard work isn't always enough. It also takes the grace of God.

Of course, we live in different times. Technology gives us the illusion that we have conquered nature and the economic process. Nonetheless, I've personally lived through the worst drought in Texas history. The sky seemed to literally dry up. Grass withered and livestock died in the pasture. It's easy to dismiss this as a temporary weather pattern, which it was. But science, once more, leaves open the possibility for action by God within the laws of nature.

Chaos theory is a field of mathematics in which very small fluctuations in initial values can have drastic impacts in dynamic systems. Chaos theory has been used to explain a host of different systems, including the weather. Indeed, chaos theory says that it's impossible to accurately make long-term weather forecasts. The sensitivity to minute changes in the starting values is too great.

Once again, I have utmost confidence that we will continue to build better forecasting models for almost everything, including the weather. Nonetheless, I once again think it entirely plausible that we will discover a degree of randomness or freedom that permits the action of God within the laws of nature.

In the Garden of Eden, God provided food for his children. The prophet Hosea lets us know that he continues to provide for us: "She did not know that it was I who gave her the grain, the wine, and the oil" (Hosea 2:10). Providing for our children is actually a share in the providence of God.

The Gift of Communication

Not long after the birth of a child, the parents start to notice that the little tyke actually takes a keen interest in them. He smiles at them—even laughs. He frequently makes interesting noises, which at times are nothing more than gas. Nonetheless, otherwise perfectly normal, rational adults start to act like . . . babies. They even begin to sound like babies. They talk baby talk. "Aren't you cute today? You know that you're cute today!"

The parents do all of this spontaneously. It's called *infant elicited responses*.[14] There's something about the sight of the baby that pulls it out of an adult. Interestingly, in the Garden of Eden, Adam was the first to talk in his face-to-face relationship with Eve (cf. Genesis 2:22–24). It's as if Eve pulled something out of Adam.

Nonetheless, scientists have discovered that baby talk is perfectly suited to teach the baby to talk. Facial expressions are exaggerated to engage the interest of the child. Speech is simplified and slowed so that the child can "follow the conversation." The vowels are elongated emphasizing the most important element of word structure. Pauses between words are lengthened, indicating to the child the place for him to enter into the conversation. Incredibly, these pauses have been timed to within 0.01 seconds of the time it would take the child to insert a simple one word response.[15] "Aren't you cute today?"—YES—"You know you're cute today!" Finally, baby talk includes the perfect blend of repetition—to reinforce learning for the child—and variation—to keep the child interested.[16]

If you are observant, you will notice that the child frequently focuses upon your mouth while you are speaking. This activates the mirror neuron system in the child's brain, including those in the Broca's area, which is a region of the brain associated with language. Baby talk is perfectly suited to teach a child to speak—and you do it all without consciously thinking!

Let's continue on. In the Garden of Eden, Adam's face-to-face communion with Eve brought meaning to his life: "Therefore a man shall leave his father and his mother and cleave to his wife" (Genesis 2:24). In many ways, this mystery is repeated in the life of the child. In his face-to-face communication with his parents, the child begins to make sense of the world.

Indeed, not long after birth, the brain of the little child attempts to figure out this big, brave world into which it has been thrust. Unfortunately, he has no experience as a frame of reference. What's a little tyke to do? Easy answer—use the experience in his parent's brain! As the baby begins experiencing life, he constantly sends signals to his parent regarding his internal state. I'm hungry. I'm scared. I'm poopy. I'm excited. I'm happy. I'm sad.

Through the mirror neuron system in the empathy regions of the parent's brain, the parent is able to perceive the internal reality of the child. They are then able to send a reality check back to the child, who uses the parent's response to help form his own thinking patterns.[17]

Oh no! Riley is not smiling. Let me make this very simple. A baby spills a glass of milk. He sees a bunch of white liquid rush out over the entire table and onto the floor. He literally doesn't know what has happened and if it is a big deal or not, but it certainly doesn't look normal. Tears well up in the child's eyes as he looks to the parent to make sense of the situation. When the parent says, "Don't cry over spilled milk," the child accepts the parent's reality check and smiles. Life is good.

This "contingent communication" happens continually between the child and the parent. So much so that the child is constantly using feedback from the parent to build models of how the world works. These models are stored in a child's implicit memory, which is the only memory active in a child during the first year of life. Since these models are not "explicit," they are largely in a person's subconscious. Nonetheless, they form the basis for the child's understanding of how the world works. In other words, they help bring meaning to the child's life.

Once more this sounds a lot like the Garden of Eden. Adam was enveloped in a deafening silence when he was alone. Locked in the isolation of self, his life had no meaning. To transform Adam, God placed him face-to-face with another person. Gazing upon Eve, Adam discovered the meaning of his existence, spoke the first words, and shattered the silence of Paradise.

God used a person to form another human person. He didn't need to do it this way. He could have created a computer chip, placed it in Adam's brain, and downloaded all the information Adam needed. Even easier, he could have simply formed the person himself, but he preferred to use another person. Why? Simply to allow us the dignity of participating in his own divine life.

A Moral Code Leading to Everlasting Life

The final aspect of the fatherhood of God that we encountered in the Garden of Eden was the moral code that God gave to Adam: "You are free to eat from any of the trees of the garden except the tree of knowledge of good and evil. From that tree you shall not eat; when you eat from it you shall die" (Genesis 2:16–17). It is obvious that God intended Adam to share this moral code with Eve.

Likewise, God expects parents to share with their children the moral code. Interestingly, the life they live is the most important way that they share this moral code with their children. Let's just take a simple example: Children of parents who smoke are three times as likely to begin smoking as children whose parents don't smoke.[18] Now I'm not going to throw you under the bus for smoking, but this illustrates a basic point. Children frequently adopt behaviors and attitudes of their parents. To a certain extent, they are primed to do so through the mirror neuron system. Every time they watch their parent consciously perform an action, they are mirroring that action in their own brain.

Nonetheless, this link between parents and children goes further. Earlier in the chapter we mentioned an exciting new field called *epigenetics*. Researchers have discovered that behavior can help determine the expression of genes, which can be passed to the next generation. Let's consider just one area, alcohol. It has long been known that children of alcoholics are more likely to become alcoholic than children whose parents are not alcoholics. Researchers have now determined that epigenetics plays a role in this relationship.[19] The alcoholism of the parent impacts gene expression, which is passed to the child. Suddenly, the ability to live a life of integrity becomes very important. We must model the behavior we wish our children to live.

By now, I'm sure a few parents are kicking themselves rather hard. But there's good news and it's easier than you think. If you wish your children to make wise choices and "turn out okay," put them in touch with God. We've seen that God makes a person's life happier, healthier, and wealthier. The easiest way to put your children in touch with God is for you to be in touch with God yourself. As can be seen in Figure 6.4, if you go to church weekly, approximately 62 percent of your children will continue going to church at least almost weekly when they are grown. That's almost two out of three. That's not bad!

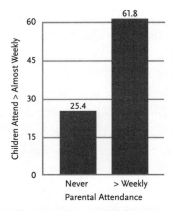

Figure 6.4: Parent and Children Prayer
Source: General Social Survey, 1972–2012.

Believe it or not, Riley is still smiling. He gets it. He just leaned over to Rose Mary and said, "It's simple. All he said is that we didn't do it by ourselves—that God helped, so go to church. I already knew that; that's why I said if you sit in church every Sunday, everything will turn out okay." Actually, I said a little more, but if Riley's happy . . .

Becoming Rich in Mercy

Before moving on to consider finding God in your life as a spouse, we need to consider the call to mercy since Christ specifically revealed the fatherhood of God to be "rich in mercy" (Ephesians 2:4). We will consider mercy in much greater detail in Chapter 8. Nonetheless, it is a very important topic right now because at least one-third of the people who read the previous section said, "Great. We went to church every week and it didn't work for us. Got any other suggestions?"

Actually, yes. Have a conversation with God who is dwelling within. Entrust to him the deepest desires of your heart and trust him to take you further in your parenting than you ever imagined. He will help you to become more merciful, which has not only transformed children but also turned their parents into saints.

If you have or had one of those kids who "just didn't seem to get it," St. Monica of Hippo is your friend. She lived during the fourth century and was the mother of St. Augustine of Hippo—that incredibly important and influential early Christian writer we have encountered on a couple of occasions. Their relationship was a bit more complex than may be indicated by the fact that both carry the distinction of "saint" in their name.

Monica and Augustine lived at the time when the Roman Empire was still straddling the fence between paganism and Christianity. Monica was a devout Christian. Augustine was happy to indulge in the pleasures offered by the pagan culture. At age seventeen, he left home and went to Carthage— the third-largest city in the Roman Empire—to study rhetoric. In short order, Augustine had an affair, begat an illegitimate son, and rejected the Christian faith of his mother. After nine years, he went to Rome to seek fame and fortune. Eventually, he moved to Milan to accept the offer of a prime teaching post.

Faced with such a son, what was a devout Christian mother to do? Of course, hound him relentlessly to clean up his act! Monica followed him from Carthage to Rome to Milan, all the while shedding copious tears and begging God to intervene in the life of her son. Eventually, Augustine met the bishop of Milan, St. Ambrose, whose words began to strike a chord in

Augustine. Not far behind, of course, was Monica. Like all good meddling mothers, she let Ambrose know that it was his job to straighten out her wayward son. Ambrose gave a most interesting reply to Monica:

> He is still unready to learn. . . . Let him be where he is . . . only pray the Lord for him. By his reading he will discover what an error . . . it all is. . . . It cannot be that the son of these tears should perish.[20]

The last sentence is an incredibly powerful statement. It implies that the conversion of Augustine was as much a result of Monica's tearful pleas to God as Ambrose's rhetorical gifts. This should give all of us hope. Our prayers can touch the heart of God so deeply that he will transform another heart!

Not long after Monica's meeting with Ambrose, Augustine had his dramatic conversion in a garden. He went on to become arguably the greatest Christian thinker in the early days of Christianity. From his pen come such memorable and poetic lines as

> Late have I loved thee, beauty ever ancient, ever new, late have I loved thee! . . . You scattered my blindness: you breathed perfume, and I drew in my breath and I pant for you: I tasted, and I am hungry and thirsty.[21]

In our lives as parents, we will at times encounter obstacles and situations that we simply cannot solve. It could be an illness or a financial situation or a wayward child or any of a million different things. Faced with these insurmountable obstacles, we turn to a power beyond ourselves. Yes, God uses these moments to transform *us*. Through them we come to understand that our parenting was never completely in our own hands. It has always been a cooperation with God.

Finding God in Your Life as a Spouse

We are called to find God not only in our life as a parent, but also in our life as a spouse. Scripture presents a very explicit and demanding standard for Christian spouses:

Husbands, love your wives as Christ also loved the church and offered himself up for her (Ephesians 5:25).

As such, we must consider Christ's life as the "divine bridegroom" of the Church. It will greatly illumine the lives we are called to live in our own marriages—lives that will only be possible if we live in union with God.

We are specifically called to imitate the moment that Christ "offered himself" for his bride. This is the moment that Christ went to the end of love: "Jesus loved his own in the world and he loved them to the end" (John 13:1). In considering this moment, we must recognize that "the end" has two meanings in this context. First, it means that Christ loved his own until the end of his life. Second, it means that Christ loved his own to the extent that it was humanly possible: "No one has greater love than this, to lay down one's life for one's friends" (John 15:13). Both of these meanings are critically important to the spousal relationship.

First, let's consider Christ's love that went until the end of his life. From a human perspective, Good Friday—the day Christ was crucified and died— was a very bad day. He was betrayed by one of his apostles, publicly denied on three occasions by the head of the apostles, and abandoned by nine other apostles. Only one apostle remained by Christ in his moment of need. On Good Friday, the apostles had a very bad day.

Nonetheless, Christ chose to continue to love them. In other words, Christ chose to love his apostles not only when they were having their best day, but also when they were having their worst. Indeed, I once heard it said that a person most needs your love when they least deserve it. This was certainly true of Christ's apostles.

We call the love offered by Jesus Christ to his apostles an "unconditional love." Many of us have heard this term but are a bit fuzzy on its meaning. It is perhaps most easily grasped in what it is not. A conditional love would be saying, "I will love you on the condition that you can make a better bacon cheeseburger than Pappas Burger and at a faction of the cost!" In other words, I have placed a requirement or condition on my love. Unconditional love means I place no requirement on my gift of love. Instead, I offer you my love not because you have earned it but because of who I am. Nonetheless, an unconditional love must go a step further.

Christ also went to "the end of love" by making the greatest sacrifice humanly possible. He offered his life. We must note that Christ chose to make this offering when he was having a really bad day: He was innocently condemned. No one came to his aid. He was scourged beyond recognition, crowned with thorns, and physically nailed to a tree. Nonetheless, Christ chose to become heedless of his own state to focus on his beloved: "Father, forgive them, for they know not what they do" (Luke 23:34). As such, Christ's love was also not conditioned by his own personal state.

In Christ's sacrifice, we see the image of truly unconditional love. We see the image of an absolutely pure love. Believe it or not, this is the demanding standard bridegroom and bride pronounce in their wedding vows:

> I, (Groom), take thee, (Bride), as my lawful wife, to have and to hold from this day forward, for better for worse, for richer for poorer, in sickness and in health, until death do us part.

Think about these vows for a moment. You promised to place your spouse above your emotional state, above your financial state, and above your physical state. There's not much left beyond these. In doing this, you pledged a love that is not conditioned by the vicissitudes of this world. You pledged to live an unconditional love.

Although this is an incredibly demanding standard, it is possible by the grace of God. Ask St. Monica. She was married to a Roman pagan, Patricius. He had a bit of a temper and some pretty dissolute habits. Furthermore, he didn't really appreciate Monica's religious sensibilities, which helps us to understand where Augustine got his wayward ways! Indeed, the entire time Monica was enduring a mother's broken heart over Augustine, she was suffering at the hands of Patricius.

Nonetheless, Monica remained a faithful, loving wife, but not in extraordinary ways. She simply remained loving and respectful and cheerful in the context of their everyday married life together. Her charity eventually touched the heart of Patricius. He was converted and baptized shortly before he died.[22] Such is the power of an unconditional love lived in everyday married life.

The Love of God Poured into Our Hearts

Believe ir or not, I actually think that the vast majority of newlyweds truly have a spontaneous desire to live such an unconditional love. Needless to say, embracing a love that goes to the end is very challenging. Indeed, it is the challenge to participate in the life of the divine bridegroom. On our own, it would not be possible. Fortunately, "God's love has been poured into our hearts" (Romans 5:5).

Indeed, when Christ went to the end of love, he allowed his heart to be opened for us: "One of the soldiers pierced his side with a spear, and at once there came out blood and water" (John 19:34). From the earliest days of Christianity, the blood flowing from the wounded heart of Christ has been considered as symbolic of the Eucharist: "There flowed from his side blood and water. . . . [The] blood symbolized . . . the holy Eucharist."[23] Many Christians—Catholic, Orthodox, and Anglican Communion[24]—believe that under the appearance of bread and wine Jesus Christ sacramentally gave to us his Body and Blood: "Jesus said to them . . . 'For my flesh is food indeed, and my blood is drink indeed. He who eats my flesh and drinks my blood abides in me, and I in him'" (John 6:53–56).

Honestly, many see this statement and belief as simply too much. Indeed, Christ himself encountered disbelief: "Many of his disciples, when they heard it, said, 'This is a hard saying: who can listen to it?'" (John 6:60) But that's the point! God's love is too much. It is excessive. It is super-abundant. The Eucharist isn't necessary. There will be countless people in heaven who have never received it. The Eucharist is pure superabundance. It is given to us so that we can tangibly experience God's superabundant love for us.

Indeed, the radical experience of God's love helped many Christians return "love for love" by offering their life for Christ. St. Ignatius of Antioch was a student of the apostle John and became the head of the Church in Antioch in the year AD 67, shortly after it was founded by the apostle Peter. On his way to martyrdom in Rome he wrote seven very important letters. In the last letter, he stated: "I have no taste for the food that perishes . . . I want the Bread of God which is the Flesh of Christ . . . and for drink I desire His blood which is love that cannot be destroyed."[25]

Since the Eucharist flows from Christ's heart that has gone to the end of love, it offers to us a very specific love from God. It is the love that refuses to die. It is a love that is victorious over betrayal, abandonment, and pain. God knows that we are all in need of this love. He knows that spouses are in need of this love if they are to fulfill their wedding vows of a love that goes to the end. For this reason, Catholic, Orthodox, and Anglican Communion spouses normally receive the Eucharist immediately after they recite their wedding vows. It is God giving them the grace that they need to participate in the life of the divine bridegroom.[26]

Riley has a very interesting look on his face. He's not upset with me. He doesn't disagree with me. He even likes it. But I don't think he's ready to jump in with both feet. Fortunately, God wants to help us. Believe it or not, we have some amazing science that helps us to grasp this mystery of super-abundant love in Christ's heart.

In the eighth century, a monk in the small town of Lanciano, situated in the rolling hills on Italy's eastern coast, was celebrating Mass while doubting the reality of the Eucharist. During the words of consecration, he witnessed the bread and wine physically change into real flesh and blood. He immediately summoned all present to witness the miraculous occurrence. The very same elements have been preserved and publicly displayed for more than twelve hundred years.[27]

In 1971 and 1981 the Benedictine monks in Lanciano consented to scientific experiments on the preserved elements, which were performed by Dr. Edward Linoli, director of the hospital in Arezzo and professor of anatomy, histology, chemistry, and clinical microscopy. He concluded that the elements were indeed human flesh and blood with blood type AB.[28] Both were "fresh," exhibiting no sign of decay—despite their age and lack of preservatives. Amazingly, the flesh was specifically identified to be flesh taken from the myocardium of the human heart. Twelve hundred years ago, medicine knew nothing of blood types or the specific flesh of the myocardium. Nonetheless, the findings of modern science perfectly reconcile with teachings dating back to the founding of Christianity. God has given us his heart to be one with our heart.

Our challenge is to profoundly unite ourselves to God dwelling within so that he can help us to participate in his own divine life. Fortunately, we have someone to show us the way. Best of all, Riley is really going to love him.

Brother Lawrence of the Resurrection was a Carmelite monk who lived in Paris during the seventeenth century. He came from a very modest background. Little money and little education. He spent time in the army and was wounded in battle before he chose to enter the religious life. Given his background, he entered the monastery as a "lay brother," which meant plenty of manual labor. He was assigned to the kitchen, which was no small task given that there were a hundred mouths to feed in the monastery. Eventually, the old war wound made it too difficult to walk around the kitchen, so he was reassigned to the sandal shop where he could sit while keeping two hundred pairs of sandals in working order.[29]

Nonetheless, this humble lay brother caught the eye of almost everyone he met. His cheerful disposition and deep recollection in the midst of demanding labors was quite impressive. Soon little Brother Lawrence was the talk of Paris. He was in demand by the rich and famous for spiritual advice. His letters on spiritual matters were cherished and saved. The words of his spiritual conversations were quickly jotted down to be preserved. When he died they were gathered together and published as *The Practice of the Presence of God*, widely recognized as one of the all-time spiritual classics of Christian literature. His simple doctrine is readily embraced by Christians of all denominations as a sure path to intimate union with God.

Brother Lawrence's "doctrine" is simple. God dwells within you. Take a moment. Turn inward and have a chat with God.

> We do not always have to be in church to be with God. We can make of our hearts an oratory [i.e., a small chapel] where we can withdraw from time to time to converse with him there. Everyone is capable of these familiar conversations with God. A brief lifting up of the heart is enough.[30]

Did you catch the profound spiritual doctrine of this all-time Christian classic? Since God dwells within you, take a moment to turn inward and talk to him. That's it! Nothing more. This is the spiritual classic Riley has been waiting for! Nonetheless, Riley remains a bit cautious. Since his feet are planted so firmly on the ground, he knows that "if something seems too good to be true, it probably is." As such, he is a bit skeptical of the impact of something so simple. Nonetheless, here's what "the practice of the presence of God" did for Brother Lawrence:

> I cannot express to you what is taking place in me at present. . . . I keep myself in his presence by . . . a quiet and secret conversation of the soul with God that is lasting. This sometimes results in interior, and often exterior, contentment and joys so great that I have to perform childish acts . . . to control them and keep them from showing out-wardly. . . . I derive greater sweetness and satisfaction than an infant receives from his mother's breast. Therefore, if I may dare use the expression, I would gladly call this state the 'breasts of God,' because of the indescribable sweetness I taste and experience there.[31]

If we consider Brother Lawrence's words for a moment, we'll discover some pretty amazing things. First, Brother Lawrence is truly driven to find union with God and he turns inward to have his desires fulfilled. God dwells "with him who is of a contrite heart and humble spirit" (Isaiah 58:15). Next, it is precisely in this union with God dwelling within that Brother Lawrence is transformed.

Believe it or not, there is some pretty amazing brain science that sounds amazingly close to the insights of Brother Lawrence. Prayer increases neural activity in the caudate nucleus region of the brain,[32] which is part of the brain's reward circuitry. It is saturated with dopamine-producing neurons originating in the ventral tegmental area. Considered as such, our brains are driven to pray and they experience something of a neurochemical high each time they do so. Furthermore, during prayer, neural activity is reduced in the amygdala and limbic system, which processes emotion. Specifically, prayer reduces fear and anxiety, thus fostering a sense of peace. This is critical. The first words Christ spoke to his apostles after he rose from the dead were, "Peace be with you" (John 20:19). When we attain union with God dwelling within, we experience peace.

If you think about it, this implies that we are called to be transformed from the inside out. Imagine how different your life would be if you were sustained by a Divine Power and a peace that transcended the vicissitudes of this world. Social upheavals would come and go. Stock markets would boom and bust. Yet you would be unmoved. You would be able to live a love that is faithful to the end, even in this ever-changing world. It would look a lot like the life of Riley, Rose Mary, and the Greatest Generation.

CHAPTER SEVEN

STEP SIX:
Find God in Other People

The sixth step to a superabundant marriage is to find God in other people. When you think about it, this is simply the natural extension of the previous step to find God in yourself. If God is dwelling within every person, then it includes the person next to you!

Interestingly, Riley has a different look in his eye. He can surprise you at times. Although he's not overtly sentimental, his heart can be touched. Of course, he would never use all the science and technical language, but he gets it. He knows that Rose Mary made his life significantly better.

They met on a blind date arranged by a friend. Riley was already a successful businessman and cut quite a dashing figure. Rose Mary was beautiful and charming and surrounded by men vying for her attention. Riley often said, "You had to get in line and take a number just to talk to her on the telephone." He was serious. She was still receiving calls from would-be suitors during the dinner party the night before their wedding!

For their first date they put on their finest clothes and went dancing in the finest ballroom in Houston. From the outset, Riley was smitten. Before long he was talking about the beautiful life he and Rose Mary would have together. Confident and self-assured, Rose Mary replied, "Then don't you think there is something you need to ask me?" Riley agreed, so he proposed on New Year's Eve, 1956.

They married four months later on April 27th. Rose Mary was every-thing Riley hoped for in a woman, wife, and mother. She was loving and beautiful and gracious. She was equally at ease on the farm or at the Four Seasons. She loved a quiet dinner for two or a gala with dignitaries. Like Riley, she was frugal to a fault and embraced the value system of the Greatest Generation. Nonetheless, she had a zest for life and could light up a room when she walked in.

Riley's work ethic and determination to escape the harsh reality of his youth could have easily trapped him in a life of endless work. Fortunately, Rose Mary could convince Riley to take time away from work, pack his bags, and set off for trips around the globe. Whether it was as an official dele-gation to communist Russia or a hunting safari to Africa or the beautiful cathedrals of Europe, you could always count on two things. First, Riley would complain about having to take time off work, pack his bags, and travel halfway around the world. Second, Riley would have the time of his life and be forever grateful that Rose Mary convinced him to go.

Likewise, Rose Mary could convince Riley to stop the yard work, take a shower, put on a tuxedo, and head out to an incredible evening. Of course he complained about the tux, the stuffy crowd, and the cost. Nonetheless, he always enjoyed himself and was glad he went—except to the opera. I don't think Riley could ever bring himself to enjoy the opera, which pre-sented me with a golden opportunity.

Houston has one of the top opera companies in the United States[1] and it was time for their fiftieth anniversary gala. Perfect opportunity to score some points with my mother-in-law. So, I invited Rose Mary to join Shelly and me for what I hoped would be a very special evening. The ladies put on their evening gowns. I put on a tux. We arrived at the gala and the headliner was . . . Elton John. Now I'm okay with Elton John—but not in evening gowns and tuxedos with my eighty-three-year-old mother-in-law! Another missed opportunity!

Rose Mary's response? Of course, she was polite and gracious. I never saw her any other way. She was truly grateful that someone loved her enough to attempt such a special evening. Indeed, Rose Mary had the unique ability to see through external superficialities to gaze upon the heart. Furthermore, she interacted with people at the level of the heart—frequently helping them to discover something within themselves that they never knew existed. If we learn her lesson, we will be able to see beyond superficial considerations to gaze upon a mystery. If we gaze intently enough, we might just glimpse the face of God.

Respecting the Dignity of a Person

When I met Shelly, she had just returned to Houston after six years. During the transition, she had moved back in with Riley and Rose Mary, which meant that every time Shelly and I went out, I had to talk to her parents. At thirty-seven years of age, the potential for awkwardness was huge. Thankfully, Shelly's mom was Rose Mary.

When I arrived, Rose Mary would answer the door and then escort me to the living room. She never left a guest unattended, so we would sit and chat until Shelly was ready. Never did she seem rushed or too busy to spend time with me. She wasn't constantly checking technology or looking past me to something or someone else. I always felt like I had her full attention. Furthermore, Rose Mary and I shared many common interests: travel, good restaurants, the arts, and our faith. So talking with Rose Mary was easy. Truth be told, I loved our chats and looked forward to seeing her while Shelly was getting ready.

Over time, I came to realize that everyone had a similar experience with Rose Mary. She had a wonderful knack for helping everyone to feel at ease. Since she took a genuine interest in others, she could draw them out of themselves. Before long, everyone was laughing and having a good time.

On the surface this may seem no more than the details of social graces. But remember, the extraordinary lies just on the other side of the ordinary. This became apparent one weekend when Riley and Rose Mary were hosting houseguests for one of Riley's business functions. One of the guests had a personality that grated on you very quickly. He knew everything about everything and was determined to let you know.

When Shelly and I arrived for dinner, it didn't take long to pick up on the issue. When we were introduced, he never bothered to make eye contact with me or interrupt the conversation he was having with the people in the other room. After a few minutes, I caught Rose Mary's eye and gave her the inquisitive look: "What's up with this guy?" I simply received a polite smile.

Before long, Rose Mary was off to the kitchen for refreshments. I offered to help and excused myself. Presented with the opportunity to speak for the first time all evening, I said, "Rose Mary, you've got to be kidding me! Has it been like this the entire weekend?" I received a nod and another polite smile before Rose Mary returned to the living room with refreshments for everyone. Indeed, the monologue continued unbroken the entire weekend. Nonetheless, the houseguests left convinced that in Riley and Rose Mary they had just made the best friends in the world.

When I saw Rose Mary's smile, it immediately reminded me of an episode from the life of St. Thérèse of Lisieux. Thérèse Martin lived at the end of the nineteenth century in northern France. She became a Carmelite nun at the tender age of fifteen. She is considered by many to be "the greatest saint of modern times."[2]

In considering life in the convent, St. Thérèse noticed that the most agreeable sisters were "surrounded with everyone's affection,"[3] while the least agreeable sisters were avoided or encountered "within the limits of religious politeness."[4] She decided to address the issue herself:

"I must seek out in recreation, on free days, the company of Sisters who are the least agreeable to me."[5]

So Thérèse sought out the Sister who had "the faculty of displeasing me in everything, in her ways, her words, her character, everything."[6] She decided to do "for this Sister what I would do for the person I loved the most."[7] Needless to say, it was a struggle. When Thérèse was most agitated by this Sister and felt the desire "to answer back in a disagreeable manner,"[8] she contented herself "with giving the Sister my most friendly smile."[9] St. Thérèse was so successful that one day the disagreeable Sister came up to her and asked, "Would you tell me, Sister Thérèse of the Child Jesus, what attracts you so much toward me; every time you look at me, I see you smile?"[10]

Welcome to the life of Rose Mary. If you think this is mundane or easy, give it a try! I have on several occasions. I'm a miserable failure. I consider it success when instead of screaming *at* you, I leave the room and scream *about* you. At least the thin air isn't offended.

The secret of success for Rose Mary and St. Thérèse is a statement by Jesus near the end of his public life: "As you did it to one of the least of these my brethren, you did it to me" (Matthew 25:40).[11] Rose Mary and St. Thérèse embraced this reality. They were able to see beyond some annoying personality traits to discover a dignity within. They related to the person at the level of that dignity.

In more recent times, Mother Teresa of Calcutta radically embraced this spiritual dignity of the person and inspired the world. She won the Nobel Peace Prize for her work picking up the "poorest of the poor" and giving them dignity while they were dying. For many it was easy to romanticize the work of Mother Teresa. The reality was much different. These were men and women discarded from society. Many had not bathed for years. They were dirty, smelly, and had hair filled with lice. Frequently, they had open sores that oozed. Many were malnourished to the point they could not walk. Many could not speak. Yet Mother Teresa picked them off the ground and gave them dignity in their final moments.

When asked how she was able to carry out her mission, Mother Teresa simply responded that each one was "Christ in distressing disguise."[12] As such, Mother Teresa was able to see beyond exterior appearances to find an inherent dignity in the soul. This dignity was not the result of what the person did; but of who the person was. In the depths of their being, they are a creature created "in the image and likeness of God" (Genesis 1:26).

Most of us will not encounter the dire circumstances of Mother Teresa. But we will encounter people whose health has deteriorated and people who are struggling financially. Both are tremendous trials for the person and those close to them. We will also frequently encounter people who are angry, rude, and obnoxious. We may even have a houseguest who can't stop talking long enough to take a breath. If we are able to see beyond the external superficialities to the true dignity of the person, it might just change their life and ours.

The Challenge to Be Charitable

The charity with which Rose Mary interacted with other people was as much a part of her moral fiber as her internal value system. Both were related to her unquestioned belief in God. In the previous chapter, we saw that Americans' belief in God and value systems have changed compared to the one embraced by Riley, Rose Mary, and the Greatest Generation. Unfortunately, so has the way in which we relate to each other.

The vast majority of Americans believe that we have a problem relating to each other in a civil manner. As seen in Figure 7.1, almost two-thirds believe we have a *major problem* with civility in modern society.[13] Seventy-one percent believe the problem has gotten worse in just the past few years.[14] Amazingly, the average American experiences seventeen uncivil acts in a given week.[15] As such, it is not surprising that 70 percent of Americans think incivility in our culture has risen to crisis levels.[16]

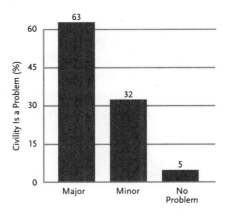

Figure 7.1: Problem with Civility
Source: Civility in America: 2013.

Numerous factors are identified as contributing to this rise in incivility. The top six factors are given in Figure 7.2. Almost all of these can be reduced to two major factors: politics and technology/media. I'm willing to tackle difficult issues—sex, money, religion—but politics? I have to draw the line somewhere! The thought of interjecting civility into our political process reminds me of the old 7 Up commercial: "Never had it. Never will."

The identification of technology/media as the second leading cause is something new. Of course, media in the form of radio, television, and the movies have been around for a long time. Furthermore, the government's

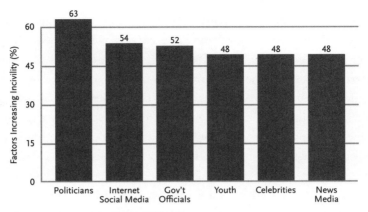

Figure 7.2: Sources Making Incivility Worse
Source: Incivility in America: 2014.

first study investigating the possible link between media consumption and negative behavior (violence) goes all the way back to 1952,[17] which was five years before the launch of *Leave it to Beaver*.

What's new is the integration of media and technology, which allows the average person to remain immersed in a multitude of media forms to an unprecedented level. The average teenager consumes more than ten hours of media every day.[18] Eighty-four percent use social media.[19] Seventy-eight percent have a cell phone from which they send 1,800 text messages a month.[20]

The immersion in media and technology is changing the way in which we interact with each other. In Chapter 3, we saw the importance of eating dinner together as a family on a regular basis. Unfortunately, the reality of the family dinner table has changed. Approximately 70 percent of 6- to 10-year-olds bring technology to the table and only 5 percent eat with no distractions.[21] Surprisingly, 73 percent of parents use a mobile device during meals.[22]

Here's the irony. Although everyone is using technology and the media on a constant basis, the vast majority is upset when someone chooses to use technology versus interacting with the live person in front of them. Eighty-seven percent of Americans consider it rude when the person you are talking with gets on their phone.[23] Eighty-six percent consider it rude when the person they are eating with talks on the phone.[24]

Notice we are not talking about random or anonymous acts of rudeness—the guy who cuts you off on the highway; or the guy screaming at a sales clerk who's just trying to do her job; or the guy talking way too loud on his cell phone in a public setting.[25] We're talking about rude behavior between friends. It is now so rampant that half of Americans say they have ended a friendship because the other person was rude.[26]

The Art of Friendship

Strained friendships simply weren't an issue impacting Rose Mary on a regular basis. She was involved in more activities and had more friends than you could imagine. These friendships were a natural fruit of Rose Mary's behavior. She genuinely respected and cared about the other person, which found expression in spontaneous acts of kindness for the other person.

It is amazing what an act of kindness can do to another person. Research indicates that simply witnessing an act of kindness leads to a state of elevation where the person witnessing the act wants to be charitable to others.[27] Furthermore, if the person is the beneficiary of the act of kindness, then he or she desires to reciprocate the act of kindness.[28]

This was my experience with Rose Mary. I really liked sitting and chatting with her while I waited for Shelly to get ready. Furthermore, this was everyone's experience with Rose Mary, which is why she had a million friends.

Having harmonious, reliable friendships is very important. Scripture says, "it is not good for man to be alone" (Genesis 2:18). A person's social network is critically important to his or her health[29] and longevity.[30] It is also critically important to his or her emotional health and happiness. Data from the General Social Survey indicates that people with a larger number of close personal friends are more likely to be happy with their lives. As seen in Figure 7.3, individuals with eight to ten close personal friends are approximately 50 percent more likely to be "very happy" with their life versus individuals with zero to two close personal friends.[31] On the other hand, individuals with zero to two close personal friends are almost three times more likely to be "not too happy" with their life versus individuals with eight to ten friends.[32]

This data raises the old chicken-and-egg question. Am I happy because

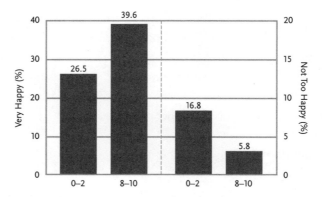

Figure 7.3: Number of Close Friends and Happiness
Source: General Social Survey 1972–2012.

I have friends, or do I have friends because I am happy? Researchers from Harvard University did some pretty amazing work to sort it out and they concluded that friendships lead to happiness. If a close personal friend of mine is happy, the probability of my happiness increases 15.3 percent.[33] If my friend lives within one mile of me, the probability of my happiness increases 25 percent.[34] Furthermore, the effect is additive. The more friends I have, the more likely I am to be happy. Each happy friend increases the probability of my happiness by about 9 percent.[35]

Now here's the really amazing part. As we just discussed, if my close personal friend becomes happy, it increases the probability of my personal happiness by 15.3 percent. Once I become happy, what happens to my other friends? It makes them more likely to be happy. Then what happens to their friends? It makes them more likely to be happy. As seen in Figure 7.4, the extent of one person becoming happy extends to a friend of a friend of a friend.[36] Amazing!

This is the life of Rose Mary. She was surrounded by family and friends and she was a very happy person. Ironically, the pathway to this superabundant personal happiness was to become self-forgetful. Rose Mary never focused on herself. She always focused on the other person. When necessary she was able to look beyond external superficialities—like a blubbering mouth—to find their dignity within. This very simple act changed their life and hers. The extraordinary lies just on the other side of the ordinary.

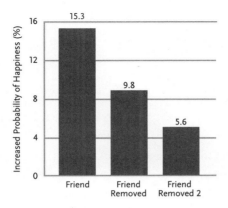

Figure 7.4: Friendship and Happiness
Source: Fowler, J. and Christakis, N.A., "Dynamic spread of happiness in a large social network: Longitudinal analysis over 20 years in the Framingham Heart Study," *BMJ* 337 (2008): art a2338.

Love as Strong as Death

Rose Mary's self-forgetfulness and love were turned first and foremost toward her own family. It found expression in the million little things that make up everyday family life. It also found expression in moments of true need. Rose Mary was an incredibly strong woman and capable of making heroic sacrifices when necessary.

One Saturday morning years ago, Riley, Rose Mary, and their four young children piled into the family station wagon and were driving to their small farm in the Texas Hill Country. As they drove out of Houston they encountered one of those thunderstorms that happen all too frequently along the Texas Gulf Coast. In a moment of time you literally cannot see five feet in front of your car. Suddenly you're struck with a dilemma: Do you stop and risk someone rear-ending you, or do you keep going and take the risk that you will rear-end someone else? On this particular Saturday morning, Riley made the same choice I've made a hundred times. He slowed down, but kept moving to avoid being rear-ended. Unfortunately, the vehicle in front of him did not make the same choice. An eighteen-wheel tractor-trailer decided to stop and pull over. However, he didn't pull entirely off the highway. Riley, Rose Mary, and their four children plowed into that tractor-trailer.

This was long before air bags. No one wore seat belts. Everyone went flying through the air. There were broken bones, cuts, bruises, and sheer panic. Rose Mary was in the front passenger seat "riding shotgun," which meant her side of the car directly hit the tractor-trailer. She went directly into the front windshield. As she lay barely conscious, trapped in twisted metal, she could hear the screams and crying of her children and the youngest daughter searching for "woof woof," the stuffed dog that had been torn from her arms. In a moment of self-forgetfulness, Rose Mary reached out to that youngest daughter, pulled her to herself, and then collapsed.

Fortunately, someone had seen the accident. They were able to remove Rose Mary from the car and rush her to a hospital. Her wounds would require reconstructive surgery. But she and the entire family would fully recover. The scars of that rainy Saturday morning would be left primarily in their minds. Years later, I asked Rose Mary how she found the strength to reach out while she was on the verge of collapse. She simply smiled and said, "That's what mothers do."

Yes, Rose Mary knew how to sacrifice for her children. She also knew how to sacrifice for her husband. I see that Riley caught my words. His head crooked a bit, but he quickly looked away. He doesn't want me to go there, but he knows I won't continue without his consent. I respect him too much. There's a pause that lingers. A tear begins to well in his eye. At length there is an almost imperceptible nod of the head.

Riley and Rose Mary were approaching their twenty-fifth anniversary. Given her flair and zest for life, Rose Mary was determined to celebrate this milestone appropriately. She rented the grand ballroom at the tennis club; selected an impressive menu; pulled together elegant decorations; booked a fabulous band; sent invitations to tons of friends; and purchased a stunning gown. Indeed, she spent as much time and care selecting that gown as most brides do selecting their wedding dresses.

For their actual anniversary, which fell on Tuesday, four days before the big party, Rose Mary planned a simple, elegant dinner at home with the family. The evening began as planned, the family enjoying a meal in the formal dining room. Before the night ended, Riley was face down on the floor. It was his second heart attack. The damage was severe. He was rushed to the hospital and immediately opened for multiple bypass surgery.

While Riley was in surgery, Rose Mary alternated her time between prayer for Riley, comfort for the children, and calls to cancel the twenty-fifth anniversary celebration—friends, caterers, florists, band. She never wore that special gown she purchased. She never returned it. It remained hanging in her closet. In time, Riley made a full recovery. It would not be inaccurate to say that Rose Mary refused to let him go. Scripture says "love is stronger than death" (Song of Solomon 8:6). Rose Mary certainly had great love and she was a very strong woman.

Finding God in Your Children

These two stories of Rose Mary take us to two very important relationships—the parent–child relationship and the spousal relationship. Interestingly enough, Scripture specifically defines God's presence in both of these relationships. Regarding the parent–child relationship, it states,

> Whoever receives one such child in my name
> receives me (Matthew 18:5).

The relationship parents have with their children is truly unique. I once took a nonscientific, random poll of several hundred couples attending one of our programs. I asked the simple question, "Who best understands your children?" Eighty-two percent of the women claimed to know their children better than anyone else. Ten percent of the women said that the fathers understood the children best, and 5 percent said that no one understands their children! These results really didn't surprise me too much. I can certainly envision my mother saying the same thing.

However, I was surprised by the response from the men. Eighty percent of men agreed that their wives know their children better than anyone else. Come on, guys! What about the good ol' father–son male bonding ritual?

Fourteen percent. What about your son's coach? Less than 1 percent. I'm not willing to relieve men of their responsibilities as fathers, which is why we run men's programs all over the country. Nonetheless, we must admit that there is something special between a mother and her child.

In the previous chapter, we saw that parents and children are able to mentally align with each other through the activation of the mirror neuron system and empathy regions of the brain. In a certain sense, parents are able to form mental models of their children in their brains. Now here's the important part. Women have larger mirror neuron systems and empathy regions in the brain.[37] Furthermore, they have larger centers for processing observation and emotion.[38] Put it all together and they're able to form really accurate pictures of their children. A mom knows!

A large portion of women I've spoken to agree with this information and find it interesting. Nonetheless, their minds spontaneously go to another place: "Of course I know my children better. I carried them in my womb for nine months!" For these women, there is something about the bond established between the mother and child during pregnancy that continues long after the child is born.[39]

It is as if the mother is still carrying a portion of her child in her womb. Believe it or not, science agrees. Research indicates that women continue to carry cells within their body from every child they have ever conceived. It is called *microchimerism*.[40] Amazingly, many women carry these cells within their brains![41] Scientists are still trying to sort out what this means—if anything.

Nonetheless, I can tell you how women I've spoken with respond to this on the emotional level. "I knew it! I always knew that my child is still part of me!" For them, there is a unique knowledge gained from the experience of deep personal union. Indeed, many cultures distinguish between experiential knowledge and intellectual knowledge.[42] This is important because when we say that we know someone, we are talking about experiential knowledge.

Let me give a simple example. If I told you that Rose Mary was born in 1922 in New Orleans; that she was 5'4" and of petite build; that she was a brunette with beautiful brown eyes; that she had a drafting degree from the

University of Houston; that she had four children and sixteen grandchildren—would you know Rose Mary? Of course not. You might know *about* Rose Mary, but you would not know her.

To know someone is to spend time with them, to experience communion with them. In this communion, you come to understand them from the inside, what makes them tick—their fears and desires, their joys and sorrows. Although this type of knowledge is not easily put into words, it is very real. Every time I discuss this topic with women, I get spontaneous agreement: "Yes. I can't put it into words, but I just know them." It is a knowledge born of communion—for a mother and child, it is knowledge that traces its roots all the way back to the womb.

For just a moment, let's think about the communion between the mother and the child in her womb. In Chapters 5 and 6 we saw that there is something in the human person that transcends his or her material body. Furthermore, we saw that this spiritual dimension of the human person must come from God. Now let me ask this simple question: "Where does this creative action of God, as it relates to the human person, occur?" In the womb of the mother. When the sperm and ovum unite, God infuses the spiritual dimension—historically called *the soul*—and a new human person is conceived.

As such, the mother has a privileged position to see the action of God in her children. Although she cannot see this action with her eyes, she can still "know" it. Remember, communication with God is not limited to our sense perception. Furthermore, in this moment the mother knows the child in the child's closest proximity to God. It is almost as if she can see the child from God's perspective—what makes the child beautiful and unique and special.

I am convinced that mothers are allowed to carry this knowledge with them their entire life. This is why the simple words "I'm disappointed in you" accompanied by a certain look can have such an effect on the child. Without being able to consciously state it, every child knows that his mother is comparing the actions in question to the mother's deepest vision of the child—a vision that traces its origin all the way back to the action of God in the womb.

Yes—But My Child Is a Gangster

Let's be honest. It's not always easy to see the innate dignity in our children. Sure, when they make straight As or hit the winning shot at the buzzer, there's no question. But what about all the times they do the very things that drive parents crazy, things inconsistent with their own dignity? Our challenge is to maintain the vision of the innate dignity of the child even when all the external indications are to the contrary. Many parents have been able to maintain this vision heroically. It frequently changes their life and that of their child.

John Pridmore was born to Brian and Joan in London's East End in 1964.[43] His father was a policeman while his mother held numerous odd jobs, mostly as a shopkeeper. Unfortunately, Brian and Joan had a very stormy marriage. One night when John was eleven, his parents informed him that they were getting a divorce and he needed to choose whom he wanted to live with. John cried that he couldn't choose between his mother and father. His life was crushed. He made the unconscious decision to never love again.

John began a rapid descent. He began stealing by age fourteen and was placed in a youth detention center the following year. By age nineteen, he was placed in an adult prison. Since he kept getting into fights with other prisoners, he was placed in solitary confinement—twenty-three hours a day in a small cell. No television. No radio. No visitors. It was designed to break a man. One of the guards told him, "You think you're tough. But when someone finally comes to visit you, you'll cry like a baby. Everyone does."

John promised that he wouldn't and he never did. The guard said, "I fear for you. I have never seen a man so hardened."

The fear was well placed. When John was released from prison he descended into London's underworld. He became an enforcer in the Mafia and controlled a good amount of the drug flow through London clubs. John's life was one of drugs, sex, and violence. He realized his life only had two possible outcomes—death or prison.

At 6'6" and a sturdy build, John was a man who commanded attention and respect. When challenged, he preferred hand-to-hand combat. He was the kind of man who could be stabbed during a fight, pause, pull out the knife, throw it on the floor, and then pummel you until you could not move. He was the kind of man who would crush a glass in your face if he didn't like the way you looked. He carried a machete in his suit jacket for good measure.

John's mother, Joan, could no longer tolerate the evil her son brought into the world. Nonetheless, she believed that he still had goodness within him. She never lost the vision of that young, innocent child. She decided to pray intently for nine days (called a *novena*) to the patron saint of hopeless cases, St. Jude. At the end of the nine days, Joan approached a statue of the Virgin Mary and said this prayer: "Now dear mother, I entrust him to you. If the only way you can keep him from bringing evil into this world is to take his life, then take his life."

John had just left a man for dead outside a London pub. He was hiding from the police. As he lay on his bed, he heard a voice telling him all the worst things he had ever done. He looked around, but saw no one. Suddenly, he thought, "It is the voice of God." The air was knocked out of him and he felt as if he were dying. He seemed to be sinking into the pit of hell. Finally, he cried out, "Give me another chance." It was granted.

John changed his life. He received permission to leave the Mafia and he embraced a life similar to a religious monk. He helped the head of the Mafia in London have a "deathbed conversion." He spoke to 400,000 youths in the presence of the Pope. He now travels the world helping youths heal broken hearts so that they do not travel the path that he did. It would have never happened but for a mother who could see through the dire circumstances of her son's life to gaze upon a spark of the divine.

Finding God in Your Spouse

Recalling the story of Riley and Rose Mary's twenty-fifth anniversary, it is easy to say Riley found God in Rose Mary. Indeed, in many ways it was the love of Rose Mary that sustained him through the heart attack and long recovery. But it would be just as easy for us to say that Rose Mary found God in Riley—in a million different ways, but above all in the love that continually placed the needs of Rose Mary and the family above his own. Indeed, it was easy for others to see that God was in the middle of Riley and Rose Mary's marriage. Scripture points to this mystery when it says,

Where two or three are gathered in my name,
there am I in the midst of them (Matthew 18:20).

At first glance, it might not be apparent how this verse relates to the spousal relationship, but recall from Chapter 2 that bridegroom and bride seal their marriages in the name of God: "Shelly, receive this ring as a sign of my love and fidelity. In the name of the Father, and of the Son, and of the Holy Spirit." Since Shelly and I sealed our marriage in the name of God, he dwells in the midst of our marriage covenant by definition.

As such, each and every time that Shelly walks up to me, God is walking up to me in her. Shelly helps me to find God. This is the essential aspect of the term "helpmate" (Genesis 2:18). Spouses are called to help each other find God. Indeed, in many ways they are on a joint journey to God. It is a journey that God himself helps to navigate.

Let's consider the life of Christ's mother, the Virgin Mary, and foster father, St. Joseph. Our first encounter with them is in the story of the Annunciation when the angel Gabriel informs Mary that she has been selected to be the mother of Jesus: "The Holy Spirit will come upon you, and the power of the Most High will overshadow you; therefore the child to be born will be called holy, the Son of God" (Luke 1:35). Christians have always believed that this miraculous event occurred the instant that Mary gave her consent: "I am the handmaid of the Lord; let it be to me according to your word" (Luke 1:38).

If we consider this scene for just a moment, it will help us to understand the pathway by which God leads couples. First, we must note that this scene occurs within the context of a legal marriage between Mary and Joseph: "A virgin betrothed to a man whose name was Joseph" (Luke 1:27).[44] Next, we note that the encounter between the angel and Mary occurred when Joseph wasn't around. Finally, it was obvious that the angel expected an immediate response from Mary. There was no option for her to say, "Let me go talk this over with my husband and then get back to you."

As such, Joseph was placed in an incredibly awkward position. There was no precedent for a virgin to give birth to a divine child. Furthermore, God could have easily avoided this awkward situation if he had sent the angel to talk with Mary when she was together with Joseph. The angel could have explained to both of them simultaneously God's plan in their life. But God chose to announce the Savior in a way that makes Joseph struggle. God wants Joseph to trust Mary, to trust that God is leading their relationship through Mary. God expects the same from Mary.

Shortly after Jesus is born, the ruler of Israel—King Herod—is told by visitors from the east that a new King of Israel has been born. King Herod cannot tolerate a rival. He therefore orders the death of all infants under the age of two. To save the Christ child, God sends an angel to tell Joseph in his sleep: "Rise, take the child and his mother, and flee to Egypt, and remain there till I tell you; for Herod is about to search for the child, to destroy him" (Matthew 2:13).

This time Mary is the one placed in an awkward position. The message was given by an angel in a dream. Trusting the content of dreams is difficult to say the least. Furthermore, the message was to pack their bags and head to Egypt, which was the place of Israel's slavery. No Jew wanted to return to Egypt. Once again, God is asking for trust between spouses. This time, God wants Mary to trust Joseph, to trust that God is working in and through him to guide their pathway to God.

God understands that trust is a very important issue in the life of a couple. Husband and wife entrust their bodies to each other to establish a "one flesh" union, which is the foundational understanding of the marriage covenant. But it goes much further. In a certain sense, husband and wife entrust the depths of their beings to each other. In my wedding vow, I promised to Shelly:

> I, Steve, receive you, Shelly, as my lawful wife, to have and to hold from this day forward, for better for worse, for richer for poorer, in sickness and in health, until death do us part.[45]

I promised to receive the fullness of Shelly's gift of herself. As we have seen on several occasions, the fullness of the human person includes that part of the person that comes specifically from God. Indeed, in Chapter 5 we saw that God has called each one of us by name (cf. Isaiah 43:1). As such, I promised Shelly that I would "have and hold" the part of her that comes from God.

This now sounds strikingly similar to our discussion regarding the special gaze that a parent is given regarding his or her child. As a parent is able to see his or her child from God's perspective, spouses are called to see each other from God's perspective. Indeed, they are called to help their spouse fulfill God's vision for them.

Needless to say, for spouses to entrust themselves to each other at this depth implies incredible vulnerability. This is the spiritual reality of being "naked and unashamed" (Genesis 2:25). We don't cover up or hide anything from our spouse. We are totally exposed. We ask our spouse "to have and to hold" this deepest part of ourselves. Trust is very important in the spousal relationship. Fortunately, God understands and has wired the spousal union to build this trust.

The trust centers in the brain include three very important regions: the amygdala, midbrain, and dorsal striatum.[46] The amygdala and midbrain regions are important in processing fear and anxiety. They must be turned down to trust someone. The dorsal striatum helps to guide future behavior based on a feedback loop that tells the brain to "repeat this behavior; it was good" or "avoid this behavior; it was bad." Amazingly, oxytocin, which is released during physical intimacy, works on all three areas. It helps to turn down the possessing of fear in the amygdala and midbrain regions while reinforcing the feedback loop in the dorsal striatum. As such, when husband and wife enter into their "one flesh union," they are releasing the oxytocin, which wires their brains to trust each other.

Yes—But My Spouse Is an Atheist

Okay. Once again let's be honest. It is easy for spouses "to have and to hold . . . for better or for worse" when you marry a spouse like Riley or Rose Mary. What happens when your spouse doesn't understand his or her own dignity? What happens when they don't recognize yours? This is obviously a very difficult situation. Nonetheless, there have been spouses able to see beyond the external difficulties to retain a belief in the innate dignity of their spouse. It certainly isn't easy, but many have transformed their spouse through this vision.

Elisabeth Arrighi and Felix Leseur were married in Paris in 1889. She had been devout from her youth. He was an intellectual and atheist. As a couple, they socially mingled with his friends. As such, Elisabeth and her faith were constantly attacked and belittled. After eight years of pressure from Felix, she abandoned it. Nonetheless, she could not long stifle the voice within. When she returned to her faith, she embraced a mission. She wanted Felix to discover in himself the spark of the divine that had attracted her to him from the beginning. Therefore, she made a pact with God:

> My God, I must have it. You must have it, this straight, true soul; he must know Thee and love Thee, and become the humble instrument of Thy glory, and do the work of an apostle. . . . Is there anything that belongs to me alone that I would not be ready to offer Thee to obtain this conversion? . . . My sweet Savior, between Thy heart and mine there must be this compact of love, which will give Thee a soul and will give me for eternity him whom I cherish, whom I want to be with me in Thy heaven.[47]

Felix and his friends renewed their pressure upon Elisabeth. Soon her health began to fail. She began to experience liver and internal problems. Eventually she developed breast cancer. Frail from infirmity, Elisabeth decided to make a pilgrimage to Lourdes in 1912. Felix accompanied her— not as a man of faith, but as a loving husband. While there, Elisabeth did not experience a physical cure, but something spiritual happened to Felix:

> I saw something of this, when, concealing myself in order not to disturb her fervor, I watched her. I had before my eyes the spectacle of something that evaded me, that I did not understand, but which I recognized clearly as being "the supernatural," and I could not withdraw my eyes from so moving a sight.[48]

Felix did not find faith, but his heart was opened. They returned to Paris and Elisabeth's health continued to deteriorate. Not long before she died, she looked Felix in the eye and declared with absolute confidence, "I shall die before you. And when I am dead, you will be converted; and when you are converted, you will become a religious. You will be Father Leseur."[49] In 1914, Elisabeth Leseur died in the arms of her beloved husband.

As Felix cleaned out Elisabeth's papers, he discovered her spiritual testament. As he read it, he once more heard of her great love for him. As he continued to clean, he discovered the secret diary she'd kept for years. Curiosity got the best of him. He read it and learned of her struggles, including the pain he caused her by continually attacking her faith. He also read of the depths of her love for him and of her assurance that they would be together forever in heaven: "Now, my beloved Felix, I tell you once more of my great love. . . . Close to God . . . we shall one day be eternally reunited. I hope for this through my afflictions offered for you and through divine mercy."[50]

Felix was instantaneously converted. He reconciled with the Church and entered the Dominican Order where he became a religious monk. He published her diary and spent the rest of his life traveling Europe and discussing Elisabeth's writings and holiness. Felix died in 1950. The cause for Elisabeth to be considered a saint was begun in 1990.

Spouses—like parents—are given a privileged position from which they are able to gaze upon a spiritual reality. Indeed, they are able to perceive something of God's gaze upon the soul. As such, they frequently see things in each other that escape the individual. When they embrace this reality, they help their spouse to become all that God created him or her to be. In the process, they transform themselves and their marriages.

CHAPTER EIGHT

STEP SEVEN:
Make It Easy to Be Good and Hard to Be Bad

We have come to our seventh and final step to a superabundant marriage: Make it easy to be good and hard to be bad.

It's amazing how quickly you can lose someone's goodwill. I've gone from hero to zero in one chapter! Riley loved it when I talked about Rose Mary and how wonderful she made his life. Now? Well, remember all the way back to the engagement party when Rose Mary hit Riley as they were sitting on the end of the couch? Riley has just returned the favor as he said, "I warned you about him. Make it easy to be good and hard to be bad. Who could even know what that means? I'll tell you what it means: It means he didn't listen when I told him how to stay happily married. I gave him a direct answer to a direct question. Problem is he doesn't listen."

Fortunately, Rose Mary has remembered our nice conversations and has been pleading my cause. It will take a moment or two, but we'll see that Riley understood and lived this step incredibly well. He simply never bothered to question things that "just make sense." Let me give you a couple of examples.

Riley ran a light manufacturing company in a very blue-collar part of Houston. Almost fifty years ago, he instituted a very generous profit-sharing plan. Indeed, it was more generous than many large corporations give to their management, and it extended to the lowest-paid hourly employee. When I asked him about it, I received a typical response from Riley: "Why wouldn't I do it? They earned it. Only makes sense that they would get part of it. Plus, it makes them loyal to you. Then they'll stay with you longer." I gently protested that since competitors weren't offering a similar plan, it wasn't necessary or competitive. Riley mumbled something along the lines of "If you're so impressed with the competitors, go work for them!"

Another time, I was out with Shelly. A nice woman walked up and politely asked, "Excuse me. Are you Riley Leggett's daughter?" Once Shelly said yes, the woman began to sing Riley's praises.

"I worked for your dad for twenty-five years, and I'd like you to know that there are only three men I've ever truly admired in my life: my father, my pastor, and your dad. No one ever knew it, but here's what your father did for us. He came around to each of the ladies in the shop and said, 'I know you need to work to make ends meet, but I also know that you have family you're trying to care for. You can take half a day off every week to tend to the needs of your family. You don't have to ask me or tell anyone else. Just do it. The only thing I ask is that you let one of the other ladies know when you're gone so that you can cover for each other.' I took that half day off for over twenty-five years. One of my saddest days was when your father retired and sold the company."

I never bothered to ask Riley about this unwritten policy. I think he would have been embarrassed that the secret was out. Of course, I've now let the secret out in a very big way, which means I'm destined to have another awkward conversation with my father-in-law in the future! Furthermore, I think I've finally learned the lesson. "It just makes sense!"

Of course, Riley is right. It does make sense. Offering your employees a generous profit-sharing plan makes them more loyal, reducing turnover, which is very important in a blue-collar industry. Furthermore, allowing employees to proactively address the needs of their families prevented much larger problems down the road and instilled tremendous gratitude. These policies set Riley up for success.

Nonetheless, we must go further. Neither of these policies were born of a cold calculation to improve the bottom line. Both had an essential element of compassion. Interestingly, compassion is related to mercy. Indeed, the word for mercy in Latin is *misericordia*, which could be translated as a suffering of the heart. Our heart goes out to those in need. As such, we need to consider the importance of mercy in the spousal relationship. We shall see that it is possible for mercy to become so superabundant that it actually envelops the soul to prevent it from falling into trouble or sin. This is the mercy that makes it easy to be good and hard to be bad. This is the mercy that helps marriages to experience a foretaste of paradise.

Hardwired for Compassion

Riley's compassion for his fellow man is certainly impressive, but not unique. Indeed, recent research indicates that people are driven to be compassionate.[1] C. Daniel Batson and his colleagues at the University of Kansas conducted thirty-one separate experiments from 1978 to 1996 in which they studied the responses of individuals to a person in need.[2] Several scenarios were devised that would resonate with college students—a freshman having trouble adjusting to college, a senior having to support her younger siblings because her parents died in a car accident, a student experiencing extreme loneliness, the pressures of taking a test.

One series of tests involved an actress—code-named Elaine—pretending to take a memory test. At random intervals throughout the test, she pretended to receive a small electrical shock. In the other room a student watched Elaine on a television monitor as she took the test. The student was told that the experiment was "studying task performance . . . under stressful conditions."[3] The stress was defined as a "moderately uncomfortable electric shock two to three times the strength of static electricity."[4] They were assured that although the shock was uncomfortable, it would cause no lasting damage. Finally, they were told that Elaine would take ten two-minute digit-recall tests.

From the outset, Elaine pretended to have great difficulty with the electrical shocks—so much so that after the second test, the researcher entered the room to talk with Elaine. She revealed that as a child she had been thrown from a horse onto an electrical fence, causing a great fear of electrical shocks. The researcher then gave Elaine the opportunity to discontinue the test. Elaine replied that although the shocks were unpleasant, she wanted to continue. "I started; I want to finish. I'll go on . . . I know your experiment is important."[5]

The researcher then entered the room with the student watching Elaine. He gave the student a few options:

- The student could continue watching Elaine receive shocks for the eight remaining memory tests.
- The student could discontinue the experiment by simply walking out, which meant that he would no longer witness the pain Elaine was experiencing.
- The student could trade places with Elaine and receive the electrical shocks in her place.

Amazingly, the majority of students chose to trade places with Elaine and receive the electrical shock for her,[6] at which time the experiment ended, and the deception was revealed. Through systematic manipulation of study variables, Batson was able to determine that the students' behavior truly revealed an altruistic motive in the human person. Humans are driven to be kind to each other. We are driven to be compassionate.

Brain imaging studies help us to understand the processes involved in this act of compassion. If we were to look into the brains of the students while they were watching Elaine, here is what we would see:

- The mirror neuron system in the students' brains would activate, allowing them to internalize Elaine's emotional state.
- Activity in the anterior cingulate would increase, making the students more empathetic and compassionate.[7]
- Activity in the caudate nucleus would increase when the students were offered the opportunity to help Elaine, which would motivate and reward them for choosing to help her.[8]

Activation of the caudate nucleus, which forms part of the brain's reward circuitry, is critical. We have already encountered this brain region on several occasions. It is also activated in human relationships. As such, we are driven to form relationships—friendships, romantic relationships, and communion with God. Putting these findings together, we see that we are driven to be compassionate in our relationships with others.

A Demanding Standard of Compassion

As I mentioned, compassion is a form of mercy. Mercy is very important in Christianity. Christ told his followers, "Be merciful, even as your Father is merciful" (Luke 6:36). He even provided a very specific standard of this mercy:

> Love your enemies and pray for those who persecute you, so that you may be sons of your Father who is in heaven; for he makes his sun rise . . . and sends rain on the just and on the unjust (Matthew 5:44–45).

Christ lived this message to the end. In his final moments he prayed for the very people who crucified him: "Father, forgive them; for they know what not what they do" (Luke 23:34). This is the love he asked us to embrace: "A new commandment I give to you, that you love one another; even as I have loved you" (John 13:34).

Is such a standard possible or is it simply a noble idea and a pious sentiment? I would like you to meet Michael Morton.[9] Michael was born in 1954. He lived a fairly normal life. He met his wife, Christine Kirkpatrick, in college. They were married and went to Disney World for their honeymoon. Although not perfect, Michael and Christine enjoyed a good marriage and an extraordinarily blessed life together.[10]

Difficulties first entered their life when their son, Eric, was born with a congenital heart defect in 1983. Eric had a hole in his heart that prevented him from getting sufficient oxygen. Suddenly, Michael and Christine's life revolved around Eric. He had to be monitored continuously to make sure that he didn't overexert himself. Needless to say, it was a great stress. Fortunately, after three years, Eric was old enough for surgery, which was successful, and life seemed to return to normal.

On August 12, 1986, Michael, Christine, and Eric went to City Grill in Austin, Texas, to celebrate Michael's thirty-second birthday. It was their last meal together. The next morning, Michael left for work at 5:30 a.m. as usual.

He didn't hear from Christine all day. He left work to pick Eric up at the babysitter's, only to find that Eric had never been dropped off in the morning. He immediately called home. A member of the county sheriff's office answered the phone. He was told to get home as fast as he could. When he arrived he discovered that his wife had been beaten to death in her bed.

Little three-year-old Eric witnessed the murder. He described the man as a "big monster with a big moustache."[11] He said that his dad was already gone, only "mommy and Eric"[12] were in the house when the monster entered. Nonetheless, the prosecuting district attorney, Ken Anderson, focused on Michael Morton as the only suspect in the crime. Six weeks later, the sheriff knocked on Michael Morton's door. "I am here to arrest you." Little Eric was pulled from Michael's arms. He screamed for his father as deputies handcuffed Michael, placed him in the car, and led him away.

Defense attorneys were denied access to key evidence, including the eyewitness testimony of Eric. A bloodstained blue bandanna found near the murder scene was never tested. Footprints indicating a man had jumped over the back fence were never mentioned. During the trial, Ken Anderson had tears streaming down his face as he told the jury that Michael was a violent, sexually depraved murderer who had killed his wife because she had fallen asleep before they had sex on his birthday. The jury convicted Michael of first-degree murder and sentenced him to life in prison.

Custody of Eric was given to Christine's sister. Michael was allowed to see him once every six months. Michael lived for those visits. They were the oxygen that kept him alive. Nonetheless, their lives grew ever further apart. They shared nothing in common.

As Eric matured, it became more and more awkward for him to visit his dad in prison for a couple of hours twice a year. Soon Eric wanted to move on with his life. He informed Michael that he was legally changing his name and never wanted to see him again. Michael said he would grant the request if Eric could look him in the eye and say that he didn't want him for a father. Eric arrived at the prison. He never raised his eyes from the floor. Michael simply asked, "Will I ever see you again after today?" Eric replied, "No." Michael looked at Christine's sister and said, "Take care of my son." He turned, walked back to his prison cell, and collapsed on the bed.

Having his wife beaten to death in their own bed did not break Michael Morton. Being wrongly charged and convicted of the murder of his wife did not break Michael Morton. Losing his freedom and being locked away for life in a maximum-security prison did not break Michael Morton. Losing his son did. It was the only thing on Earth that linked him to a life that predated the nightmare he had entered.

Michael Morton was not a religious man, but that night he cried out to God. He felt nothing. Ten days later, as he was preparing for bed, he heard beautiful harp music from a classical music station coming through his headphones. Suddenly, he was bathed in golden light and seemed to be floating above his bunk. He felt a limitless love focused on him. He knew that he was in the presence of God. Once again, Michael's life was changed in a moment. The dagger piercing his heart was removed. The anger and bitterness left. The plans of revenge disappeared.

Michael's original defense attorney, Bill Allison, continued to believe in Michael's innocence. He continued to work for years without pay to gain access to evidence he believed would free Michael. Eventually he teamed with John Raley, an attorney specializing in DNA testing, and Barry Scheck and Nina Morrison from The Innocence Project. Their requests for DNA testing of the bloodstained blue bandanna were blocked for seven years by one of Ken Anderson's protégés, District Attorney John Bradley.

At last, a court granted a freedom of information request to access the original investigator's report on the murder. The testimony of Eric was discovered. DNA testing followed. It definitively cleared Michael Morton and identified the true killer. A hearing was scheduled and Michael was set free almost twenty-five years after he had been wrongly convicted.

Amazingly, when Michael Morton was released from prison, he was not an angry or bitter man. He did not seek revenge or retribution. Indeed, when the original prosecutor, Ken Anderson, was tried and convicted for tampering with evidence, Michael appealed on his behalf for mercy: "Your honor . . . I ask that you do what needs to be done, but at the same time, be gentle to Judge Anderson."[13]

Through his ordeal, Michael learned a critical lesson about mercy in an almost inconceivable way. Michael's freedom was never in the hands of Ken

Anderson. He carried it in his own hands. When he forgave those who had wronged him, he gained a freedom that no one could take from him: "Now everything is different for me. . . . I understand suffering and unfairness. I can't think of anything better to receive than that. I'm good with this world. What's happened to me. Where I'm going. What I'm doing. I know three little simple things because of that: One, God exists; two, he is wise; and, three, he loves me."[14]

The Choice to Forgive or to Hold a Grudge

Fortunately, very few people will ever experience the extreme injustice that Michael Morton received. Nonetheless, all of us will experience situations where we believe that we have been wronged. For most of us, these small injustices are much more mundane, even comical in the scheme of things. Someone ate the last scoop of milk-and-cookies ice cream and didn't replace it (which is actually quite serious). Someone didn't offer help when I needed it. Someone betrayed my confidence—which should be excusable if it is a well-intended son-in-law trying to help other people (just in case Riley is still listening)!

Although they are mundane, these little perceived injustices introduce stress into the individuals involved and their relationships. This stress leads to a host of immunological, physical, and emotional issues.[15] In one test, researchers asked seventy-one college students to recall an interpersonal offense and then imagine either forgiving the offender or holding a grudge. Stress was measured on the basis of skin conductance, heart rate, and blood pressure. In all cases, the choice to hold a grudge led to an increase in stress.[16] Since stress eventually takes a toll on a person's physical and emotional health, it is not surprising that researchers have linked an unwillingness to forgive to compromised health from almost every possible angle—physical symptoms currently experienced, medications being taken, fatigue, sleep quality, and somatic complaints.[17]

Fortunately, there is a stress-release valve in interpersonal relationships. It is called *mercy*. Interestingly, when a person believes that he or she has been wronged, the two little words "I'm sorry" are more important to preserving or restoring the relationship than retribution or restoration. In one test, customers who were dissatisfied with their service on an online auction site were offered three solutions—an apology, monetary compensation of €2.50, or monetary compensation of €5.00. As seen in Figure 8.1, twice as many people were willing to withdraw their complaints when offered an apology versus a monetary compensation.[18] Obviously, the apology must be perceived as sincere, which frequently implies an honest attempt to either resolve the problem or ensure that it will not be repeated in the future.

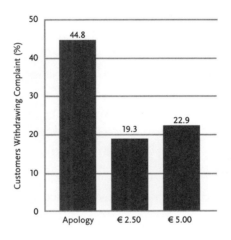

Figure 8.1: The Power of Apology
Source: Abeler, J. et al. "The Power of Apology," *Economics Letters* 107 (May 2010): 233–235.

Although the simple words "I'm sorry" have incredible power to preserve or restore a friendship, there is some brain chemistry that makes it very difficult to speak these words. When a person does something he perceives to be wrong, he experiences shame, which increases activity in the amygdala[19]—the part of the brain processing emotions such as fear. As such, the guilty person is more inclined to run and hide than he is to step forward and say, "Sorry."

This is exactly what Adam and Eve did in the Garden of Eden. As soon as they ate the forbidden fruit, they "hid themselves from the presence of the Lord God among the trees of the garden" (Genesis 3:8). God had a solution. Although he was the one offended, he stepped forward to initiate the reconciliation. "The Lord God called to the man, and said to him, 'Where are you?'"

(Genesis 3:9). In his encounter with Adam and Eve, God assured them that although they would suffer the consequences of their actions, that subtle serpent would one day be defeated: "He shall crush your head" (Genesis 3:15).

This is the exact behavior we see in Jesus Christ. When Judas leads the band of soldiers to arrest Christ in the Garden at Gethsemane, Jesus Christ steps forward to encounter Judas (cf. John 18:4). Furthermore, even while Judas is in the act of betrayal, Jesus Christ calls him "friend" (cf. Matthew 26:50). This is the merciful love we are asked to practice: "Love one another, even as I have loved you" (John 13:34). When we do, we are the ones who reap the reward.

Researchers investigating the relationship between justice and forgiveness discovered that an act of unsolicited forgiveness by the victim was frequently more beneficial to the victim than bringing the offender to justice. Researchers asked participants to imagine several scenarios surrounding the burglary of a residence. Among others, these scenarios included

- the offender remaining at large,
- the offender being convicted and sentenced to jail,
- the offender being ordered to make restitution to the victim, and
- the victim deciding to offer an unsolicited act of forgiveness.

The scenario most beneficial to the victim was when the victim offered an unsolicited act of forgiveness. A reduction in stress was measured in terms of smaller heart rate changes and less tension around the eyes and brows. Indeed, even when the offender remained at large, if the victim offered an unsolicited act of forgiveness, the victim experienced substantial benefits in terms of stress reduction.[20]

Mercy in the Spousal Relationship

Although the ability to forgive is important to all relationships, studies indicate that the closer the relationship, the more critical mercy becomes.[21] Indeed, forgiveness is more critical to the spousal relationship than any other relationship.[22] When the relationship ties are very strong, our expectations of the other person are also strong, making it easy to have our feelings hurt.

Indeed, in a nonscientific survey of participants attending a religion-based couples' enrichment program, 76 percent of the husbands and 69 percent of the wives said their spouses held grudges at least occasionally.[23]

This is a massive problem. Research indicates that the disruption of the spousal bond causes more personal stress than any other issue.[24] Indeed, the top three issues causing personal stress—as measured by the Social Readjustment Rating, which measures the time it takes to adjust to a life event—relate to the spousal union: the death of a spouse; divorce from a spouse; or separation from a spouse. As shown in Figure 8.2, each of these issues is more stressful than being sentenced to jail.

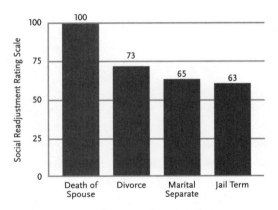

Figure 8.2: Personal Stress and Marital Problems
Source: Holmes, T., and Rahe, R. H. "The Social Readjustment Rating Scale," *Journal of Psychosomatic Research* 11 (1967): 213–218.

As such, there is tremendous need for mercy in the spousal relationship. Fortunately, when the relationship ties are very strong, we are more motivated to be forgiving as a means of maintaining the long-term integrity of the relationship.[25] Realistically, it is frequently the offended party that must step forward to begin the process of reconciliation.

Christ understood the special need for this proactive mercy in the spousal relationship. Indeed, from a spiritual perspective, Christ even experienced this reality. Obviously, Christ was not married in the same way that we are. Rather, throughout history, the Church has been considered to be the mystical bride of Christ: "Let us rejoice . . . for the marriage of the Lamb has come, and his Bride has made herself ready" (Revelation 19:7).[26]

In reality, the members of Christ's Church have caused him as much pain as any person has received from his or her spouse. Let us just consider Good Friday. Jesus was betrayed by one of his apostles. He was publicly denied on three occasions by the head of the apostles. Nine other apostles abandoned him. The very people who hailed him as king a week 'earlier called for his execution. Christ knew the pain of a heart wounded by unreturned love. Nonetheless, Christ responded with mercy, which transformed the Church:

> Christ loved the church and gave himself up for her, that he might sanctify her . . . that he might present the church to himself in splendor, without spot or wrinkle or any such thing, that she might be holy and without blemish (Ephesians 5:25–28).

This sounds amazingly like the science we have just discussed. Christ was the person offended. Nonetheless, he stepped forward to offer an unsolicited act of forgiveness. When he did, it transformed the situation. As such, it is not surprising that Christ's command to "love one another as I have loved you" (John 13:34) finds a specific fulfillment in marriage: "Husbands, love your wives, as Christ loved the church and gave himself up for her" (Ephesians 5:25).

Mercy as the Foundation of Marriage

This need for mercy in the spousal relationship is so great that I would even say that mercy is the very foundation of marriage. We see this illustrated in the very first Christian marriage—St. Joseph and the Virgin Mary. Let us go back and consider the Annunciation from the angel Gabriel once again.

In the previous chapter, we saw that the angel announced the coming of Christ to Mary when she was alone. Joseph was not to be found. Furthermore, the angel let Mary know that Joseph would not be the physical father of Jesus: "The Holy Spirit will come upon you, and the power of the Most High will overshadow you; therefore the child to be born will be called holy, the Son of

God" (Luke 1:35). Finally, the angel obviously expected an immediate reply from Mary. No option to wait and talk it over with Joseph. When Mary gives her consent, the Christ child is incarnate in her womb.

Imagine Joseph's predicament as he listened to Mary relate the account of the angel's appearance. The Jews were not anticipating a divine messiah[27] so there was no expectation of the need for a divine birth. I'm certain that Joseph prayed intensely about the situation, but God did not immediately resolve his questions. Rather, God wished Joseph to struggle to come to a decision on his own, which he did: "Joseph her husband, since he was a righteous man, yet unwilling to expose her to shame, decided to divorce her quietly" (Matthew 1:19). This decision sheds considerable light on the importance of mercy in Christian marriage.

First, we must note that Joseph is identified as a righteous or just man. In Judaism, a just or righteous man was someone who followed the law Moses received from God. Regarding a betrothed woman who was found to be pregnant with another man's child, the law was very clear: "If there is a betrothed virgin, and a man meets her in the city and lies with her, then you shall bring them both out to the gate of that city, and you shall stone them to death" (Deuteronomy 22:23). When Joseph chose not to "expose" Mary "publicly," he made the decision to not fulfill the dictates of the law regarding Mary—very unusual behavior for a "righteous man."

Next, we must note that Joseph chose to "divorce her quietly." In other words, Joseph was not going to tell anyone the reason he was divorcing Mary, which would have exposed her to the law. As such, the natural assumption on the part of most people would be that Joseph did not have a good reason for divorcing Mary. Furthermore, since most people would have believed that Mary was pregnant with Joseph's child, it would look like he was walking out on his family precisely when his wife was pregnant with his firstborn son. Needless to say, most people would consider Joseph to be a real loser.

Despite his own innocence, Joseph was willing to experience public shame to protect Mary from being exposed to the law. This decision is consistent with the mandate we just discussed: "Husbands, love your wives, as Christ loved the church and gave himself up for her" (Ephesians 5:25). Furthermore, once Joseph chooses to place mercy at the heart of his relationship with Mary, God sends an angel to illuminate the entire situation and Joseph brings Mary into his home (cf. Matthew 1:24). Mercy placed at the heart of the relationship between bridegroom and bride is called to be the foundation of the home.

Mercy and the Promise of Heaven

At this point Riley is scratching his head. He doesn't disagree. He's just a little unsure of how this deep theology relates to real life. I think I can help if I give him a simple story.

Katie lived a pretty typical life with her parents and little brother in a suburb of Denver, Colorado.[28] She did what most teenage girls do—go to school, hang out with friends, talk about boys. Unfortunately, the normalcy of her life was upset one day when her father left a note for her mother stating he wasn't sure if he loved her any more. He needed time in the mountains away from the family to sort things out. After he left, the family discovered that he had not gone into the mountains for a little discernment by himself. He was living with another woman.

Not surprisingly, Katie's family went into a tailspin. Katie did her best to help hold the family together spiritually, emotionally, and financially. She took a part-time job to help make ends meet. She was especially focused on the needs of her younger brother—helping with meals and homework and providing for his lunch money out of her small part-time salary. Through it all, she did her best to hold herself together.

Under such circumstances, Katie could easily have traveled a path all too familiar: She could have dropped out of high school, succumbed to substance abuse, initiated early sexual activity, become an unwed mother, and sunk into a life of poverty without much hope. Fortunately, she chose to travel a different path. She relied on the youth minister at her local parish and friends in the youth group to sustain her. Most importantly, she refused to let die her dreams for herself and the family she one day wanted.

One weekend while she was attending a youth retreat a thought suddenly hit her: "If I'm going to be married in the future, then my future husband is alive on Earth today. I know how hard things are for me and my friends. He must be facing issues as well." On that very day, Katie decided to "go to war for my future husband" by praying for all his needs and struggles—although she didn't know who he was or the struggles he was facing.

She also began writing him letters. She discussed her own life and struggles. She talked about the life she hoped they would live together. She opened her heart about her dreams for a better future. Since she could not attach a name or a face to her future husband, she simply addressed her letters, "Dear HTB," which stood for "Dear Husband To Be."

During this time, Mark Hartfiel was living in Houston, Texas. His life looked radically different from Katie's. He had a wonderful family. His mother was devout and his father was one of the most successful coaches in Texas high school basketball history. Indeed, Mark and his brother started on one of those teams alongside a future NBA All-Star. Mark enjoyed the "fringe benefits" of being a high school sports star. He spent plenty of time at parties and knew lots of girls. He would later confide that his outlook on life was defined by one word—pleasure.

Katie faithfully continued her prayers for her HTB and all his issues until she once again found herself on a retreat. She felt very distinctly that her HTB was experiencing a very strong struggle "right now." She began praying incredibly intensely for him. Back in Houston, Mark was struggling with his faith. His life was not consistent with the devout faith of his mother. Then, as he was taking a shower before bed, not consciously thinking about anything, he suddenly felt "the rush of the Holy Spirit." He was instantaneously converted. He knew that he had to change his life. He also knew that someone must have been praying for him.

Mark radically changed his life. He turned down the chance to play basketball in college. Instead, he enrolled in a small Catholic college called Franciscan University not far from Pittsburgh. On the first day of class a young girl caught his eye—Katie. After a few days of the obligatory awkwardness, Mark finally approached her. They hit it off immediately. Before long, they were in love. They shared their stories about their journey to Franciscan, which for Mark included the story of his instantaneous conversion. Before long they realized that his conversion occurred precisely during the time Katie was on retreat and praying intensely for her HTB.

Through the years Katie had continued her journal—always addressing her letters, "Dear HTB." She decided it was time to make a change and began addressing her letters, "Dear Mark." She was right. They graduated and were married. As a wedding present, she presented Mark with a binder immediately following the rehearsal dinner the night before their wedding. Her words were simple, "Open it and you will understand." In it, Mark found all the letters that Katie had written through all the years, including the last letter, which reads in part:

> I can't believe I am writing my last letter. I have been waiting a long time for this moment, and here it is. If you are reading this it means that tomorrow we will be man and wife . . . Many of the letters in the first half of my journal . . . are full of whining and venting. . . . I considered removing some of them . . . [but] I give you all of my past, present and future. . . . You will meet me as a 17-year-old . . . and watch me grow into Mrs. Mark Hartfiel. I've been yours for longer than you could possibly imagine. . . . I've loved and respected you since before you had a face. . . . You make me want to be holy. As we give each other everything tomorrow, let's give each other the promise of heaven as well. Know that I am praying for you. I have waited and I am so glad that I don't have to wait anymore. I love you.[29]

Wow! What a way to start a marriage! Mark was so overwhelmed that he refused to read the letters all at once. Instead, he read them very slowly— only a couple of letters a year. He never wanted it to end. These letters and Mark and Katie's story are chronicled in her book, *Woman in Love: Redefine the Journey Toward Your Husband to Be*.

This is certainly a wonderful story. But I would like us to think about Mark's conversion for just a moment. He did not on his own recognize the error of his ways, ask for mercy, and convert his life. As such, Mark's conversion was not simply the forgiveness of his sins when he asked for mercy. Rather, it is as if mercy found Mark. Katie's prayers obtained for him the gratuitous, spontaneous gift of mercy. This is getting very close to the mercy we need to practice in our marriages, but we need to take one more step.

The Possibility of Superabundant Mercy

St. John Bosco took this concept of gratuitous mercy a step further.[30] Don Bosco, as he is commonly called, was born into a poor farming family just outside of Turin, Italy, in 1815. His father died shortly after John's second birthday. Raised by his devout mother and grandmother, John showed signs of a special calling from a young age. At the age of nine his future vocation was revealed to him in a dream:

> He was in a field surrounded by a crowd of boys. Some . . . were fighting and using bad language. . . . In the middle of this ruckus appeared a noble-looking Man. . . . 'Come here,' he said. . . . 'You will never help these boys by beating them. Be kind to them, lead them, teach them that sin is evil and that purity is a precious gift.'[31]

Don Bosco understood that his life mission would be to help young boys in trouble. He lived during the time of the industrialization of Italy. Countless young boys were leaving the farms and flocking to the large cities looking for work. Since the boys had no money, no education, and no place to stay, the conditions were ripe for major problems. Crime and violence were common. Don Bosco waded into the worst areas of Turin to take thousands of homeless boys off the streets and provide them with food, clothing, and shelter. He gave them an education and taught them a trade. He found them employment and turned them into model citizens.

To achieve his remarkable results, Don Bosco developed a new method for the formation for youth, which he called the *Preventive Method*. The goal was to place the youth "in the impossibility of committing faults"[32] by having them "at all times under the vigilant eye of the Rector, who like loving fathers, talk with them, guide them in any difficulty, and give them advice and correction in a kind manner."[33] They treated the youth "entirely [with] reason and religion, and above all [with] kindness."[34]

Don Bosco's preventive system was incredibly successful. On one occasion Don Bosco asked the government for permission to take three hundred inmates from the local prison eight miles into the countryside of Turin to visit an abandoned hunting lodge.[35] He was adamant that no prison guards could accompany him. Don Bosco and a few of his aides would accompany the inmates on their sixteen-mile walk. Although government officials were certain that not a single inmate would return, they eventually granted Don Bosco's request when he promised to go to prison in the place of any inmate that escaped. To the government's great surprise, the entire day was filled with song and joy and laughter and every single prisoner returned. The minister of the interior begged Don Bosco, "Show me how one can gain such control over boys."[36]

The simple answer to the minster of the interior was mercy—superabundant mercy. Indeed, Don Bosco took the mercy we encountered in Mark and Katie's story a step further. Mark had sin in his life when Katie's prayers obtained for him the gift of mercy. Don Bosco did not wait for his boys to commit sin before asking for mercy. His prayers—and actions—obtained for the boys a mercy so superabundant that it spontaneously went to the boys and enveloped them to help prevent them from committing sins. Indeed, it was Don Bosco's kindness and love that enveloped them so that it was easy to be good and hard to be bad.

The 7 Steps to a Superabundant Marriage are absolutely consistent with Don Bosco's Preventive Method:

- Reason is included in Step 4: Set your mind on the things above.
- Religion is included in Step 3: Give God some of your time.
- Kindness is included in Step 6: Find God in other people.

In considering Don Bosco's Preventive Method, the hidden ingredient that made it so successful was the gift of time. It is implied by the fact that the youth were to be "at all times under the vigilant eye of the Rector." There was nothing more important for Don Bosco than to be with "his boys."[37] The gift of time is also the secret ingredient that will help marriages to become truly superabundant.

The Time for Love

Time is a major issue within marriages and families today. Indeed, we saw in Chapter 3 that many Americans are working longer and harder than ever. In Chapter 6, we saw that stress is making it harder for us to relate to each other with civility. Worst of all, this lack of time and stress is making it harder than ever for us to treat each other with mercy and compassion.

Researchers at Princeton tested the willingness of seminary students to help a stranger in need. The students were asked to go across campus to deliver a talk. As they walked to the site of the talk, they passed a man slumped over in need of help. As shown in Figure 8.3, the degree that a student felt rushed had a major impact on his willingness to help the stranger. Sixty percent of the students who were *not* in a hurry stopped to help the individual. Only 10 percent of those very hurried stopped to help—and that's among seminary students!

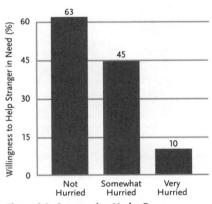

Figure 8.3: Compassion Under Pressure
Source: Darley, J., and Batson, D., "'From Jerusalem to Jericho': A Study of Situational and Dispositional Variables in Helping Behavior," *Journal of Personality and Social Psychology* 27 (1973): 100–108.

The "Good Samaritan Study" was completed at Princeton in 1973. At the time, researchers had to create a scenario to artificially induce a hurried state among the study's participants. Today, the typical family is in a perpetual race against the clock and in a constant state of stress. Many couples spend their entire day simply checking off a long list of things that need to get done and have little or no time for each other, which is incredibly troubling since the entire reason the couple got married was so that they could spend their entire lives together. Nonetheless, there is something more at work.

Surveys indicate that married couples spend approximately two hours per day in leisure time together, time not dedicated to checking off the million things needing to be done.[38] Unfortunately, as shown in Figure 8.4, the majority of this leisure time is spent watching television. I say unfortunately because studies indicate that watching television—like using the Internet—is an isolating activity.[39] When time spent watching television is excluded, couples spend less than one hour per day in leisure time together. This is a

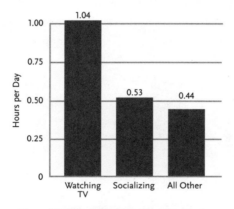

Figure 8.4: Spousal Leisure Time Together
Source: Fein, D., "Spending Time Together: Time Use Estimates for Economically Disadvantaged and Nondisadvantaged Married Couples in the United States" (working paper, US Department of Health and Human Services, 2009).

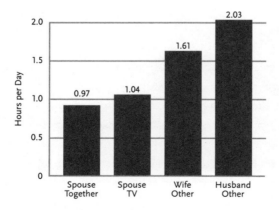

Figure 8.5: Total Spousal Leisure Time
Source: Fein, D., "Spending Time Together: Time Use Estimates for Economically Disadvantaged and Nondisadvantaged Married Couples in the United States" (working paper, US Department of Health and Human Services, 2009).

major issue since studies indicate a couple's time together is a major determinant of marital stability.[40]

I certainly understand the time challenge that couples face today. Furthermore, the mobile 24/7 world has certainly made things even more difficult. Nonetheless, we need to be honest. Couples are taking leisure time, just not with each other. As seen in Figure 8.5, wives take approximately 1.61 hours of leisure per day separate from their husbands and husbands take approximately 2.03 hours of leisure per day separate from their wives.[41] As such, something more must be at work.

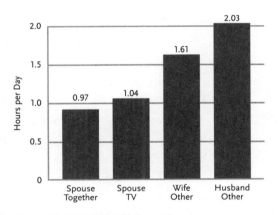

Figure 8.5: Total Spousal Leisure Time
Source: Fein, D., "Spending Time Together: Time Use Estimates for Economically Disadvantaged and Nondisadvantaged Married Couples in the United States" (working paper, US Department of Health and Human Services, 2009).

To understand the true issue, think about the moment a couple first falls in love. Most people aren't just sitting around keeping a couple of hours a day free so that "when I meet the right person I won't have difficulty working him or her into my schedule." Rather, when people fall in love they willingly rearrange their schedules so that they can spend time together. They even do things they really have no interest in so long as they can spend time together.

Riley and Rose Mary certainly did. Their second date was to the Cotton Bowl in Dallas. Early in the morning, they hopped onto a bus with a bunch of other couples, drove to Dallas, watched the game, and drove home—all before midnight! When Riley and Rose Mary told me about it, I cracked up laughing: "Rose Mary, I had no idea you liked football so much!" She just smiled.

Over time it is very easy to stop doing things as a couple—like make a daytrip to watch the Cotton Bowl in Dallas. Too far. Too expensive. Too tiring. Don't really like football. Lot of other things I need to get done. These things are all true, but they are no more true today than they were when the couple first fell in love. The issue is that many couples allow the flames of that first love to grow dim. Scripture encourages us: "I hold this against you: you have lost the love you had at first. Realize how far you have fallen . . . and do the works you did at first" (Revelation 2:4–5).

Not surprisingly, Riley and Rose Mary were able to keep their first love strong. A few years after I found out about their second date being to the Cotton Bowl, I was at dinner and Rose Mary mentioned that she liked the Houston Astros' new uniforms. I said I didn't realize they had new uniforms and asked if they brought back the old "Astro rainbow." She laughed. "They did that a couple of years ago. I'm talking about the new alternate uniform they wear on away games for this year." She then proceeded to walk me through all six of the Astro uniforms, including when they wore them and which ones she liked best. I was amazed and said, "Rose Mary, you must watch a lot of baseball." She simply smiled. So I followed with another one, "Rose Mary, I had no idea you liked baseball so much." She smiled once again.

Keeping the first love alive and strong is absolutely dependent upon a couple of critical things. First is the willingness to forgive. Holding grudges is incredibly destructive to the individual and spousal union. For most couples the issues will not be massive injustices like the one Michael Morton suffered. They will be the small things of everyday life. Frequently, it is the offended party that must step forward to initiate the process of reconciliation.

Second is the willingness to make the gift of time to your spouse. Indeed, day in and day out, this is the greatest gift we can make. It is a gift because once you give your time away, you never get it back. Spontaneously step forward. Offer your spouse the gift of your time and spend an abundance of time together. It will transform your life and marriage. At the very least, it will make it easy to be good and hard to be bad.

CHAPTER NINE

Marriage as a Foretaste of Paradise

It's been quite a journey, but we've made it through all seven steps and I'm really proud of Riley. We took him deeper than he wanted to go on a couple of occasions and I wasn't sure if he would stay with us, but he did. Truth be told, he enjoyed the journey. Nothing like seeing a not-so-young son-in-law jump through hoops just to show Riley he was right all along. Indeed, he's waiting for me to sheepishly approach and say, "Sorry, Riley. I should have believed you from the outset"—which I now respectfully offer.

Nonetheless, I can see that he and Rose Mary have moved down to the end of the couch by themselves. I won't make the same mistake that started all my troubles. At the engagement party, they were sitting quietly at the end of the couch while the party swirled around them. Naïve Steve thought they were feeling left out, so I walked up and started a conversation from which I have never fully recovered. I didn't realize they were sitting quietly by themselves by choice. Riley and Rose Mary had seen plenty of parties in their day. They just wanted to go home and go to bed, but thought it impolite to leave too early.

I know that Riley and Rose Mary once more need to go, but I've asked them to linger for just a moment. We need the benefit of their wisdom. We need to go beyond studies and surveys and brain scans. We need a vision that transcends the limits imposed by this physical world because the desires of the human heart know no such limits. Indeed, the love in the human heart is called to pass from this world to the next. Riley and Rose Mary are close enough to see it. We shall allow them to lead us there.

The Pathway to Happiness

Before we allow Riley and Rose Mary to help us develop a vision that touches the divine, we need to answer the question, "What difference do the 7 Steps to a Superabundant Marriage make to my life in this world?" We began with a very bold claim. We said that the 7 Steps would not only help to divorce-proof your marriage but also place superabundant happiness within your reach. We need to consider if we have fulfilled that bold claim.

To determine the impact of the 7 Steps on the probability of divorce, let's look at some data from the General Social Survey, which covers several questions that harmonize very well with the 7 Steps.[1] For individuals who had been married at some point in their life, 28.2 percent have experienced a divorce. This number is considerably lower than the 40 percent divorce rate frequently cited because this survey included a broader cross-section of society. As such, it included couples newly married. Undoubtedly, over time some of these marriages will fail, increasing the overall divorce rate. To see the impact of the 7 Steps, I would like to start adding steps and see what happens to the probability of divorce in this cross-section of the population.

We considered the first step—honor your wedding vows—in the second chapter. We saw that it included fidelity to your spouse both before and during marriage and the need to avoid "virtual infidelity"—e.g., pornography. For individuals who did not cohabitate before marriage and were never unfaithful to their spouse during marriage, the chance of divorce decreased from 28.2 percent to 11 percent, as seen in Figure 9.1. The radical reduction in the probability of divorce related to sexual issues is consistent with the data presented in Chapter 2. Since the quickest route to the divorce lawyer is sexual infidelity,[2] the best way to lower the probability of divorce is sexual exclusivity.

Since the General Social Survey did not have a question that easily related to the impact of finances on marital stability, let's jump to the third step—give God some of your time. In Chapter 4, we saw that attendance at weekly church services lowered the probability of divorce by changing the behaviors that lead to divorce.[3] We also saw that a robust, well-structured prayer life

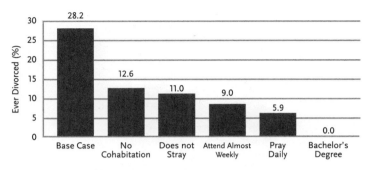

Figure 9.1: The 7 Steps and the Probability of Divorce
Source: General Social Survey, 1994.

would give God a portion of every unit of time—day, week, month, year, and lifetime. The two most fundamental aspects of a well-structured prayer life are weekly worship, which is to honor the Sabbath, and daily personal prayer. Adding weekly public worship and daily personal prayer to our previous two actions further lowers the chance of divorce from 11 percent to 5.9 percent.

We considered the fourth step—set your mind on the things above—in Chapter 5. Among other things, we saw that this included the integration of modern science with Scripture and the teachings of Christianity. This integration required the study of the findings of modern science, the reading of Scripture, and much personal prayer. We already covered personal prayer in the previous step. Data in the General Social Survey does not allow us to simultaneously investigate the impact of reading Scripture and secular studies. Therefore, we will consider a college degree—combined with personal prayer from the previous step—as a proxy for "set your mind on the things above." If we add a college degree—bachelor's or higher—to our previous four items, the probability of divorce is reduced to zero. Indeed, as seen in Figure 9.1, the chance of divorce in this survey was 0 percent.

We need to briefly pause to consider this result. I personally know individuals who did the five things we mentioned—didn't cohabit, didn't stray, went to church every week, prayed every day, and had a college degree—and yet got divorced. As such, the probability isn't truly 0.0 percent. Instead, we need to recognize that we are talking about population samples, which imply

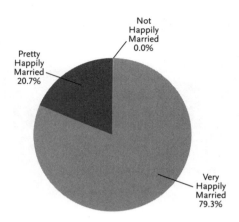

Figure 9.2: The 7 Steps and Marital Happiness
Source: General Social Survey, 1972–2012.

a host of issues including survey bias, sample error, confidence intervals, etc. Such factors can lead to survey results that differ from reality. Furthermore, the only year in which the General Social Survey asked questions relating to all five of the items mentioned above to the same sample group was 1994. We do not have more recent data to cross-check these results.

Nonetheless, other studies have also identified the very large impact sexual exclusivity (both before and after marriage), religious attendance, and education have on the probability of divorce.[4,5,6] Although the 7 Steps cannot claim to truly reduce the probability of divorce to 0 percent, they can claim to *radically* reduce the probability of divorce. As such, we have certainly fulfilled our claim that they help to divorceproof your marriage.

However, our bold claim went even further. We claimed that the 7 Steps would put you on the path to truly superabundant happiness. Data from the General Social Survey indicates that this claim is absolutely true. Considering just those couples fulfilling the five items we mentioned— those who didn't cohabit, didn't stray, went to church every week, prayed every day, and had a college degree—not only were they all still married, but they were all happily married. As seen in Figure 9.2, almost four out of five couples were in the highest possible category of marital happiness. They were very happily married. One in five couples were happily married and no one claimed to be unhappily married. Once again, the survey said 0 percent. Obviously, all of the same caveats from above apply once again. Nonetheless, we are talking about superabundant happiness.

This superabundant marital happiness is absolutely critical on the personal level. To a large extent, your personal happiness is tied to your marital happiness. As can be seen in Figure 9.3, individuals who are very happily married are significantly more likely to be personally happy than those who are unhappily married. Indeed, almost six out of ten individuals who are very happily married are also very happy in their personal lives, and fewer than 5 percent report being personally unhappy. When you consider individuals that are not happily married, the numbers are almost flipped—only 5.7 percent are personally very happy while over half are personally unhappy. Taken together, these results indicate that we have fulfilled our very bold claim. The 7 Steps not only radically reduce the probability of divorce, they radically increase the probability of a happy marriage, which leads to personal happiness.

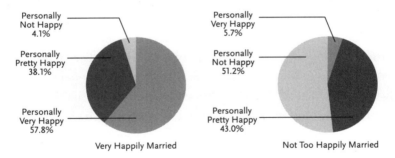

Figure 9.3: Marriage and Personal Happiness
Source: General Social Survey, 1972–2012.

The 7 Steps and the Life of the Holy Family

Given the dramatic impact of the 7 Steps, it is absolutely appropriate to ask, "Why are these seven steps so effective?" To answer this question, I would like to take a look at the very first Christian family—the Holy Family. The home of Jesus, Mary, and Joseph in Nazareth holds a very unique position in Christian tradition. Indeed, it has even been described as "a paradise on earth."[7] Before we simply dismiss such talk as poetic license, let's pause to look more deeply.

In the Garden of Eden, the greatest gift that Adam and Eve enjoyed was intimacy with God, who would stroll through the garden "at the afternoon air" (Genesis 3:8). When Adam and Eve ate the forbidden fruit this intimacy was destroyed. They began to hide "from the presence of the Lord God among the trees of the garden" (Genesis 3:8). In short order, they were expelled from the Garden. Ever since, humanity has longed for the day that it could return to its primordial intimacy with God.[8] Indeed, the great promise of heaven is that we will see the face of God (cf. 1 John 3:2).

Now think of the life of the Holy Family in Nazareth. Every day Mary and Joseph dwelt in the presence of God and gazed upon his face. As funny as it sounds, every day Mary and Joseph could wake Jesus and say, "Good morning, God." If Paradise is defined as the intimate presence of God, we need to take a serious look at the Holy Family.

The Holy Family stands at the intersection of the Old Testament and the New Testament. As such, it is simultaneously a devout Jewish family and the first Christian family. If we look intently enough, we will discover that the most important elements defining the life of the Holy Family have been hidden within the 7 Steps to a Superabundant Marriage.

As I begin talking with couples about the Holy Family, I frequently have a little fun. I begin by asking, "Would you agree that life in your home is pretty much defined by how things are going in your spousal relationship, what's happening at the dinner table, and the events of your social calendar?" After reflecting for just a second or two, I normally receive a bunch of nods in agreement. So I follow with, "Okay. Who in your family has control of these three things?" I now receive instantaneous responses that range from polite chuckles to howls of hysteria. Everyone knows that women control all three of these things.

Of course, God knows it too. Therefore, it is not surprising that the Mosaic Law specifically entrusts to women these three areas of the home. Mosaic Law essentially requires that a portion of each of these areas be "set aside" for the Lord, which is to sanctify them and make them holy.[9] When these laws are followed, the home is sanctified and the family becomes holy. Let us look at these three areas and see how they relate to the 7 Steps.

The Niddah laws (cf. Leviticus 15:19–24; 18:19) regulated the sexual relationship between husband and wife. The Jewish woman was required to undergo a ritual immersion in a mikvah seven days following the conclusion of her menstrual cycle before she could resume sexual relations with her husband.[10] As such, the couple set aside their sexual relationship during this interval as a gift offered to God. For us, the first step—honor your wedding vows—regulates the sexual relationship between husband and wife, who are called to remain faithful to the vows offered at the foot of the altar. By following God's intent for sexual relations, they offer themselves and their spousal union to God.

The Kosher laws governing Jewish dietary practices are perhaps the most easily identifiable aspect of Jewish life. These laws govern essentially every aspect of the Jewish table and are incumbent on both men and women. Regarding the dinner table, the issue specifically entrusted to women was the "separation of the challah" (cf. Number 15:20–21). This law required the woman to set aside a portion of the dough to be given as an offering in the temple.[11] In an agrarian society, food is money. The Jewish home was called to share their bread with others. For us, the second step—use money for others—requires us to set aside a portion of our financial resources for the benefit of others.

The Nerot laws regulated the Sabbath observance (cf. Exodus 20:8) and required the woman to light two candles at least eighteen minutes before sundown on the Sabbath (i.e., Friday night).[12] The lighting of the Sabbath candles ushered the Sabbath into the Jewish home, which was a day totally set aside for the Lord. For us, the third step—give God some of your time—calls us to build an authentic prayer life by setting aside a portion of each unit of time (day, week, month, year, and lifetime) for God.

Living as observant Jews, Mary and Joseph would have followed these dictates—recognizing that the majority of Christians do not believe that Mary and Joseph had a sexual relationship.[13] Into this very Jewish home, God sent the angel Gabriel with a message: "The angel said to her, '. . . Do not be afraid, Mary, for you have found favor with God. And behold, you will conceive in your womb and bear a son, and you shall call his name Jesus. He will be great . . . and the Lord God will give to him the throne of his father

David, and he will reign over the house of Jacob forever'" (Luke 1:30–33). In other words, the angel helped Mary and Joseph understand God's action in their lives. For us, the fourth step—set your mind on the things above—calls us to ponder God's action in the world and our lives personally.

The angel Gabriel specifically told Mary that she would find God dwelling within her: "Behold, you will conceive in your womb and bear a son. . . . The Holy Spirit will come upon you, and the power of the Most High will overshadow you; therefore the child to be born will be called holy, the Son of God" (Luke 1:31–35). For us, the fifth step—find God in yourself—asks us to turn inward to find God dwelling within.

An angel was sent to Joseph and informed him that he would find God in Mary: "Behold, an angel of the Lord appeared to him in a dream, saying, 'Joseph, son of David, do not fear to take Mary your wife, for that which is conceived in her is of the Holy Spirit'" (Matthew 1:20). For us, the sixth step—find God in other people—asks us to go beyond external appearances and find God dwelling in other people. Like Joseph, we are called to find them in the members of our family in a special way.

Finally, as we saw in the previous chapter, Joseph placed mercy at the heart of his relationship with Mary. He chose to "send Mary away quietly" (Matthew 1:19) as opposed to fulfilling the dictates of the law, which required Mary to be stoned to death (cf. Deuteronomy 22:23). Since Joseph planned to divorce Mary without telling anyone the circumstances, most people would have assumed that Joseph divorced his wife without sufficient cause when she was pregnant. Joseph would have been held in very low esteem. He was truly self-sacrificial for the sake of his bride. Indeed, he made mercy the foundation of the Holy Family. For us, the seventh and final step—make it easy to be good and hard to be bad—asks us to embrace a mercy so superabundant that it actually envelops a soul to help prevent it from sinning.

Considered from this perspective, it is easy to see that the 7 Steps are profoundly related to the Holy Family. They help us to enter into and live the life that the Holy Family lived in Nazareth. This is really good news because the life within the Holy Family was a type of Paradise.

The Holy Family was a heaven, a paradise on earth, endless delights in this place of grief; it was glory already begun in the . . . lowliness of their life (Monsieur Jean-Jacques Olier).[14]

The Divine Lesson in Love

Suddenly, we are standing at the gates of Paradise. When we briefly considered the mystery of Paradise in Chapter 1, we saw that God gave humanity a divine lesson in the science of love. He worked to expand the human heart beyond the confines of this material world—beyond mere sensual pleasure, beyond success and achievement, beyond power and domination. Only after Adam's heart expanded to embrace the way of love did God place Adam into that sleep where he could create Eve from the love in his heart. Together, Adam and Eve were to become one and journey beyond the limits imposed by this material world to touch God himself (cf. Genesis 1:28).

Unfortunately, this noble vision of marriage did not long endure. Using very symbolic language, Scripture reveals a primordial temptation experienced by humanity (cf. Genesis 3:1–5). When Adam and Eve ate the forbidden fruit, their union was distorted and filled with tension: "Your desire shall be for your husband and he shall rule over you" (Genesis 3:16). They pulled back from each other by placing something in their union that did not previously exist: "They sewed fig leaves together and made themselves aprons" (Genesis 3:7). Furthermore, their communion with God was filled with shame and fear.[15] They hid from him "among the trees of paradise" (cf. Genesis 3:8).

Separated from their spouse and God, Adam and Eve are once more alone, which was their state before God led them through the divine lesson in the science of love. As such, we see that Adam and Eve have lost their lesson in love. In the end, they are expelled from the Paradise where they received this divine lesson and where they were called to live the way of love. At last, an angel is sent to guard the way to the tree of life with a "flaming sword" (cf. Genesis 3:24). Such was the unhappy lot of humanity.

Fortunately, God had an answer. Jesus Christ would enter into the depths of humanity's fallen state and journey back to Paradise for us. To understand this journey, we will need to stretch our spiritual legs and consider some of the beautiful mystical theology of the past two thousand years.

Oh no! I think I pushed Riley one time too many. He just got up, grabbed Rose Mary's hand, and said, "I think it's time for us to go"—and I don't think he is talking about the kitchen! If Rose Mary can convince him to hang on for a few minutes, this is not as hard as it sounds. It is certainly not as hard as making six days equal 13.8 billion years!

Some of the earliest and most influential thinkers in the Christian era used a process called *biblical typology*, where one story is used to shed spiritual light on a different story by considering the parallels between the stories. We specifically want to investigate the unique relationship that exists between Adam and Jesus Christ since Scripture says, "Adam was a type of the one who was to come [i.e., Jesus]" (Romans 5:14).

It is significant that Christ began his Passion in a garden (cf. John 18:1). Early Christianity saw a spiritual link between Christ's agony in a garden and the Garden of Eden. Alcuin, a towering figure in eighth-century England, stated that Christ entered "where there was a garden, that the sin which was committed in a garden, he might blot out in a garden."[16]

Next, we note that Jesus is arrested, tried and convicted, scourged, crowned with thorns, and robed in a purple garment. As such, he is stripped of all his glory. From the earliest days of Christianity, this was seen as a manifestation of Adam and Eve being striped of their original innocence and clothed in a fallen nature. St. Ephrem the Syrian is one of the most illustrious saints in Orthodox Christianity. In the fourth century he stated, "All these changes did the Merciful One make, stripping off glory and putting on a body; for He had devised a way to reclothe Adam in that glory which he had stripped off."[17]

Next, we note that this "descent of Christ" is related to his willingness to take on the sins of the world: "Surely he has borne our griefs . . . he was wounded for our transgressions, he was bruised for our iniquities" (Isaiah 53:4–5). Once again, special recognition was given to the relationship with Adam. Romanos the Melodist, one of the Eastern Orthodox saints of the sixth century famous for writing hymns, captured this analogy very well: "Take courage . . . I shall come to show you from what suffering I liberated Adam and how much I sweated for his sake."[18]

Next, Christ was made to carry his own cross (cf. John 19:17). Christ's cross has always been symbolically related to both the tree of knowledge of good and evil and the tree of life. Regarding its relationship to the tree of the knowledge of good and evil, Theodore the Studite, an eighth-century abbot from Eastern Orthodoxy, stated, "This was the tree upon which the Lord . . . healed the wounds of sin that the evil serpent had inflicted on our nature. A tree once caused our death, but now a tree brings life. . . . What an astonishing transformation!"[19]

Finally, Christ was crucified at "the place of a skull, which is called in Hebrew Golgotha" (John 19:17). Many early Christian commentators identified "the skull" with Adam's skull. As such, Calvary was seen as the burial place of Adam. Origen, an important third-century scholar from Alexandria, wrote, "I have received a tradition to the effect that the body of Adam, the first man, was buried upon the spot where Christ was crucified."[20]

Pulling all of this together, we are able to paint a spiritual picture of Christ on Calvary as follows: Jesus has returned to the garden from which Adam has been exiled. He has accepted Adam's guilt and entered into his fallen state. His hand is fastened to the tree from which Adam was forbidden to eat. He has been judged as guilty and deserving of death.

In the Garden of Eden, it was precisely at this moment that Adam pulled back from the way of love. He experienced shame and hid from God and, to a certain extent, separated himself from Eve. As such, Adam was once more alone. On Calvary, Christ entered into Adam's solitude. He has been abandoned, denied, and betrayed by his own apostles. He has given away his last earthly possession—his mother (cf. John 19:26). He feels abandoned and separated from God: "My God, my God, why have you forsaken me?" (Mark 15:34). In Christ, humanity is ready for another divine lesson in the science of love. This message will essentially relate to mercy.

The Divine Lesson in Mercy
One of the most famous parables in Scripture is the parable of the prodigal son:

There was a man who had two sons; and the younger of them said to his father, "Father, give me the share of property that falls to me." And . . . not many days later the younger son gathered all he had and took his journey into a far country, and there he squandered his property in loose living. When [the younger son] had spent everything, a great famine arose in that country, and he began to be in want. So he went and joined himself to one of the citizens of that country, who sent him into his fields to feed swine . . .

He came to himself and said, "How many of my father's hired servants have bread enough and to spare, but I perish here with hunger. I will arise and go to my father, and I will say to him, 'Father, I have sinned against heaven and before you; I am no longer worthy to be called your son; treat me as one of your hired servants.'" And he rose and came to his father. But while he was yet at a great distance, his father saw him and had compassion, and ran and embraced him and kissed him . . . [and] said to his servants, "Bring quickly the best robe, and put it on him; and put a ring on his hand, and shoes on his feet; and bring the fatted calf and kill it, and let us eat and make merry; for this my son was dead, and is alive again; he was lost, and is found" (Luke 15:11–24).

Interestingly, many of the earliest Christian commentators understood this parable based upon the typology between Adam and Christ. The younger son who left his father's house was a seen as a symbol of Adam: "There are some who say of these two sons, that . . . the younger [is] man, who departed on a long journey, when he fell from heaven and paradise to Earth; and they adapt what follows with reference to the fall or condition of Adam."[21] Unfortunately, outside of the father's house, the younger son loses his dignity and ends by feeding swine. This represents Adam's loss of his original innocence.

Now comes the critical point. It is not Adam in his fallen nature that comes to his senses. Adam remains forever afraid of the father. Rather, it is Christ who brings humanity to its senses: "The Lord coming called the race of man to repentance, because he saw that to return of their own accord to whence they had fallen had never been in their thoughts."[22] Since Jesus Christ is from the "bosom of the Father" (John 1:18), he understands that the Father is "rich in mercy" (Ephesians 2:4). As such, even in our fallen state we are able to hope for communion with God. Man does not need to be afraid of the Father. He does not need to be alone.

Suddenly, the human heart can once more expand to all that it was created to be. Jesus Christ, the prodigal Adam, cries, "I thirst" (John 19:28). It is the thirst for communion.[23] From the very depths of humanity's fallen state, Christ offers himself to find communion with God: "Father, into your hands I commit my spirit" (Luke 23:46). When Christ rises from the dead in a garden (cf. John 19:41–42), he completes humanity's return to the Paradise from which we had been exiled.

The Return to Paradise

I can see Riley reaching for his keys. He seriously wants to go. If I can just get him to hang on for one more minute, we'll be standing in Paradise. Unfortunately, he couldn't care less about standing in Paradise at this point. He prefers to be lying on his bed. Nonetheless, there's a ray of hope. Rose Mary is having trouble finding her coat.

We need to consider this garden in which Christ rose from the dead. Since Christ has conquered death, in this garden "death shall be no more" (Revelation 21:4). As such, this garden not only takes us back to the Garden of Eden that began Scripture, but also takes us forward to the garden that brings Scripture to its close. Like the Garden of Eden, this garden has a tree of life (cf. Revelation 22:2), fountain of living water (cf. Revelation 22:1), and the abiding presence of God (cf. Revelation 22:4). Indeed, this is the ultimate Paradise to which the Garden of Eden pointed.

Jesus Christ wants us to be with him in this ultimate Paradise: "I wish that where I am they also may be with me" (John 17:24). He wants us to make the journey together with him. During his journey, Jesus was sustained by a love that was stronger than death (cf. Song of Songs 8:6). For us to accompany Jesus on his journey, we must be sustained by the same love.

As such, when Jesus goes to the very end of love (cf. John 13:1), he allows his heart to be opened for us: "One of the soldiers pierced his side with a spear, and at once there came out blood and water" (John 19:34).

We need to briefly consider this moment. We have already encountered the thought of the great Eastern Church father, St. John Chrysostom, on many occasions. He placed special emphasis on this moment when Christ's heart was wounded:

> There flowed from his side blood and water. Beloved, do not pass over this mystery without thought; it has yet another hidden meaning, which I will explain to you. I said that water and blood symbolized baptism and the holy Eucharist. From these two sacraments the Church is born . . . since the symbols of baptism and the Eucharist flowed from his side, it was from his side that Christ fashioned the Church.[24]

These three realities—the Church, baptism, and the Eucharist—became incredibly important for early Christian commentators. Indeed, they were seen to mystically represent Paradise: "What then was Paradise is now represented by the Church."[25] The waters of baptism were seen as the restored spring of water that brought life to Paradise (cf. Genesis 2:6): "This gift of the spirit . . . is in her a fountain of living water springing up unto everlasting life."[26] The Eucharist was seen as the restored tree of life: "The assembly of the saints bears resemblance to Paradise: in it each day is plucked the fruit of Him who gives life to all; in it, my brethren, is trodden the cluster of grapes, to be the Medicine of Life."[27]

Born of Christ's wounded heart, the Church is born in the moment of passage. Jesus has already remained faithful until death, but he has not yet risen from the dead. Jesus is the Passover lamb (Cf. John 1:29). As such, the Church still experiences the reality of this fallen world, but it already has a foretaste of the Paradise that is to come.[28]

Marriage and the Mystery of Paradise

I know that Riley thinks that I've gotten lost in a deep thicket from which I will never emerge, but this concept of Paradise is absolutely critical to the marriage of husband and wife. Indeed, the nuptial blessing given to Catholic couples proclaims these amazing words:

> Father, by your plan man and woman are united, and married life has been established as the one blessing that was not forfeited by original sin or washed away in the flood.[29]

"The one blessing not forfeited by original sin." Considered as such, the nuptial blessing takes us back once more to the gates of the Garden of Eden. Although Catholic, Orthodox, and Protestant wedding ceremonies are very different, each evokes the mystery of Paradise in some way. Common to all three is the fact that the couple comes to the church to get married. Since the Church represents Paradise, bridegroom and bride return to Paradise to enter into marriage as had been intended from the beginning. Catholic and Protestant ceremonies begin in a similar fashion.

- The ceremony begins with the bridegroom standing at the foot of the altar while the bride is outside the sanctuary. In Paradise, Adam was "alone" (cf. Genesis 2:18).
- The priest or pastor stands next to the bridegroom. God was present with Adam in Paradise. God said, "It is not good that the man should be alone" (Genesis 2:18).
- The bride enters the church and walks up the aisle. In Paradise, God brought the woman to the man (cf. 2:22).
- At the sight of the bride, the congregation stands and the fanfare in "Canon in D" sounds. It is as if the congregation were participating in Adam's joy in Paradise when he exclaimed, "This, at last, is bone of my bones and flesh of my flesh; she shall be called woman because she was taken out of man" (Genesis 2:23).

In Catholic weddings, once the bride joins the bridegroom at the altar, the priest asks them three questions. The first question, "Have you come here freely and without reservation to give yourselves to each other in marriage?"[30] confirms that the couple wishes to form a Christian marriage. Once they answer "yes," the priest asks two additional questions, which explicitly take us back to the mystery of Paradise.

Scripture contains two stories of humanity in its innocence—the story of creation in Genesis chapter 1 and the story of the Garden of Eden in Genesis chapter 2. Both of these stories end with a revelation about the union of man and woman. Bridegroom and bride are asked if they are willing to live the vision of marriage contained in these two stories:

- "Will you love and honor each other as man and wife for the rest of your lives?"[31] The final vision we have of humanity in its innocence is the "one flesh" union of man and wife revealed in the story of the Garden of Eden: "Therefore a man leaves his father and his mother and cleaves to his wife, and they become one flesh" (Genesis 2:24). The priest asks the couple if they are willing to embrace this vision.

- "Will you accept children loving from God and raise them according to the laws of Christ and his Church?"[32] This question finds its origin in God's original blessing to humanity in its innocence, "God blessed them, and God said to them, 'Be fruitful and multiply, and fill the earth and subdue it; and have dominion over the fish of the sea and over the birds of the air and over every living thing that moves upon the earth'" (Genesis 1:28). The priest asks the couple if they wish to receive the "one blessing not forfeited by original sin."

Once the bridegroom and bride respond "yes" to each of these questions, they pronounce their vows and a Christian marriage is formed as had been intended "from the beginning." Unfortunately, the bridegroom and bride retain their fallen state. As such, the vows are much easier to pronounce than they are to live.

Recognizing this reality, Catholic, Orthodox, and Anglican Communion couples normally immediately turn to receive the Eucharist. It flows from Christ's wounded heart, from a love that was faithful until the end. Furthermore, Jesus gives us the Eucharist as the food for our journey from this fallen world to that Paradise yet to come.[33] As such, for Catholic,

Orthodox, and Anglican Communion Christians, Jesus's presence in the Eucharist is critical to marriage.[34] Sustained by his grace, couples can experience a love that soars above the limits of our broken, wounded world.[35] Indeed, this is the spiritual reality underlying the data regarding marriage, happiness, church attendance, and prayer. Indeed, this is a large part of the secret for Riley and Rose Mary.

They certainly embraced their own advice. They sat in church together as a family every Sunday. Their marriage certainly radiated something of the joy of Paradise—even if it included struggles in this fallen world. Indeed, the family wants me to let you know that Riley and Rose Mary were not perfect nor would they appreciate me building them and their marriage up so much. (I guess I'm destined to have yet another awkward conversation with my father-in-law in the future!) But that's the point. Precisely because Riley and Rose Mary weren't perfect, what they had is within our grasp and it was beautiful. If I could just convince them to stay and share it with us; but Riley said it is time to say, "Goodbye."

Riley and Rose Mary's Goodbye

When Shelly and I married, Riley and Rose Mary were already well into their golden years. As such, a true fear for Shelly was that her parents would die before they held our first child. When Shelly and I received our nuptial blessing and I heard the words "May they live to see their children's children,"[36] I turned to look at Rose Mary. I told Shelly that my wedding prayer for her was that both of her parents would hold our first child. I am grateful that this prayer was granted.

Nonetheless, after a few years, their strength and energy began to fade. Rose Mary began to have a series of accidents. She went to Toys "R" Us to buy a gift for a grandchild and tripped on a rug. Her head hit the floor and she "got blood all over." Shortly thereafter, she was taking a shower and slipped and fell through the glass shower door. Since it was an older home, the glass was not tempered. Rose Mary severed a nerve and lost the use of one of her arms.

Soon the family began to worry that something more serious was wrong. Rose Mary had a series of diagnostic tests run and she was diagnosed with

ALS, or Lou Gehrig's disease, which meant that over the course of the next few years she would lose the use of all of her limbs and her ability to communicate. Rose Mary would require around-the-clock care. At the time of the diagnosis, Riley told Shelly, "I feel better than I've felt in years. I think that I'm going to live to be a hundred. I think that I'm up to the challenge of caring for Rose Mary."

The following week, as Rose Mary was completing her diagnostic work, Riley was walking across the hospital lobby, tripped, and hit his head on the marble floor. He was in Methodist Hospital in Houston, which is rated as one of the top five hospitals in the United States. If you're going to hit your head on a marble floor, that is a good place to do it. He was rushed to the emergency room. CAT scans revealed a very small aneurysm. Doctors assured him that he would make a complete recovery. Nonetheless, he was checked into the hospital for observation as a precautionary measure.

Over the next four days, Riley slowly became incoherent. Along the way, he was telling everyone goodbye, but in his own way.

At the end of Rose Mary's last visit, Riley flashed that infectious smile and said, "Hey kid, we had a good time, didn't we?" She nodded and smiled and then allowed them to roll her away in a wheelchair.

To Shelly, he said, "I'm doing my best not to die for the sake of your mother."

While his son and another daughter were in the room, Riley was rambling incoherently. Suddenly, he became absolutely lucid. He looked into a corner of the room near the ceiling and said, "Do you see that beautiful woman dressed in white?" His eyes followed from one corner of the room to the other. Then he said, "Oh well. She's gone." He immediately began to ramble incoherently once again.

After four days, the family was exhausted. Rose Mary needed around-the-clock care. Although Rose Mary had limited help, Riley had been her primary caregiver, which meant the family now had to step in. At the same time, they needed to keep someone with Riley at all times. Each of us had families with young children needing attention. Finally, the children decided to hire a sitter to stay with Riley for just one night. She was given explicit instructions to call at the first sign of trouble. All of the families were within fifteen minutes of the hospital, which is pretty good for Houston.

I was the last family member to see Riley alive. When I got home I told Shelly, "They did another CAT scan today and the doctor says your dad is going to be just fine. I'll trust him because he's the doctor, but I have to say that your dad looks like he is in real trouble."

At 4:00 a.m., a call was received from the hospital with the simple message: "We are sorry to inform you, but your father is dead." This man, who was so beloved by his family that every one of his children named their first-born son after him,[37] died alone in a hospital room.

The family gathered at Rose Mary's house. They woke her and let her know: "Mom, Dad is gone." As she burst into tears, her only words were, "I never got to say goodbye."

After Riley's funeral, Rose Mary was adamant that she wanted to remain in her home. It was incredibly challenging, but the family pulled together. The three daughters each took at least one night a week with Rose Mary. The son took care of the house and finances and yard. It took a small army of additional helpers, but the family was able to pull together 24/7 care for Rose Mary in her own home.

At the same time Shelly and I began to pray intently for the circumstances surrounding Rose Mary's passage. We could not bear the thought that she might die alone like Riley. Over the next eighteen months, Lou Gehrig's disease took its toll. Rose Mary lost the use of all of her limbs. She could no longer speak. She communicated by an ever-so-small nod or simply blinking her eyes. She eventually needed to have a feeding tube inserted.

As Rose Mary's eighty-fourth birthday approached, the family desperately wanted to do something special for Rose Mary. It would undoubtedly be their last celebration together. Nonetheless, Rose Mary was adamant that she wanted absolutely nothing for her birthday. No one could argue with her logic. She couldn't eat or drink anything special because she was limited to her feeding tube diet. She had lost the use of her limbs and was no longer able to leave the house. In her words, "Anything you bring in this house for me now, you will just have to clean out when I'm gone in a couple of months."

Unwilling to let Rose Mary's last birthday pass without ceremony, we racked our brains for a suitable send-off. Suddenly, an idea hit. Four years earlier, the family had attempted to produce a special video for Rose Mary's eightieth birthday celebration. All the kids and grandkids had taped wonderful messages of love and thanksgiving to Rose Mary. Unfortunately, a technologically incompetent but well-meaning son-in-law never completed the video, so the footage remained buried in a desk drawer. We quickly hired someone, and a beautiful video was produced for Rose Mary's birthday.

The entire family gathered together to watch the video. At its conclusion, everyone received a big surprise. Since the original footage had been recorded four years earlier, Riley also had a chance to wish Rose Mary a happy birthday. When Riley appeared on screen, a hush overtook the room. He had a beautiful message. At the end, he spoke words that took on a whole new meaning:

"Rose Mary, I hope that one day you can get to where I am. It won't be easy, but hang in there, kid. Happy Birthday."

Something changed in Rose Mary that day. She couldn't speak, so we'll never know for sure, but perhaps there was a change from the acceptance of the end to a longing for the end. In any event, her health rapidly deteriorated. Just two weeks later, it was Shelly's turn to spend the night with her mom. As was frequently the case, I decided to join her, along with our four-year-old daughter.

We had a little routine that was quite amusing. Shelly would put her mom to bed. At the same time, I would put our four-year-old daughter to bed. Then Shelly and I would meet to chat and have tea in the kitchen. Afterward, she would go to bed with her mother and I would go to bed with our four-year-old daughter. It's important to keep a sense of humor during difficult times!

On this particular evening, our daughter was already asleep, so I was in the kitchen preparing the tea. A baby monitor was picking up the sound of Shelly working with Rose Mary. At this point, Rose Mary's primary means of communication was looking at a large poster board with the alphabet. The caregiver would guess which letter Rose Mary was looking at until Rose Mary had spelled a word.

Shelly was doing her best to make out the first letter of the first word that

Rose Mary was trying to communicate, but she couldn't do it. After more than five minutes, I stopped making the tea and just listened. I could not believe how difficult it was. After more than ten minutes, Shelly had not made out the first word and Rose Mary just gave up. I walked into the room next door and stood in front of a bust of Riley. Before long, I said this simple prayer, "Riley, things are so difficult. Can't you just take Rose Mary to where you are?"

The next morning, I left for work and dropped our daughter at pre-school. Shelly stayed with her mother all day, telling me, "Something is just not right." Finally, when it was time for dinner, Shelly still did not want to leave her mother.

I pleaded with her, "You have to eat anyway. We will go out to eat. After dinner, you can go back to be with your mom if you want."

Shelly consented, so we went to a local Italian restaurant where we bumped into her brother and his family. It was one of those glorious fall nights in Houston. The kids played games outside while we waited for our table. We had a great meal and for the space of about an hour and a half, all the struggles of the past two years seemed to fade into the background.

When we arrived home, the phone was ringing as we walked into the door. "Shelly, get over here right away. It's your mother. She's having trouble breathing."

The family quickly gathered together. It was obvious that Rose Mary's time had come. Rose Mary had left instructions that she wanted a priest, but it was hard to contact one on Friday night. Finally, the family called the local seminary. Unfortunately, the only number they had was for the receptionist, who was long gone. Fortunately, a visiting priest happened to be walking by at just the right moment and decided to pick up the phone. He took the message, but had no idea who the Leggett family was or where they lived. He was convinced there was nothing he could do.

As he opened the door to leave the lobby, he literally ran into Fr. Brendan Cahill, the Rector or head of the seminary.[38]

"Fr. Brendan, I just took a call from a Leggett family. They say Rose Mary is in her final minutes and they're not far from here. You know anything about that?"

Fr. Brendan replied, "Know anything! They're great friends. I grew up with the Leggetts since I was a kid. I'll be at their house in less than five minutes."

Fr. Brendan arrived and gave Rose Mary the Last Rites. He led the family through the Rosary. As they prayed, Rose Mary closed her eyes and drifted away in the arms of her children.

The Great Mystery of Marriage

I dare say that when she opened her eyes, Riley was standing there to greet her—flashing that big infectious smile. Rose Mary lost Riley on their twenty-fifth anniversary, but she got him back again. At the end of life, they replayed the story once again. However, this time she'll never lose him again.

Marriage is a great mystery (cf. Ephesians 5:32). It not only points back to the original Paradise as "the one blessing not forfeited by original sin," but also points forward to that Paradise that is yet to come. In this Paradise, we once more find a wedding ceremony: "Let us rejoice and exult and give him the glory, for the marriage of the Lamb has come, and his Bride has made herself ready" (Revelation 19:7). Indeed, in our marriages on Earth we are prepared for the one that is yet to come.

In his first letter to the Corinthians, St. Paul speaks of the way of love: "Love is patient and kind; love is not jealous or boastful . . . Love never ends" (1 Corinthians 13:4–13). These words match the desires of the bridegroom and bride so perfectly that they are very frequently read at weddings. The last verse is absolutely critical: "So faith, hope and love abide, these three; but the greatest of these is love" (1 Corinthians 13:13). More than poetic language, these words speak an essential truth.

Our faith will one day come to an end. When we die, we will see what is on the other side. Either we are right or we are wrong, but we won't need faith. Likewise, our hope will one day come to an end. Either we will attain our heart's desire in a Paradise where "death shall be no more, neither shall there be mourning nor crying nor pain any more" (Revelation 21:4), or we won't. But we won't need hope.

What about love? It "is as strong as death" (Song of Solomon 8:6). Indeed, love passes through the grave to find its fulfillment in heaven. The love we live in this life will accompany us on our journey to the next life. Here is the mystery. In Paradise, God created man and woman to be a "unity of the two." For this reason, I left my father and mother and am clinging to my spouse. When we die, we go back into the ground as a "unity of the two." The vast majority of people will not be buried with their parents, or siblings, or children. They will be buried beside their spouse. Together they await the marriage feast of the Lamb.

When it comes, we pay it forward once again. In the normal course of events, the husband precedes the wife in death. He enters into the Paradise of heaven to dwell in the presence of God. There he waits until God says, "It is not good for man to be alone." Then he rejoices as his bride once more comes to him: "At last!"

Marriage is a great mystery. It is a great blessing. God does not want you to struggle through twenty, thirty, forty, or fifty years of a difficult marriage. He wants you to experience superabundance. These 7 Steps are a sure guide to help get you there.

God has such wonderful plans for your life. So much love. So much joy. Even in the midst of this fallen world.

Live the love. It's real.

It won't be easy, but it will be worth it.

A Special Note to Those Not Yet Married

When I present the 7 Steps to a Superabundant Marriage, the most frequent response I receive by far is, "Please take this to young couples—newlyweds who have just begun their marriages or engaged couples before they even begin. Help them to begin their marriages with the right foundation so that they avoid the issues that cause so much pain and are so difficult to resolve once they have begun."

This is certainly our great desire. We have programs to help parishes and churches use the 7 Steps to a Superabundant Marriage in marriage preparation and for couples in the first few years of their marriage. We even have materials for those who do not belong to a parish or church to help them integrate the 7 Steps into their marriages. I also let them know that they can be a great aid in this endeavor. They can contact their pastor or priest or those responsible for marriage preparation and let them know about the 7 Steps. They can give the materials to young couples who are seriously considering marriage or just beginning their journey.

This desire to help get the 7 Steps into the hands of engaged couples or those seriously considering marriage frequently leads to a question, "Can these 7 Steps be lived by someone who is not yet married? If so, how?"

The simple answer is yes. The 7 Steps can easily be adapted and lived by those wanting to help place their future marriages on a strong foundation. For that matter, they can be lived by anyone wanting to live a life that leads to happiness, health, and sufficient financial resources. The means of living these steps as a single person contemplating entering into a future marriage are actually included in the steps themselves. I would summarize them as follows:

Step One: Honor Your Wedding Vows

In Chapter 2, we saw that fidelity to your spouse actually begins before marriage. Indeed, we saw statistics that premarital sexual activity and cohabitation substantially increase the probability of getting divorced in the future. As such, a tremendous gift you can give to your future spouse is to begin being exclusive to him or her today—which was once called "saving yourself for marriage." This includes not consuming pornography or other sexually explicit materials, which are a form of virtual infidelity.

Step Two: Use Money for Other People

In Chapter 3, we saw that preexisting debt brought into a marriage is a major source of marital conflict for newlyweds. When one person brings preexisting debt into a marriage, his or her past behaviors limit possibilities for the couple as they begin their life together. As such, an excellent gift you can make to your future marriage is to live your life in such a way that you avoid debt and actually bring savings into marriage. This will not only help you avoid the issue of preexisting debt but will also help you to develop thinking patterns and a lifestyle compatible with the demands of marriage. Since a large portion of young people need to borrow money to get a college education, the amount of student loans should be kept to the absolute minimum.

Step Three: Give God Some of Your Time

In Chapter 4, we saw that giving time to God transforms the person. Indeed, it specifically changes those behaviors that most frequently lead to divorce. This reality is certainly true long before a person gets married. As such, an excellent gift you can make to your future marriage is to develop a relationship with God today. The two most important steps you can take are to go to church on a weekly basis and to begin praying to God on a daily basis. Our website has many suggestions for developing a well-structured prayer life.

Step Four: Set Your Mind on the Things Above

In Chapter 5, we saw that it is possible to reconcile faith and science regarding the three significant issues: the creation of the universe; the creation of the human person; and the formation of the spousal bond. In the process, we discovered that the extraordinary lies just on the other side of the ordinary. This process involved three things: the study of secular science, the reading of Scripture, and personal prayer. As such, the prayerful reading of Scripture—with an openness to the findings of modern science—is an excellent way to form the mind to find God in the everyday things of marriage and family life.

Step Five: Find God in Yourself

In Chapter 6, the discussion of finding God in yourself began with a discussion of the moral code that Riley, Rose Mary, and the Greatest Generation lived. It also showed that a strong relationship with God helps to strengthen the individual to actually live the moral code they espouse. One of the most essential gifts you can give to your future spouse is to become a person of integrity today. I would suggest that the foundation for a personal moral code is the Ten Commandments (cf. Deuteronomy 5:4–21). Different religions have slight variations in the way the Ten Commandments are numbered, but they are as follows:

1. You shall have no false gods before me nor carve a graven image that you bow down before.
2. You shall not take the name of the Lord in vain.
3. Honor the Sabbath.
4. Honor your father and your mother.
5. You shall not kill.
6. You shall not commit adultery.
7. You shall not steal.
8. You shall not bear false witness against your neighbor.
9. You shall not covet your neighbor's wife.
10. You shall not covet your neighbor's property.

Step Six: Find God in Other People

In Chapter 7, we saw that God is coming to us through other people, especially the members of our own family. As such, we should treat everyone with dignity and respect. We also saw that we have a crisis in civility in modern culture. In very close relationships, the small things of interpersonal relationships become more important, not less. As such, treating every person with dignity and respect now is an excellent means of preparing yourself for the intimacy of married life. Furthermore, we must remember that a person most needs our love when they least deserve it. We must practice being kind and generous to other people when they are having their most difficult moments.

Step Seven: Make It Easy to Be Good and Hard to Be Bad

In Chapter 8, we considered a mercy so superabundant that it went out to envelop the soul and help prevent it from falling into sin and other difficulties. There we heard the story of Mark and Katie, where Katie's prayer for her HTB (husband to be) obtained for him the grace to transform his life and set their marriage on the road to superabundance. One of the best gifts you can give to your future spouse is to begin praying for him or her today. Pray for all his or her needs and struggles. This prayer begins before marriage, but lasts to the end of your life.

Finally, the greatest suggestion that I would give to newlyweds—indeed all couples—is to give time to each other every single day. In Chapter 8, we saw that time was the secret ingredient in Don Bosco's Preventive Method. Nonetheless, the secret of time goes much further.

Time is also a secret of Lourdes. In the stories of Alexis Carrel and Felix and Elisabeth Leseur, we saw "miraculous healings" associated with their visits to Lourdes, France. Indeed, we saw healing on every level: physical healing in the cure of Marie Bailly's tuberculosis peritonitis; spiritual healing in the (eventual) conversion of Alexis Carrel; and the healing of the marriage of Felix and Elisabeth Leseur. One of the most amazing things about Lourdes is that people still take time for each other, especially for those who are in need.

Finally, believe it or not, time is the secret ingredient in Riley's simple advice: Sit in church with your family every Sunday and have dinner with your family every night. Okay, Riley. I give. You were right all along.

Notes

1. The percentage of individuals "Not too happy" with their lives is as follows: married, 7.7; divorced, 19.3; separated, 29.4; never married, 14.6. General Social Survey, 1972–2012.

2. Ibid.

3. Department of Health and Human Services, *National Vital Statistics Reports* 61 (4) Deaths: Final Data for 2010, May 8, 2013, Table I-7.

4. J. Wilmoth et al., "Does Marital History Matter? Marital Status and Wealth Outcomes Among Preretirement Adults," *Journal of Marriage and Family* 64 (February 2002): 254–268, Table 3.

5. Ibid.

6. Ibid.

7. Ibid.

8. United States Census Bureau, "Number, Timing and Duration of Marriages and Divorces, 2009" (May 2011), Figure 5.

9. Ibid.

10. Approximately 39 percent of second marriages end by the fifteenth anniversary versus 33 percent of first marriages. Department of Health and Human Services, "Cohabitation, Marriage, Divorce and Remarriage in the United States," *Vital and Health Statistics,* series 23, no. 22 (July 2002), Table 21 and Table 41.

11. US Census Bureau, "Number, Timing and Duration."

12. The National Center on Addiction and Substance Abuse at Columbia University (CASA), "The Importance of Family Dinners II" (September 2005): 8.

13. General Social Survey, 1972–2012.

14. In the United States, the battle between educators and many religious leaders over the theory of evolution was particularly intense. One of the most famous court cases in the twentieth century was the "Scopes Monkey Trial," formally known as *The State of Tennessee v. John Thomas Scopes* in 1925. The Butler Law in made it illegal to teach human evolution in Tennessee. John T. Scopes, a high school math and science teacher, was accused of breaking this law. The entire nation was riveted

on Dayton, Tennessee, as some of the biggest legal names in the country fought for eight days. Scopes lost the trial in Dayton. In 1968, the US Supreme Court ruled in *Epperson v. Arkansas* that states could not establish laws such that "teaching and learning must be tailored to the principles or prohibitions of any religious sect or dogma." State laws prohibiting the teaching of human evolution were considered to be primarily religious in nature and, therefore, violated the First Amendment.

15. Galileo is considered one of the greatest scientists of the sixteenth and seventeenth centuries. His support of heliocentrism (the belief that Earth orbits the sun) got him in trouble with Pope Urban VIII, the Inquisition, and the Jesuits. He spent the last nine years of his life under house arrest. Pope John Paul II publicly apologized in 1992 for the way in which members of the Catholic Church handled the Galileo case.

16. St. Augustine, Sermon Mai 126.6, quoted in *The Essential Augustine,* Ed. by V. Bourke. (Indianapolis, IN: Hackett Publishing, 1974), 123.

17. Pope John Paul II, "The first meaning of man's original solitude is defined on the basis of a specific test, or examination, which man undergoes before God (and in a certain way also before himself)," October 10, 1979.

18. Considering Scripture's vision of humanity in its innocence, it is to be noted that God blesses the "one flesh union" of man and woman with fruitfulness: "And God blessed them and God said to them, 'Be fruitful and multiply, and fill the earth and subdue it'" (Genesis 1:28). Since God creates the soul of every human being, the blessing of a child implies an encounter with God. We will see some amazing science in Chapter 5 relating to this reality.

19. The Scriptural account indicates that the "six stone jars . . . each holding twenty or thirty gallons" were for the Jewish rite of purification (Cf. John 2:6). This rite required Jewish persons who came into contact with a corpse to be cleansed with water on the third and seventh day after touching the corpse. See Numbers 19:11–22.

20. The Catholic Encyclopedia, citation for Cana of Galilee, accessed online at http://www.newadvent.org/cathen/03226a.htm on May 12, 2015.

21. "[Mary] is attentive, she discreetly notices that they wine has run out. Wine is a sign of happiness, love and plenty. How many of our adolescents and young people sense that there is no longer any of that wine to be found in their home?" (Pope Francis, Homily, Samanes Park, Guayaquil, Ecuador, July 6, 2015).

CHAPTER TWO: STEP 1: HONOR YOUR WEDDING VOWS

1. The Book of Common Prayer, Anglican Communion. Its most popular version was from 1662, but it dates to 1549.

2. See *The Rites of the Catholic Church* v. 1, Study Edition (New York: Pueblo Publishing, 1990), 728–729.

3. Ibid., 728.

4. P. Amato et al., "A Longitudinal Study of Marital Problems and Subsequent Divorce," *Journal of Marriage and Family* 59 (August 1997): 612–624.

5. The Gallup Poll, "Americans, Including Catholics, Say Birth Control is Morally OK—Birth Control has the broadest acceptance among 18 behaviors" (May 22, 2012).

6. General Social Survey, 1972–2012.

7. Ibid.

8. Data from the General Social Survey indicates that the sexual revolution definitely had an impact on marital infidelity. Only 6.1 percent of individuals married during the 1930s were unfaithful to his or her spouse. However, 21.8 percent of the individuals married during the 1960s were unfaithful to his or her spouse.

9. US Department of Health and Human Services, "Fertility, Family Planning, and Women's Health: New Data from the 1995 National Survey of Family Growth," series 23, no. 19, (May 1997).

10. US Department of Health and Human Services, "Teenagers in the United States: Sexual Activity, Contraceptive Use and Childbearing, 2002," series 23, no. 24 (December 2004), Figure 2.

11. E. Laumann et al., *The Social Organization of Sexuality: Sexual Practices in the United States* (Chicago: University of Chicago Press, 1994), p. 207, Table 5.8.

12. Ibid., p. 504, Figure 13.6.

13. For an excellent discussion of the history of pornography and technology's role, see Frederick Lane, *Obscene Profits: The Entrepreneurs of Pornography in the Cyber Age* (New York: Routledge, 2000).

14. General Social Survey, 1972–2012.

15. Ibid.

16. Gallup Poll, "Americans, Including Catholics, Say Birth Control is Morally OK."

17. The sample included 250 couples for the original taping of "The Choice Wine," Creighton University, Omaha, Nebraska, February 14–15, 2014.

18. General Social Survey, 1972–2012.

19. "Is the Internet Bad for Your Marriage? Online Affairs, Pornographic Sites Playing Greater Role in Divorces," http://www.prnewswire.com /news-releases/is-the-internet-bad-for-your-marriage-online-affairs-pornographic-sites-playing-greater-role-in-divorces-76826727.html, accessed on June 9, 2014.

20. For a good review on the neurological aspects of pornography consumption see William Struthers, *Wired for Intimacy—How Pornography Hijacks the Male Brain*, (Downers Grove, Illinois: IVP Books, 2009), especially Chapter 4, "Your Brain on Porn," 83–111.

21. Fisher, H. *Why We Love—The Nature and Chemistry of Romantic Love* (New York: Henry Holt, 2004), 67–76.

22. M. Robinson et al., "Cupid's Poisoned Arrow—Porn-Induced Sexual Dysfunction: A Growing Problem," *Psychology Today* (July 11, 2011).

23. J. Schneider, "Effects of Cybersex Addiction on the Family: Results of a Survey," *Sexual Addiction and Compulsivity* 7 (2000): 31–58.

24. General Social Survey, 1972–2012.

25. L. Brizendine, *The Male Brain* (New York: Broadway Books, 2010), 110.

26. See J. Geller, *Titanic: Women and Children First* (New York: W.W. Norton, 1998), 66–70.

27. Ibid., 85–87.

CHAPTER THREE: STEP 2: USE MONEY FOR OTHERS

1. Data is used for individuals married during the 1970s so that we have the opportunity to look at their behavior across most of their adult life. Data is taken from the General Social Survey, 1972–2012.

2. NPR/Robert Wood Johnson Foundation/Harvard School of Public Health, "The Burden of Stress in America" (2014).

3. D. Schramm et al., "After I Do: The Newlywed Transition," *Marriage and Family Review* 38 (2005): 45–67.

4. L. Skogrand et al., "The Effects of Debt on Newlyweds and Implications for Education," *Journal of Extension*, 43, no. 3, (June 2005): art. 3RIB7.

5. L. C. Allum, "AARP Bulletin Survey on Budgeting and Credit Card Use," 2012.

6. B. Knutson et al., "Neural Predictors of Purchases," *Neuron* 53 (January 4, 2007): 147–156.

7. Ibid.

8. Associated Press–AOL Health Poll: Credit Card/Debt Stress Study, 2008.

9. J. Dew, "Two Sides of the Same Coin? The Differing Roles of Assets and Consumer Debt in Marriage," *Journal of Family Economic Issues* 28 (2007): 89–104.

10. Associated Press–AOL Health Poll: Credit Card/Debt Stress Study, 2008.

11. Quoted in J. Marshall et al., "Newlywed Debt: The Anti-Dowry," *The Forum for Family and Consumer Issues* 9, no. 1 (March 2004).

12. The Gallup Poll, "The '40-Hour' Workweek is Actually Longer—by Seven Hours," August 29, 2014.

13. Federal Reserve Bank of St. Louis, Economic Research, Average Annual Hours Worked by Persons Engaged in the United States, 2011, accessed online at https://research.stlouisfed.org/fred2/series/AVHWPEU-SA065NRUG on December 10, 2014.

14. N. McCarthy, "Americans Work Nights and Weekends More than Anyone Else," *Forbes* (October 8, 2014).

15. R. Ray et al., *No-Vacation Nation USA—a comparison of leave and holiday in OECD countries, European Economic and Employment Policy Brief* no. 3 (European Trade Union Institute, 2007).

16. The National Center on Addiction and Substance Abuse at Columbia University, "The Importance of Family Dinners VIII" (September 2012).

17. Ibid.

18. Ibid.

19. Survey, "Good Technology," July 2, 2012, http://www1.good.com /about/press-releases/161009045.html.

20. Pew Research, "Networked Workers," September 24, 2008.

21. Survey, "Good Technology," July 2, 2012.

22. Pew Research, "Networked Workers," September 24, 2008.

23. See J. Coates, *The Hour Between Dog and Wolf: How Risk Taking Transforms Us, Body and Mind* (New York: Penguin, 2012), 27–28 and 179–190.

24. UBS Investor Watch, "What is 'Wealthy'?" 3Q2013.

25. Ibid.

26. E. Diener, "Beyond Money: Toward an Economy of Well-Being," *Psychological Sciences in the Public Interest* 5, no. 1 (2004): 1–31.

27. T. DeLeire and A. Kalil, "Does Consumption Buy Happiness? Evidence from the United States," *International Review of Economics* 57, no. 2 (2010): 163–176.

28. Diener, "Beyond Money."

29. General Social Survey, 1972–2012.

30. Diener, "Beyond Money."

31. Shelly and I never had a son. Nonetheless, long before Riley passed away, we let him know that if we ever did, the first one would be named after him.

32. Associated Press/MTV Youth Happiness Poll, Ages 13–24, April 16–23, 2007.

33. W. Harbaugh et al., "Neural Responses to Taxation and Voluntary Giving Reveal Motives for Charitable Donations," *Science* 316, no. 1622 (2007): 1622–1625.

34. E. Dunn et al., "Spending Money on Others Promotes Happiness," *Science* 319, no. 5870 (March 2008): 1687–1688.

35. L. Aknin et al., "Giving Leads to Happiness in Young Children," *PLOS ONE* 7, no. 6 (June 2012): art. e39211.

36. L. B. Aknin et al., "Prosocial Spending and Well-Being: Cross-Cultural Evidence for a Psychological Universe," *Journal of Personality and Social Psychology* 104, no. 4 (April 2013): 635–652.

37. W. M. Brown et al., "Altruism Relates to Health in an Ethnically Diverse Sample of Older Adults," *Journals of Gerontology* 60B, no. 3 (May 2005): P143–P152.

38. E. Dunn et al., "On the Costs of Self-Interested Economic Behavior: How Does Stinginess Get under the Skin?" *Journal of Health Psychology* 15, no. 4 (May 2010): 627–633.

39. Z. Chance and M. I. Norton, "I Give, Therefore I Have: Giving and Subjective Wealth" (working paper, Yale University and Harvard Business School).

40. Bureau of Labor Statistics, Consumer Expenditure Survey, 2012, Table 1300.

CHAPTER FOUR: STEP 3: GIVE GOD SOME OF YOUR TIME

1. For a good summary and discussion of studies investigating the link between religious practice and marital stability, see Harold Koenig, *Handbook of Religion and Health, 2nd Edition*, chapter 13, Oxford University Press, 2012.

2. General Social Survey, 1972–2012.

3. Andrew Newberg, MD, is the Director of Research at the Myrna Brind Center of Integrative Medicine at Thomas Jefferson University Hospital and an Adjunct Professor of Religious Studies and an Associate Professor of Radiology at the University of Pennsylvania School of Medicine.

4. See *The Mystical Mind: Probing the Biology of Religious Experience* (1999); *Why God Won't Go Away: Brain Science and the Biology of Belief* (2002); *Why We Believe What We Believe: Our Biological Need for Meaning, Spirituality, and Truth* (2006); *How God Changes Your Brain: Breakthrough Findings from a Leading Neuroscientist* (2009); *Principles of Neurotheology* (2010); *Words Can Change Your Brain: 12 Conversation Strategies to Build Trust, Resolve Conflict, and Increase Intimacy* (2012).

5. Andrew Newberg, *How God Changes Your Brain: Breakthrough Findings from a Leading Neuroscientist* (New York: Ballantine Books, 2010), 50.

6. Ibid., 52–53.

7. Ibid., 51–52.

8. For a good summary and discussion of relevant material, see Harold Koenig, *Handbook of Religion and Health*.

9. The results include the average amount of time spent on all forms of prayer. The daily average of 8.4 minutes equates to a weekly average of approximately one hour. Bureau of Labor Statistics, U.S. Department of Labor, American Time Use Survey—2012 Results, Table 1.

10. Ibid.

11. Ibid.

12. Approximately three out of four (74 percent) Americans profess belief in God. Harris Poll, November 13–18, 2013.

13. Bureau of Labor Statistics, U.S. Department of Labor, American Time Use Survey—2012 Results, Table 1.

14. Ibid.

15. Newberg, *How God Changes Your Brain*, 50.

16. Catechism of the Catholic Church #2653: St. Ambrose, *De officiis ministrorum* 1, 20, 8, PL 16, 50.

17. Recommended Bibles are *Ignatius Catholic Study Bible—New Testament* (with footnotes by Dr. Scott Hahn) and *The Catholic Study Bible: New American Bible* (2nd Edition).

18. Many excellent daily meditation books are available. Frequently, the writings and talks of the Pope are organized into daily meditation books. There are several based on the work of Pope St. John Paul II. More recently, the work of Pope Francis has appeared in books such as *A Year of Mercy with Pope Francis: Daily Reflections* (2014) and *Through the Year with Pope Francis: Daily Reflections* (2013).

19. The Divine Office is a means of praying Scripture, especially the Psalms, at different intervals throughout the day. It takes its inspiration from a verse in the Psalms: "Seven times a day I praise thee" (Psalm 119:164). As early as the sixth century, St. Benedict divided the 150 Psalms into groups that his monks would pray seven times a day. In the course of a week, they completed the entire 150 Psalms. Although it has been modified throughout the centuries, the Divine Office is still the foundation for prayer in monasteries. Many individuals working in the world enjoy saying Morning and Evening or Night prayers from the Divine Office.

20. The practice of saying the Rosary dates to the early thirteenth century and St. Dominic. It is a means of meditating on the life of Christ while saying prayers, especially the Our Father and Hail Mary. Many individuals benefit from using a book to help them meditate on the mysteries of the Rosary. Recommendations include *Praying the Rosary with Pope Francis*, United States Conference of Catholic Bishops, 2014; *The Rosary: Chain of Hope*, Fr. Benedict J. Groeschel, (San Francisco: Ignatius Press, 2003); *Rosary Meditations from Mother Teresa of Calcutta: Loving Jesus with the Heart of Mary*, Missionaries of the Blessed Sacrament, 1984.

21. See http://en.wikipedia.org/wiki/Classical_planet.

22. The derivation of the names for the days of week is best seen in Latin or a romantic language that ties to Latin (such as French). Sunday is dedicated to the Sun or Sol (Latin). In French, it is *Dimanche*. Monday is dedicated to the moon or Luna (Latin). In French, it is *Lundi*. Tuesday is dedicated to Mars. In French, it is *Mardi*. Wednesday is dedicated to Mercury or Mercurius (Latin). In French, it is *Mercredi*. Thursday is dedicated to Jupiter or Iuppiter (Latin). In French, it is *Jeudi*. Friday is dedicated to Venus. In French, it is *Vendredi*. Saturday is dedicated to Saturn or Saturnus (Latin). In French, it is *Samedi*.

23. In 1 Kings 6:1 we learn that King Solomon began construction of the

Temple in Jerusalem in 480 BC after the Exodus. The Temple was constructed in approximately 966 BC.

24. See Koenig, *Handbook of Religion and Health*, Chapter 11: Drug and Alcohol Use.

25. Even in a country as secular as modern France, a majority of the public holidays are rooted in the liturgical calendar. Of the eleven public holidays in France, seven have an origin in the liturgical calendar: Easter Monday (the Monday after Easter), Ascension Day (forty days after Easter), Whit Monday (Monday after Pentecost), Assumption of the Blessed Virgin Mary (August 15), All Saints Day (November 1), Christmas Day (December 25), and St. Stephen's Day (December 26).

26. See Koenig, *Handbook of Religion and Health*, Chapter 6: Well-Being and Positive Emotions.

27. Newberg, *How God Changes Your Brain*, 51–52.

28. J. P. Griffin, "Changing Life Expectancy throughout History," *Journal of the Royal Society of Medicine*, December 1, 2008, 101(12): 577, Table 1.

29. Newberg, *How God Changes Your Brain*, 52–53.

30. The Holy Land is where Jesus physically lived while he was alive on earth. Pilgrims visit the Holy Land to retrace the steps of Jesus—from his birth to his Passion, death, and Resurrection. Modern Israel is approximately the size of New Jersey. With the exception of a few years in Egypt during his infancy, Christ spent his entire life in the Holy Land.

31. Jesus lived and Christianity was founded during the time of the Roman Empire. The Apostles Peter and Paul were martyred in Rome. Many early Christians were martyred in Rome. During the Renaissance, great basilicas were constructed on the most important sites in Rome. Today, Rome continues to be the residence of the Pope and the center of the Roman Catholic Church.

32. Believed to be the burial place of the Apostle James. In the middle ages, routes to Santiago de Compostela crisscrossed all of Europe. Pilgrims walked hundreds of miles to the basilica. It has experienced a revival in the past few decades.

33. Catholics believe that Christ's mother, the Blessed Virgin Mary, appeared to a young French girl, Bernadette Soubirous, eighteen times between February 11, 1858, and July 16, 1858. On February 25, 1858, Mary revealed a hidden spring to Bernadette. Since then, numerous documented miracles have been attributed to the water from Lourdes.

34. Catholics believe that Christ's mother, the Blessed Virgin Mary,

appeared to three young peasant children six times between May 13, 1917, and October 13, 1917. These apparitions were made famous by Pope John Paul II when the assassination attempt occurred on May 13, 1981, the anniversary of the first apparition.

35. General Social Survey, 1972–2012.

36. Ibid.

37. For an excellent overview of Alexis Carrel's life, see the introduction by Stanley L. Jaki in Alexis Carrel, *The Voyage to Lourdes* (Fraser, MI: Real View Books, 1994).

38. Ibid.

39. Ibid., 94.

40. Eugenics is the belief that humanity can improve its genetic stock by selective reproduction. Individuals of "superior qualities"—such as intelligence, athletic ability, general health, and appearance—are "allowed" to reproduce while those of "inferior qualities" are not. In its most radical form, there are efforts to "proactively" remove "inferior individuals" from the "human gene pool." In other words, individuals not deemed worthy by some authority are exterminated. The concept of eugenics has been embraced by a large array of individuals in the modern era. Charles Darwin stated: "If the various checks specified in the two last paragraphs, and perhaps others as yet unknown do not prevent the reckless, the vicious and otherwise inferior members of society from increasing at a quicker rate than the better class of men, the nation will retrograde, as has occurred too often in the history of the world" (Charles Darwin, *The Descent of Man*, London: John Murray, 1882, Chapter 5, p. 218). Eugenics found its most radical proponent in Adolf Hitler: "It is a half measure to let incurably sick people steadily contaminate the remaining healthy ones. . . .The demand that defective people be prevented from propagating equally defected offspring is a demand of the clearest reason. . . . If necessary, the incurably sick will be pitilessly segregated—a barbaric measure for the unfortunate who is struck by it, but a blessing for his fellow men and prosperity." *Mein Kampf,* Trans. Manheim, R. (Boston, MA: Houghton Mifflin Company, 1971), p. 255.

41. In *Man, the Unknown*, Dr. Carrel advocated euthanasia (killing) of criminals: "Those who have murdered, robbed while armed with automatic pistol or machine gun, kidnapped children, despoiled the poor of their savings, misled the public in important matters, should be humanely and economically disposed of in small euthanasic institutions supplied with proper gases. A similar treatment could be advantageously applied to insane, guilty of criminal acts" (New York: Halcyon House,

making their world a little softer

Joanna Andersen

our unconditional guarantee

If you're unhappy with a product at any time for any reason, just bring or send it back to us, and we'll refund the purchase price or replace the item. It's as simple as that.

return policy

We will be glad to credit you in the same form of payment with which your purchase was made. Cash refunds over $30 will be issued via refund check. Without a receipt, we will exchange the merchandise or issue a gift card.

price adjustment

One adjustment will be made within 14 days from the original date of purchase. This adjustment policy is not effective during end of season Hanna Sale time periods.

making their world a little softer

Joanna Andersen

our unconditional guarantee

If you're unhappy with a product at any time for any reason, just bring or send it back to us, and we'll refund the purchase price or replace the item. It's as simple as that.

return policy

We will be glad to credit you in the same form of payment with which your purchase was made. Cash refunds over $30 will be issued via refund check. Without a receipt, we will exchange the merchandise or issue a gift card.

price adjustment

One adjustment will be made within 14 days from the original date of purchase. This adjustment policy is not effective during end of season Hanna Sale time periods.

hanna Andersson

GIFT RECEIPT

Transaction #:   5159
Date: 6/24/2016   Time: 01:58:14 PM
Cashier: Shauna   Register: 2

Item	Description
33080-DF4-70	BBY PRNT SLPR DINOFRIEND

5 1 5 9
VISIT US ONLINE
www.HannaAndersson.com
(800) 222-0544
Thank You
Shauna

1938), 318–319. Although Dr. Carrel is an advocate for eugenics, he is explicit that they should be "voluntary" (300) and cannot be applied indiscriminately (except for convicted criminals): "We cannot prevent the reproduction of the weak when they are neither insane nor criminal. Or destroy sickly or defective children as we do the weaklings in a litter of puppies. . . . Of course, the reproduction of human beings cannot be regulated as in animals" (296, 300). Nonetheless, the Nazis used *Man, the Unknown* to help justify their T-4 Euthanasia program, which began as early as 1939. It found its full expression in the attempt to exterminate the Jews in extermination camps "supplied with proper gases." For more on the Nazi T-4 Euthanasia program, see Ian Kershaw, *Hitler: 1936–1945 Nemesis* (New York: W.W. Norton, 2001), 259–261.

42. Carrel, *Voyage to Lourdes*, 35.

43. Ibid., 35–36.

CHAPTER FIVE: STEP 4: SET YOUR MIND ON THE THINGS ABOVE

1. Quoted in Peter Seewald, *Benedict XVI: Light of the World: The Pope the Church and the Signs of the Times—A Conversation with Peter Seewald* (San Francisco: Ignatius Press, 2010), 168.

2. For a summary of the current understanding of the creation of the universe, see Neil deGrasse Tyson, *Origins: Fourteen Billion Years of Cosmic Evolution* (New York: W. W. Norton, 2005 and 2014).

3. St. Augustine, "The City of God," Book XI, Chapters 6–7, The Catholic University of America Press, "The Fathers of the Church Series," v. 14, 1952, p. 196.

4. Jewish commentary on creation in Genesis also pointed to a much deeper understanding. "Know that . . . the six days of creation represent all the days of the world." Ramban Nahmanides, *Commentary on the Torah*, v. 1, Genesis, Trans. Chavel, C. (Brooklyn, NY: Shilo Publishing House, Inc., 1999), 61. "The secret of the years of the world is alluded to in this place." Ibid., 416.

5. St. Augustine sees hidden within the six days of creation an understanding for six ages of the human person and six ages of the world. See "Against the Manichees," Book 1, Chapter 23, The Catholic University of America Press, "The Fathers of the Church Series," v. 84, 1991, pp. 83–88 and "The City of God," Book XXII, Chapter 30, The Catholic University of America Press, "The Fathers of the Church Series," v. 24, 1954, pp. 510–511.

6. G. Schroeder, *The Science of God—the Convergence of Scientific and Biblical Wisdom* (New York: Free Press, 1997) Chapter 3.

7. The theory of relativity allows for the "dilation of time" based upon two factors—gravity (gravitational redshift) and the stretching of time (cosmological redshift). The difference in time between the sun and Earth is a result of the gravitational redshift since the sun's gravity is 27.9 times stronger than Earth's gravitational pull.

8. *Genesis and the Big Bang* (New York: Bantam Books, 1990); *The Science of God* (New York: Free Press, 1997); *The Hidden Face of God* (New York: Free Press, 2001); *God According to God* (New York: Harper One, 2009).

9. Note that Schroeder has corrected the calculations presented in the third and fourth chapters of *The Science of God* to account for the fact that the expansion of the universe is actually accelerating. The corrected calculations can be found on his website, geraldschroeder.com, at the end of the article, "The Age of the Universe: One truth as seen from two vastly different perspectives and both true—literally," October 2013.

10. Schroeder, *The Science of God*, 58.

11. Jean Baptiste Lamarck proposed the transmutation of species in *Philosophie Zoologique* in 1809. There are important differences between Darwin's theory of evolution and discussion of transmutation of species, but the possibility of species evolving over time was becoming more openly discussed in academic circles during the nineteenth century.

12. Charles Darwin, *The Origin of Species* (New York: Random House, 1993), 19.

13. Ibid.

14. Charles Darwin, *The Autobiography of Charles Darwin*, Ed. by Nora Barlow (New York: W. W. Norton, 1958/2005), 72.

15. St. John Chrysostom, Homilies on Genesis, #13, The Catholic University of America Press, "The Fathers of the Church Series," v. 74, 1986, p. 173.

16. John C. Eccles, *How the Self Controls Its Brain* (New York: Springer, 1994), Preface, xi.

17. Ibid., 9.

18. Although unseen with the human eye, the cell phone wave is part of the physical world. The brain is a purely spiritual reality.

19. St. John Chrysostom, Homilies on Genesis, #13, The Catholic University of America Press, "The Fathers of the Church Series," v. 74, 1986, pp. 171–173

20. For Catholics, Pope Pius XII defined the Church's teaching on the possibility of evolution in his encyclical *Humani Generis*: "The teaching

authority of the Church does not forbid that . . . research and discussion . . . take place with regard to the doctrine of evolution, in as far as it inquires into the origin of the human body as coming from pre-existent and living matter—for the Catholic faith obliges us to hold that souls are immediately created by God" (*Humani Generis*, August 12, 1950, #36).

21. The most important remaining elements are nitrogen, calcium, phosphorus, potassium, sulfur, sodium, chlorine, and magnesium.

22. *The Rites of the Catholic Church*, v. 1, Study Edition (New York: Pueblo Publishing, 1990), 730.

23. Homily for the Jubilee of Families, October 15, 2000.

24. For a summary of the attraction between men and women, see H. Fisher, *Why We Love—The Nature and Chemistry of Romantic Love* (New York: Henry Holt, 2004), 104–110; L. Brizendine, *The Female Brain* (New York: Broadway Books, 2006), Chapters 3 and 4; L. Brizendine, *The Male Brain* (New York: Broadway Books, 2010), Chapters 3 and 4.

25. For a good summary of the neurochemistry of attraction see Fisher, *Why We Love*, 51–76.

26. L. J. Young, "Increased Affiliative Response to Vasopressin in Mice Expressing the V_{1a} Receptor from a Monogamous Vole," *Nature*, August 19, 1999, 766–768.

27. Z. Wang et al., "Neurochemical regulation of pair bonding in male prairie voles," *Physiology and Behavior*, 2004.

28. B. Acevedo et al., "Neural correlates of long-term intense romantic love," Oxford Journals, *Social Cognitive and Affective Neuroscience*, 2011.

29. A. Aron et al., "Romantic Relationships from the Perspectives of the Self-Expansion Model and Attachment Theory—Partially Overlapping Circles," *Dynamics of Romantic Love* (New York: Guilford Press, 2006), 371.

30. Ibid., 369.

31. For the theologically minded, Pope John Paul II is not implying an "ontological" union—nor am I.

CHAPTER SIX: STEP 5: FIND GOD IN YOURSELF

1. Tim Russert, *Wisdom of Our Fathers—Lessons and Letters from Daughters and Sons* (New York: Random House, 2007), 42–43.

2. Josephson Institute, Center for Youth Ethics, "2010 Report Card on the Ethics of American Youth," 2011, Data Tables.

3. The National Center on Addiction and Substance Abuse at Columbia University, "Wasting the Best and Brightest: Substance Abuse at America's Colleges and Universities," March 2007, p. 53.

4. Ibid.

5. Ibid., 52.

6. University Health Services at Berkeley, "Sexual Assault/Rape: Alcohol and Other Drugs," at http://www.uhs.berkeley.edu/home/healthtopics/sexualassault/saalcohol.shtml, accessed on April 23, 2015.

7. E. Laumann, et al., *The Social Organization of Sexuality* (Chicago: University of Chicago Press, 1994) 186–190.

8. E. Carter et al., "Religious people discount the future less," *Evolution and Human Behavior* 33 (2012): 224–231.

9. My mother was an identical twin. She and her sister enjoyed playing practical jokes, including occasionally switching dates! Nonetheless, when I was young and first learned that my mom and aunt were identical twins, I refused to believe it. In my mind, they didn't look anything alike.

10. N. Carey, *The Epigenetics Revolution: How Modern Biology is Rewriting our Understanding of Genetics, Disease and Inheritance* (New York: Columbia University Press, 2012).

11. Most translations have "from whom every family in heaven and earth is named." However, the Greek is "patria"—father.

12. L. Brizendine, *The Male Brain* (New York: Broadway Books, 2010), 83–84.

13. Ibid., 84.

14. D. Stern, *The First Relationship: Infant and Mother* (Cambridge, MA: Harvard University Press, 1977), 29–33.

15. Ibid., 24.

16. Ibid., chapter 2, for the science behind baby talk.

17. Excellent resources for the organization of an infant's mind include D. Siegel, *The Developing Mind: How Relationships and the Brain Interact to Shape Who We Are*, 2nd Edition, (New York: Guilford Press, 2012) and D. Siegel et al., *Parenting from the Inside Out* (New York: Jeremy P. Tarcher/Penguin, 2003).

18. See M. Vuolo et al., "Parent and Child Cigarette Use: A Longitudinal, Multigenerational Study," *Pediatrics* 132, no. 3, (September 2013): 1–10.

19. See S. Moonat et al., "Neuroscience of alcoholism: molecular and cellular

mechanisms," *Cellular and Molecular Life Sciences* 67, no. 1 (January 2010): 73–88.

20. Augustine of Hippo, "Confessions," Book III, Chapter 21, Saint Augustine, *Confessions*, Trans. Chadwick, H., Oxford World's Classics (Oxford, UK: Oxford University Press, 2008).

21. Ibid., Book X, Chapters 27–28.

22. Ibid., see Books I–II.

23. St. John Chrysostom, "Catecheses," quoted in the Liturgy of Hours, Office of Readings for Good Friday.

24. Christianity is divided into three main branches—Catholic (50.1 percent), Orthodox (11.9 percent), and Protestant (36.7 percent). The Catholic and Orthodox branches believe in Christ's Real Presence in the Eucharist. As a generalization, the Protestant branch does not believe in Christ's Real Presence in the Eucharist. However, Christians in the Anglican Communion, which is usually considered part of Protestant Christianity, believe in Christ's Real Presence in the Eucharist. The theological discussion of this topic is beyond the scope of this book. The percentages for the three main Christian branches are taken from Pew Research Center, "Global Christianity—A Report on the Size and Distribution of the World's Christian Population," December 19, 2011.

25. St. Ignatius of Antioch, Letter to the Romans, #7, *The Apostolic Fathers, The Fathers of the Church*, v. 1 (Washington, DC: Catholic University Press, 1946), 111.

26. Regarding the relationship between the spousal bond and the Eucharist, Pope John Paul II made an incredibly strong statement: "The Eucharist is the very source of Christian marriage. . . . In this sacrifice of the New and Eternal covenant, Christian spouses encounter the source from which their own marriage covenant flows, is interiorly structured and continuously renewed" (Pope John Paul II, *Familiaris Consortio*, #57).

27. For information on the Eucharistic Miracle of Lanciano see R. Burke et al., *The Eucharistic Miracles of the World* (Bardstown, KY: Eternal Life Publications, 2009), 122–123, and J. Carroll Cruz, *Eucharistic Miracles* (Rockford, IL: TAN Books and Publishers, 1987), 3–18.

28. Interestingly, this is the same blood type found on the Shroud of Turin. See Burke, *Eucharistic Miracles of the World*, 123.

29. For biographical information on Brother Lawrence, see Brother Lawrence of the Resurrection, "The Practice of the Presence of God," Trans. Sciuba, S. (Washington, DC: ICS Publications, 1994), xvii–xxiii.

30. Ibid., 107.

31. Ibid., 53–54.

32. U. Schjodt et al., "Rewarding Prayers," *Neuroscience Letters* 443 (2008): 165–168.

CHAPTER SEVEN: STEP 6: FIND GOD IN OTHER PEOPLE

1. It is the only opera company in the United States to have won a Tony Award, a Grammy Award, and an Emmy Award. It is always included in the list of premier opera companies.

2. Statement of Pope St. Pius X taken from *Story of a Soul—The Autobiography of St. Thérèse of Lisieux*, 3rd Edition, Trans. Clarke, J. (Washington, DC: ICS Publications, 1996), 287.

3. Ibid., 246.

4. Ibid.

5. Ibid.

6. Ibid., 222.

7. Ibid.

8. Ibid., 223.

9. Ibid.

10. Ibid.

11. Ibid., 247. St. Thérèse explicitly ties her charitable behavior toward disagreeable sisters to this statement of Christ.

12. Mother Teresa quoted in B. Kolodiejchuk, *Mother Teresa: Come Be My Light—The Private Writings of the "Saint of Calcutta"* (New York: Doubleday, 2007), 146.

13. Weber Shandwick et al., "Civility in America: 2013," 3, online at https://www.webershandwick.com/uploads/news/files/Civility_in_America_2013_Exec_Summary.pdf, accessed July 1, 2015.

14. Ibid.

15. Ibid.

16. Ibid.

17. Keisha L. Hoerner, "The Forgotten Battles: Congressional Hearings on Television Violence in the 1950s," accessed online at www.scripps.ohiou.edu/wjmcr/vol02/2-3a-B.htm on July 22, 2015.

18. Kaiser Family Foundation, "Generation M2: Media in the Lives of 8 to 18 Year Olds" (2010).

19. Pew Research, "Social Media Update: 2013" (December 30, 2013).

20. Pew Research, "Teens, Smartphones & Texting" (March 19, 2012).

21. R. Brown, "Seven out of ten Cambridge children use technology at the dinner table but want to spend more time with parents, study finds," *Cambridge News* (May 28, 2014).

22. J. Radesky et al., "Patterns of Mobile Device Use by Caregivers and Children During Meals in Fast Food Restaurants," *Pediatrics*, (March 10, 2014).

23. Weber Shandwick, *Civility in America: 2013* (New York: Weber Shandwick, 2013), 5.

24. Ibid.

25. Ibid. Seventy-six percent of individuals consider it rude when someone else speaks loudly on a cell phone in a public setting.

26. Ibid., 3.

27. S. Algoe et al., "Witnessing excellence in action: the 'other-praising' emotions of elevation, gratitude, and admiration," *The Journal of Positive Psychology* 4, no. 2, (2009): 105–127.

28. Ibid.

29. L. Berkman, "Assessing the Physical Health Effects of Social Networks and Social Support," *Annual Review of Public Health* 5 (1984): 413–432.

30. L. Berkman et al., "Social Networks, Host Resistance, and Mortality: A Nine-Year Follow-Up Study of Alameda County Residents," *American Journal of Epidemiology* 109, no. 2, (1979): 186–204.

31. General Social Survey, 1972–2012.

32. General Social Survey, 1972–2012.

33. J. Fowler et al., "Dynamic Spread of Happiness in a Large Social Network: Longitudinal Analysis over 20 Years in the Framingham Heart Study," *BMJ* 337 (2008): art. a2338.

34. Ibid.

35. Ibid.

36. Ibid. Fowler et al., "Dynamic Spread of Happiness."

37. Brizendine, *The Male Brain*, xv–xvi. Brizendine, *The Female Brain*, 14–15.

38. Ibid., both sources.

39. "Every person's history is written first of all in his own mother's heart." (Pope John Paul II, Homily, Opening of the Holy Door at St. Mary Major, January 1, 2000).

40. Chimerism is when one organism is composed of genetically different cells. An example would be the recipient of an organ transplant. The donated organ would have the genetic profile of the donor while the rest of the recipient's body would have its naturally occurring genetic profile. Microchimerism is when an organism has a limited number of genetically different cells within its body. Studies indicate that women continue to carry within their bodies cells from every pregnancy they have conceived. These cells are genetically different from the mother's cells since they are the offspring of the genetic fusion of the father's sperm and mother's ovum. See H. S. Gammill and J. L. Nelson, "Naturally acquired microchimerism," *The International Journal of Developmental Biology* 54 (2010): 531–543.

41. W. Chan et al., "Male Microchimerism in the Human Female Brain," PLOS ONE 7, no. 9 (2012): art. e45592. doi:10.1371/journal. pone.0045592.

42. Many cultures distinguish between experiential knowledge, which is how we would come to know a person, and intellectual knowledge. French: *connaitre* vs. *savoir*. Spanish: *conocer* vs. *saber*. German: *kenntnis* vs. *wissenschaft*.

43. John Pridmore, *Gangland to Promised Land—One Man's Journey from the Criminal Underworld to Christ* (Sycamore, IL: Lighthouse Catholic Media, 2011).

44. At the time of Christ, marriages within Judaism involved two steps—the betrothal and the bringing into the home of the bride. The legal union was formed at the time of the betrothal so that a divorce was required to become "unbetrothed." At the time of the Annunciation, Mary and Joseph were betrothed. As such, the legal union was already formed.

45. The English rendition of the vows is "I, Steve, take you, Shelly, to be my lawful wife . . ." However, in Latin, the key word is "accipere," which could more accurately be translated as "accept" or "receive." Thus, the vow becomes "I, Steve, receive you, Shelly, to be my lawful wife . . ."

46. T. Baumgartner et al., "Oxytocin Shapes the Neural Circuitry of Trust and Trust Adaptation in Humans," *Neuron* 58 (May 22, 2008): 639–650.

47. Elisabeth Leseur, *The Secret Diary of Elisabeth Leseur* (Manchester, NH: Sophia Institute Press, 2002), 122.

48. Ibid., xxxviii–xxxix.

49. Ibid., xli.

50. Ibid., 145.

CHAPTER EIGHT: STEP 7: MAKE IT EASY TO BE GOOD AND HARD TO BE BAD

1. For a good summary of relevant research see *The Compassionate Instinct*, Edited by D. Keltner et al. (New York: W. W. Norton and Company, 2010).

2. The results of all relevant studies are summarized and discussed in C. Daniel Batson, *Altruism in Humans* (New York: Oxford University Press, 2011).

3. Ibid., 98.

4. Ibid., 99.

5. Ibid., 100.

6. Ibid., appendices B–G, pp. 275–302.

7. D. Keltner, "The Compassionate Instinct," in *The Compassionate Instinct*, 10.

8. Ibid.

9. For details regarding the Michael Morton story, see Michael Morton, *Getting Life: An Innocent Man's 25-Year Journey from Prison to Peace* (New York: Simon & Schuster, 2014). See also the documentary *An Unreal Dream: The Michael Morton Story*, First Run Features, 2014.

10. Morton, *Getting Life: An Innocent Man's 25-Year Journey*

11. *An Unreal Dream: The Michael Morton Story.*

12. Ibid.

13. Ibid. Ken Anderson was removed from his seat as district judge. His license to practice law was revoked. He was fined $500 and sentenced to ten days in county jail and 500 hours of community service. After five days in jail, he was released for good behavior and is eligible to have his law license renewed in five years.

14. Ibid.

15. J. Kiecolt-Glaser et al., "Psychoneuroimmunology: Psychological Influences on Immune Function and Health," *Journal of Consulting and Clinical Psychology* 70, no. 3, (2002): 537–547; N. Schneiderman et al., "Stress and Health: Psychological, Behavioral and Biological Determinants," *Annual Review Clinical Psychology* 1 (2005): 607–628.

16. C. V. O. Witvliet et al., "Granting Forgiveness or Harboring Grudges: Implications for Emotion, Physiology, and Health," *Psychological Science* 12, no. 2 (March 2001): 117–123.

17. K. Lawler et al., "The Unique Effects of Forgiveness on Health: An Exploration of Pathways," *Journal of Behavioral Medicine* 28, no. 2 (April 2005): 157–167.

18. J. Abeler et al., "The Power of Apology," *Economics Letters* 107 (May 2010): 233–235.

19. P. Michl et al., "Neurobiological Underpinnings of Shame and Guilt: A Pilot fMRI Study," *Social Cognitive and Affective Neuroscience* 9, no. 2 (2014): pp. 150–157.

20. C. V. O. Witvliet et al., "Retributive Justice, Restorative Justice, and Forgiveness: An Experimental Psychophysiology Analysis," *Journal of Experimental Social Psychology* 44, no. 1 (Jan. 2008): 10–25.

21. J. Karremans et al., "When Forgiving Enhances Psychological Well-Being: The Role of Interpersonal Commitment," *Journal of Personality and Social Psychology* 84, no. 5 (2003): 1011–1026.

22. Ibid.

23. Couples attending The Choice Wine. Survey results for men regarding their wives holding grudges: Never, 24%; Sometimes, 56%; Usually, 14%; Always, 3%; Even when I'm innocent, 3%. Survey results for women regarding their husbands holding grudges: Never, 31%; Sometimes, 58%; Usually, 6%; Always, 4%; Even when I'm innocent, 1%.

24. T. Holmes et al., "The Social Readjustment Rating Scale," *Journal of Psychosomatic Research* 11 (1967): 213–218.

25. Karremans, "When Forgiving Enhances Psychological Well-Being," 1011–1026.

26. "The Church . . . is described as the spotless spouse of the spotless Lamb, whom Christ 'loved and for whom He delivered Himself up that He might sanctify her,'" Lumen Gentium, #6, Second Vatican Council, November 21, 1964.

27. "On one point the Rabbis were unanimous, [the Messiah] would be just a human being divinely appointed to carry out an allotted task. The Talmud nowhere indicates a belief in a superhuman Deliverer as the Messiah," A. Cohen, *Everyman's Talmud* (New York: Schocken Books, 1949/1975) 347.

28. For the story of Mark and Katie Hartfiel see Katie Hartfiel, *Woman in Love: Redefine the Journey Toward Your Husband To Be* (Katy, TX: Hearts United, 2012).

29. Ibid., 12–13.

30. P. Lappin, *Give Me Souls—The Life of Don Bosco* (New York: Salesiana Publishers, 1986).

31. Ibid., notably "The Lady and the Dream," prior to Chapter 1.

32. G. Lemoyne, *The Biographical Memoirs of St. John Bosco*, v. 4 (New York: Salesiana Publishers, 1967), 381.

33. Ibid.

34. Ibid.

35. Ibid., 164–167.

36. P. Lappin, *Give Me Souls—The Life of Don Bosco*, 167.

37. Don Bosco "was convinced that 'round the clock' supervision was both reasonable and preventive . . . telling the catechists . . . never leave the boys to themselves; keep an eye on them, always and everywhere." In J. Morrison, *The Educational Philosophy of St. John Bosco* (New York: Salesiana Publishers, 1979/1997), 92.

38. D. Fein, "Spending Time Together: Time Use Estimates for Economically Disadvantaged and Nondisadvantaged Married Couples in the United States," working paper, US Department of Health and Human Services, 2009.

39. R. Kraut et al., "Internet Paradox: A Social Technology that Reduces Social Involvement and Psychological Well-Being?" *American Psychologist* 53, no. 9 (September 1998): 1017–1031.

40. M. Hill, "Marital Stability and Spouses' Shared Time: A Multidisciplinary Hypothesis," *Journal of Family Issues* 9, no. 4 (December 1988): 427–451.

41. Fein, "Spending Time Together."

CHAPTER NINE: MARRIAGE AS A FORETASTE OF PARADISE

1. Data is taken from the General Social Survey for 1994. It is the only year in which all the relevant questions were asked of the same population sample.

2. P. Amato et al., "A Longitudinal Study of Marital Problems and Subsequent Divorce," *Journal of Marriage and the Family* 59 (August 1997): 612–624, Table 2.

3. Ibid., Table 4.

4. E. Laumann, *The Social Organization of Sexuality—Sexual Practices in the United States* (Chicago: University of Chicago Press, 1994), 504, Figure 13.6.

5. "Marriage and Cohabitation in the United States: A Statistical Portrait Based on Cycle 6 (2002) of the National Survey of Family Growth," U.S. Department of Health and Human Services, Vital and Health Statistics, series 23, no. 28 (February 2010).

6. "Cohabitation, Marriage, Divorce, and Remarriage in the United States," Department of Health and Human Services, Vital and Health Statistics, series 23, no. 22 (July 2002).

7. Monsieur Jean-Jacques Olier, quoted in A. Doze, *Saint Joseph: Shadow of the Father*, Trans. Audett, F. (New York: Alba House, 1992), 52.

8. One of the most famous examples of this is Augustine's statement, "O Lord, you have made us for yourself, and our hearts are restless until they rest in thee." See "Confessions," Book 1, Chapter 1, Saint Augustine, *Confessions*, Trans. Chadwick, H., Oxford World's Classics (New York: Oxford University Press, 2008).

9. In Judaism, special attention is given to the derivation of words in Hebrew, which helps to illumine their inner meaning. The word for "holy" in Hebrew is qadosh (שׁ דֹזָק), which is derived from the word for "consecrated," qadash (שׁ.דָק), which is itself derived from the word "to be set aside," qodesh (שׁ דֹ.ק). As such, something is holy when it has been set aside as consecrated to God.

10. H. Nonin, *To Be a Jew: A Guide to Jewish Observance in Contemporary Life* (New York: Basic Books, 1972), 136–139.

11. E. Kitov, *The Jew and His Home—A Guide to Jewish Family Life* (New York: Feldheim Publishers, 1957/2004), 231.

12. H. Nonin, *To Be a Jew: A Guide to Jewish Observance in Contemporary Life* (New York: Basic Books, 1952), 72–74.

13. Catholic, Orthodox, and Anglican Communion Christians profess believe in the perpetual virginity of Mary: "The deepening of faith in the virginal motherhood led the Church to confess Mary's real and perpetual virginity even in the act of giving birth to the Son of God made man" (Catechism of the Catholic Church, #499). Nonetheless, it is to be expected that Mary followed the Niddah laws.

14. Monsieur Jean-Jacques Olier, quoted in A. Doze, *Saint Joseph: Shadow of the Father* (New York: Alba House, 1992), 52.

15. Recall the neurological science regarding shame presented in Chapter 8. Shame leads to an increase in fear and anxiety, hence the desire to hide.

16. Quoted in Thomas Aquinas, *Catena Aurea*, V. 4, Part II (Albany, NY: Preserving Christian Publications, Inc., 1995), 546.

17. St. Ephrem the Syrian, Nativity Hymn, XXIII.13, quoted in *Hymns on Paradise* (Crestwood, NY: St. Vladimir's Seminary Press, 1990), Hymn VI.8, p. 69.

18. Romanos the Melodist, "Mary at the Cross," quoted in L. Gambero, *Mary and the Fathers of the Church—The Blessed Virgin Mary in Patristic Thought* (San Francisco, CA: Ignatius Press, 1999), 336.

19. Theodore the Studite, Sermon, "Oratio in adorationem crucis," PG 99, 691–699, taken from the Office of Readings, Friday, Second Week of Easter.

20. Origen, "Commentary on Matthew," 126: PG 13, 1777. It should be noted that the identification of Calvary with the burial spot of Adam was never universally accepted. Notably, St. Jerome explicitly rejected it, preferring the explanation that it was the spot for the execution (beheading) of criminals (cf. Aquinas, *Catena Aurea*, V. I, Part II, p. 948). The former interpretation is accepted here for two reasons. First, the identification of the place of Christ's crucifixion with "Golgotha, the place of the skull" is one of the few passages contained in all four Gospels. As such, this designation was of considerable importance to the Gospel writers and early Christian community. The fact that Christ was executed as a criminal together with other criminals is already contained in the Gospel narrative and does not seem to merit such emphasis. Second, each of the Gospels refers to the term in the singular, i.e., "the skull," pointing to the identification of a unique skull and/or person.

21. St. John Chrysostom quoted in Aquinas, *Catena Aurea*, V. III, Part II, p. 530.

22. Ibid.

23. Meditating on the words "I thirst" spoken by Christ from the cross, Mother Teresa stated: "Jesus wants me to tell you again. . . . how much is the love He has for each one of you—beyond all what you can imagine. . . . Not only He loves you, even more—He longs for you. . . . He thirsts for you. . . . His words . . . are not from the past only, but alive here and now, spoken to you." In Kolodiejchuk, *Mother Teresa: Come Be My Light*, 42.

24. St. John Chrysostom, "Catecheses," quoted in the Liturgy of Hours, Office of Readings for Good Friday.

25. St. Augustine, "Contra Litterani Petiliani Donatist AE Cortensis, Episcopi," Book 22, Chapter 87, *Nicene and Post-Nicene Fathers*, V.4 (Peabody, MA: Hendrickson Publishers, 1995), 307.

26. Ibid., "Contra Fastum Manichaeum," Book 2, Chapter 13, 536.

27. St. Ephrem the Syrian, *Hymns on Paradise*, Hymn VI.8, p. 111.

28. "Through her liturgical actions the pilgrim Church already participates, as by a foretaste, in the heavenly liturgy" (Catechism of the Catholic Church, #1111).

29. Nuptial blessing given at the end of the Catholic Nuptial Mass. See *The Rites of the Catholic Church* v. 1, Study Edition (New York: Pueblo Publishing Company, 1990), 730.

30. Ibid., 726.

31. Ibid.

32. Ibid.

33. The Jewish exodus from Egyptian slavery to the Promised Land was seen as a foreshadowing of the Christian journey from this world to heaven. The Jews were sustained on their pilgrimage by manna—bread from heaven. Jesus declared the Eucharist to be the Christian manna: "Your ancestors ate the manna in the desert, but they died; this is the bread that comes down from heaven so that one may eat it and not die" (John 6:49–50).

34. Pope John Paul II, "The Eucharist is the very source of Christian marriage. . . . In this sacrifice of the New and Eternal covenant, Christian spouses encounter the source from which their own marriage covenant flows, is interiorly structured and continuously renewed" (Familiaris Consortio, #57).

35. "The grace which you received in marriage remains with you through the years. Its source is in the pierced heart of the Redeemer, who sacrificed himself on the altar of the Cross for the sake of the Church, his Spouse . . . This grace remains ever close to that source: it is the grace of self-sacrificing love, a love which both gives and forgives. It is the grace of a selfless love which forgets the hurt it has suffered, a love faithful unto death, a love bursting with new life" (Pope John Paul II, Address to the Fourth World Meeting of Families, January 25, 2003).

36. See *The Rites of the Catholic Church* v. 1, 730.

38. Shelly and I never had a son. Nonetheless, long before Riley died, we told him that if we ever did, the first one would be named after him.

38. Brendan Cahill is now the Bishop of the Diocese of Victoria in Texas.